Dostoevsky's Dickens

*FOR
ADA NISBET*

DOSTOEVSKY'S DICKENS

A Study of Literary Influence

Loralee MacPike

1981
BARNES & NOBLE BOOKS
Totowa · New Jersey

First published in the USA 1981 by
Barnes & Noble Books
81 Adams Drive
Totowa, New Jersey 07512

ISBN 0-389-20062-X

CONTENTS

A NOTE ON TRANSLITERATION AND EDITIONS

The transliteration system used is that suggested by Thomas Shaw in *The Transliteration of Modern Russian for English-Language Publications* (Madison: Univ. of Wisconsin Press, 1967). With the exception of commonly established spellings such as Dostoevsky and Tolstoy, I transliterate all Russian words and names according to this system. This causes some discrepancies between my work and quoted material, much of which was done earlier under the French system of transliteration which has given us 'Dostoievski', 'Tolstoi' and 'Tourgenieff'. These discrepancies have been ignored in the text to avoid the distracting use of 'sic'.

In addition, discrepancies arise due to uncoordinated book title translations. *Besy* is variously translated as *The Possessed* and *The Devils*, the latter of which is closer to a literal translation; however, I retain the former as the more widely known English version. Likewise, *The Insulted and Injured* has often been translated as *The Humiliated and Offended*, or *Humility and Offence*, from the original French translations of the title.

There are two good editions of Dostoevsky's works, both in translations by Constance Garnett. William Heinemann published in England simultaneously with Macmillan in New York. Garnett's translations remain the best overall in my opinion, being more literal and frequently more accurate than even the most recent translations.

Citations from Dickens are from the *New Oxford Illustrated Dickens* edition (London: Oxford University Press).

The following abbreviations have been used in textual citations:

BK   *The Brothers Karamazov* (Macmillan, 1912)

CP   *Crime and Punishment* (Macmillan, 1914)

EH   *The Eternal Husband and Other Stories* (Macmillan, 1917)

FF   *The Friend of the Family and Other Stories* (Macmillan, 1920)

II   *The Insulted and Injured* (Macmillan, 1923)

P   *The Possessed* (Macmillan, 1923)

RY   *A Raw Youth* (Macmillan, 1916)

DW   *Diary of a Writer*, trans. Boris Brasol (New York: Braziller, 1954)

WN   *White Nights and Other Stories*

Pis'ma Letters *(Pis'ma)*, ed., A. C. Dolinin (Moscow: Goslitizdat, 1928–1930).

I have used my own translations of Dostoevsky's letters and of Russian critical works.

ACKNOWLEDGEMENTS

The research for this study was supported by a grant from the American Association of University Women which enabled me to visit the Lenin Library in Moscow, the Public Library (Saltykov-Shchedrin Library) in Leningrad, and the Shevchenko and Communist Party Libraries in Kiev, as well as the British Museum. This invaluable aid allowed me to examine materials unavailable outside the Soviet Union. Research time granted by the University of Hawaii allowed for writing the manuscript.

For the ideas I present here there are many to thank. To Ada Nisbet, whose incisive thinking and vast bibliographical knowledge of Dickens have shaped my ideas and research beyond all possibility of documentation, go my deepest thanks. Joan Hodgson, Interlibrary Loan Librarian at the University of California at Santa Cruz, again and again exhausted American library resources in a devoted effort to place obscure Russian criticism at my disposal. Michael Hollington has been a steady and helpful critic who has in more than one instance held me to my path when I would have wandered. Barbara Fox, James Allsup, Diane Dreher, Janette Lewis, Ann Rayson, Glenn Mann and Joan Robins have kept me going. And Loretta MacPike, my typist, has brought it all to fruition. This volume stands as my thanks for the unstinting help and encouragement I received at every step.

by Dmitri's imprisonment. What did Dostoevsky see in Dickens that made possible such recognizable yet inconceivably oppugnant metamorphoses? Were these metamorphoses inherent in the Dickens Dostoevsky read? One thing is certain: through Dostoevsky's reading of Dickens we find a Dickens invisible to the eye of the critic who focuses on the English author alone.

It has, fortunately, become a commonplace of literary criticism to compare Dostoevsky to Dickens and to explore ways in which Dickens influenced the Russian master. I say 'fortunately' because such comparisons by their very nature must quickly become diffuse and allusive if they are to do more than stand as mere lighthouses of fact. Fortunately for both Dickens and Dostoevsky, the often sterile influence-hunting of the 1940s and 1950s, largely abandoned now among English-speaking critics, seems to have bloomed into vital studies of these two writers and led thence to that elusive search for the creative mind itself, beyond if not outside of the physical works it produces. And so the contemporary critic has the benefit of one book-length study in English, two major articles, and two dissertations devoted to the influence of Dickens on Dostoevsky; one Russian critic has also compared the two at length.[2] In addition, literally dozens of writers discuss the fact of influence. In most of these studies, however, emphasis is placed upon the achievements of the writer who absorbed the influence: N. M. Lary, in *Dostoevsky and Dickens*, finds Dickens a Dostoevsky manqué; Donald Fanger's *Dostoevsky and Romantic Realism* traces in Dostoevsky the culmination of Dickens' attempts to romanticize and thus transform reality; Stefan Zweig, in *Three Masters*, sees Dostoevsky as the acme of psychological realism and Dickens as but an intermediate step.[3] Even the late Igor Katarsky, whose primary interest is Dickens, finds it necessary in *Dickens in Russia* to treat Dostoevsky as an advancement over the earlier writer.

While these are important studies, and while their results help us toward an understanding of Dostoevsky, it remains to ask what can be learned about Dickens through his influence on Dostoevsky. In one sense this work is a reverse influence study, turning the fact of influence back upon the writer whose influence was absorbed and asking what such absorption can tell us about hitherto neglected or overlooked aspects of a master whose importance to the world of literature has still not been fully plumbed.

It is indisputable that Dostoevsky knew Dickens well. In fact, all of nineteenth-century Russia knew Dickens well. For a long time Russia had been far more familiar with Western literature than the West with Russian literature. Not only were English works widely available beginning in the 1820s, but it was fashionable to read them. Thus Dickens appeared upon a scene well prepared to receive and appreciate him.

Even the briefest look at Dickens' Russian literary reputation bespeaks the broad extent of writers' and readers' familiarity with him. On 20 July 1844 the *Petersburg Literary Gazette* stated that 'the name of Dickens is more or less well known to any educated person among us,' and in 1891 the same idea was echoed in an anonymous editorial in the newspaper *Russian Thought*: 'The name of C. Dickens is well known to any slightly-educated Russian reader.' Vissarion Belinsky, Russia's foremost nineteenth-century literary critic, said in 1844 that 'everyone' had read *Nicholas Nickleby*, *Oliver Twist*, *Barnaby Rudge*, and *The Old Curiosity Shop*.[4] Even Dickens' first important translator, Irinarkh Vvedensky, wrote Dickens in June 1849: 'For about ten years your name has enjoyed enormous fame in Russia and you are read with great zeal from the banks of the Neva to the remotest limits of Siberia.'[5] As Igor Katarsky, a leading Soviet bibliographer, biographer, and critic of Dickens, observed, 'in all probability there was not a single Russian writer, artist, publisher, or educator of the nineteenth century who remained indifferent to Dickens' works, and the best of them prized him especially.'[6]

Translations of Dickens began coming out almost as soon as the novels were written. *Pickwick Papers* was first translated (from the French translation by Eugenie Boyet) in 1838 and *Nicholas Nickleby* in 1840, both in abbreviated form. Several of the *Sketches by Boz* appeared in various periodicals in 1839. The first complete and fairly accurate translation was of *Oliver Twist*, published in 1841, and it was with this novel that Dickens' permanent popularity in Russia was firmly established. After this, translations followed very closely the appearance of the novels in England—the Russians waited as eagerly as the Americans for each installment of *The Old Curiosity Shop* and all the novels that followed. *Dombey and Son*, translated simultaneously in 1947 by Vvedensky in a free translation and by A. I. Butakov in a more literal version, was enthusiastically received by Belinsky, upon whose favour a writer's popularity in Russia largely depended. Two works, *Barnaby Rudge* and *American Notes* (the latter in excerpts only), were even published in English in the *St Petersburg English Review of Literature, the Arts and Sciences* in 1842.

In addition to Russian versions there were, of course, French and German translations of Dickens circulating in Russia to supplement, for those able to read them, the lack or the incompleteness of available Russian translations. Dickens' popularity in Russia was so widespread that it would be possible to assume Dostoevsky had read him even if he had left no record of the fact. In a time and a country in which every educated man could be assumed to have a broad knowledge of Dickens and of English literature in general, a voracious reader like Dostoevsky would be certain to have known him.[7]

But we need not conjecture, for Dostoevsky often mentions Dickens. He refers to him directly in his novels, letters, notebooks, and prose writings. Members of his family tell us in their journals of reading he had done or planned to do. His novels contain frequent oblique references to specific topics whose striking similarity of expression and idea almost verifiably identify them as Dickensian in origin.

Dostoevsky's specific references to Dickens begin with his remembrance that Dickens appeared in Russia 'about the middle of the Thirties' (*DW* 345–46), simultaneously with George Sand, and end after his death with the discovery in his personal library of copies of *Bleak House* and *Dombey and Son* in French editions.[8] Throughout his lifetime he often and fondly referred to his English counterpart as 'the great Christian—Dickens' (e.g.,

DW 347). During his imprisonment and exile (1849–59) Dostoevsky, so his brother tells us, 'refused even to read the books brought to him and only twice became interested in *David Copperfield* and "Posthumous notes of the Pickwick Club" by Dickens, in Vvedensky's translation, and took them to the hospital for reading.'[9]

Dostoevsky's novels often mention or mirror Dickens. The Nellie Valkovsky sub-plot of *The Insulted and Injured* parallels Little Nell's saga in *The Old Curiosity Shop*. *The Idiot* has long been associated with Dickens because of Dostoevsky's avowed attempt to fashion Myshkin after Don Quixote and Pickwick. He wrote to his niece Sofia Aleksandrovna on 1 January 1868, about his plan to create in *The Idiot* a 'perfectly beautiful man':

> Of all the noble figures in Christian literature, I reckon Don Quixote the most perfect. But Don Quixote is beautiful only because he is at the same time comic. And Dickens' Pickwick (an endlessly weaker idea than Don Quixote, but nonetheless huge) is also comic, and this gives him his value. (*Pis'ma* II, 71)

Pickwick was one of Dostoevsky's models in his lifelong attempt to create a genuinely good man. There are specific references to Dickens in *The Eternal Husband* (1870), *The Possessed* (1872), and *A Raw Youth* (1875).[10] *Diary of a Writer* records Dostoevsky's claims to a particularly deep Russian understanding of Dickens:

> We, however, understand Dickens, when rendered into Russian, almost as well as the English—perhaps, even all nuances. Moreover, we love him—perhaps, not less than his own countrymen. And yet, how typical, original and national is Dickens! What can be derived from this?—Is such an understanding of alien nationalities a special gift of the Russians, as compared with Europeans? (*DW* 75)[11]

Again in The *Diary* for 1873 Dostoevsky tries to define genre and uses Dickens as an example:

Indeed, Dickens is genre, too, nothing but genre. But Dickens created Pickwick, Oliver Twist, and grandfather and grand-daughter in the novel *The Old Curiosity Shop*. No, our genre is still a long way off: it still stands on its 'hunters' and 'nightingales'. Dickens has them, too, in secondary places. Judging by certain indications, I am inclined to think that at the present juncture of our art Pickwick and the grand-daughter would seem something ideal to our genre. ... What is genre, in substance? Genre is an art of portraying contemporaneous, current reality which the artist has personally felt and seen with his own eyes, as distinguished, for instance, from historical reality which cannot be beheld with one's own eyes, and which is being portrayed not in a fluent but completed state. (I will make a *nota bene*: we say: 'beheld with his own eyes.' But Dickens had never seen Pickwick with his own eyes, merely perceiving him in the diversity of the reality observed by him; he created a character and presented him as a result of his observations. Thus, this character is as real as an actually existing one, even though Dickens had merely taken an ideal of the reality.) (*DW* 82–83)

Dostoevsky's idea of the ultimate reality of the best artistic creations was not new; Ruskin also spoke of it in *Modern Painters*:

The whole power, whether of painter or poet, to describe rightly what we call an ideal thing, depends upon its being thus, to him, not an ideal, but a *real* thing. No man ever did or ever will work well, but either from actual sight or sight of faith. ... [Great men] do not know or care whether the things they describe are vulgarities or not. They *saw* them; they are facts of the case. If they had merely composed what they describe, they would have had it at their will to refuse this circumstance or add that. But they did not compose it. It came to them ready fashioned; they were too much impressed by it to think what was vulgar or not vulgar in it.[12]

Although Ruskin spoke of painters and Dostoevsky of writers, they were talking about the same thing: an ability to create a real character from an inner vision of reality which makes of the thing created something 'perfectly typical' in the German sense of the word 'ideal'—a physical more than a moral ideal. This is the 'ideal' Dostoevsky finds in Little Nell. Dostoevsky himself creates in much the same way; he says of Prince Myshkin: 'Is not my fantastic *Idiot*, the very dailiest truth?' (*Pis'ma* II, 170). *The Idiot* is closely connected with Pickwick, and like him Myshkin was conceived through what Ruskin calls the 'sight of faith'.

Dostoevsky was well aware of the problem of creating the ideal out of the real without destroying or distorting the real. In *The Old Curiosity Shop*, Nell and her grandfather were so typical that they became ideal in Dostoevsky's mind: it was this Trishatov saw in his recollection in *A Raw Youth* of the child and the old man:

There's one passage at the end, when they—that mad old man and that charming girl of thirteen, his grand-child, take refuge after their fantastic flight and wandering in some remote place in England, near a Gothic mediaeval church, and the little girl has received some post there, and shows the church to visitors ... [sic] then the sun is setting, and the child in the church porch, bathed in the last rays of light, stands and gazes at the sunset, with gentle pensive contemplation in her child soul, a soul full of wonder as though before some mystery, for both alike are mysteries, the sun, the thought of God, and the church, the thought of man, aren't they? Oh, I don't know how to express it, only God loves such first thoughts in children.... While near her, on the step, the crazy old grandfather gazes at her with a fixed look ... [sic] you know there's nothing special in it, in that picture of Dickens, there's absolutely nothing in it, but yet one will remember it all one's life, and it has survived for all Europe—why? It's splendid! It's the innocence in it! And I don't know what there is in it, but it's fine. (*RY* 434–35)

The incommunicable idea Trishatov remembers from Dickens' novel is the perfect representativeness of Nell and her grandfather. They stand for an ideal which may exist only in the human mind but which is nonetheless completely real to every seeker after the ideal. It is this use of absolute reality to picture to each reader his ideals that Dostoevsky recognized in Dickens and sought for in his own works.

At the same time Dostoevsky was aware that neither he nor Dickens would ever be able to achieve the ideal. In his recently published notebooks of 1875–1876 Dostoevsky gives his random thoughts about what he was reading and writing in those years, and Dickens' name appears four times:

The beautiful ones in our century: Pickwick, Notre Dame, Misérables. The first tales of George Sand, Lord Byron (lame-leg), Lermontov, Turgenev, *War and Peace*, Heine, Pushkin ... Walter Scott.*

[The New Times of 12 March 1875] speaks of the extraordinary people ... [sic] Where have they gone? Where are the good people? Where the ideals [sic] The good people are contiguous with ideals. In France—in Misérables. In stable England, Dickens' ideal is too modest and elementary.†

I read about Copernicus formerly. I read 'The Voice' (about a bunch of facts), I read about the extra-ordinary ones. Everything about ancient literature (worship). About the newest things, about the literature of despair, about the universal truths of Lev Tolstoy. Note: About Don Quixote. About Shakespeare, *Dickens*. 'Misérables' (the sole ideal), in Dickens it is all ideal, we have 'Adolescence,' Turgenev has 'A Nest of Gentlefolk.'‡

N.B. Consciousness and love, which are, perhaps, one and the same thing, because you cannot be conscious of anything without love, but with love you are conscious of everything. ...

On the other hand [you have] conventionality: Artem'eva, Dickens.[13]§

These jottings show Dostoevsky's awareness of some of Dickens' shortcomings. He sees both Dickens' conventionality, which sometimes causes him to create from wish rather than from felt reality, and the resultant extremes of idealism which falsify his perceptions. He sees the precariousness of the ideal, yet in his own creations he tries to capture what he sees Dickens attempting and often realizing.

The last reference to Dickens in Dostoevsky's writings occurs near the end of his life (18 August 1880), when all of Dickens had been translated and published in Russia. He writes to N. L. Osmidov, in answer to a request for a reading list for Osmidov's daughter. In addition to Scott, Pushkin, Gogol, and the general classics, Dostoevsky says, 'Let her read through all of Dickens without exception' (*Pis'ma* IV, 196). As Angus Wilson pointed out in 'Dickens and Dostoevsky', Dostoevsky was not the sort of person to advise reading books he himself had not read; therefore one can presume that he had read all of Dickens in some form or other.

Typical of Dostoevsky's outspoken love for Dickens is an anecdote told by a friend, Anna Ivanovna Suvorina, who breakfasted with the writer and a group of other friends one morning:

Suddenly F.M. turned to me with a question: How did I like Dickens? I said to him, shamefully, that I had not read him. He was surprised and fell silent. The conversation went along other lines. Again completely unexpectedly, F.M. loudly said: 'Friends, we have among us the happiest of mortals!' I looked around at all our company wonderingly. These were all rather elderly people, and I saw no special joy in their faces. After a short silence Dostoevsky said: 'My neighbour Anna Ivanovna.'

*†‡§Dostoevsky was notoriously inconsistent in the notebooks and used all sorts of strange shorthand. This is the form in which the editor transcribed them.

I gave a start, from the unexpectedness of it ... [sic] 'Yes, yes!
She! Friends, lucky Anna Ivanovna has not yet read Dickens,
and she, fortunate one, still can experience this happiness! Ah,
how I would like to be in her place! And read again *David
Copperfield* and all of Dickens!' I explained to him why,
reading so much, I had not read Dickens; that I had tried but I
just could not read him through, that is, I positively could not
read of the suffering of children or animals, and the godfather
of my child, Ivan Fedorovich Gorbunov, added that I only
liked the sufferings of lovers. ... Dostoevsky laughed and said:
'That is very interesting, but nonetheless you must read
Dickens. When I am very tired and feel on bad terms with
myself, no one can calm or gladden me like this peaceful
writer!' I promised to read him.[14]

In addition to Dostoevsky's own references to Dickens, his
family adds to our knowledge both of what he read by Dickens
and of how he felt about him. His wife's diaries tell us that he
read *Nicholas Nickleby*, *The Old Curiosity Shop*, *David
Copperfield*, and *Little Dorrit*, the latter in French translation. He
must have read *David Copperfield*, for Anna Grigor'evna
Dostoevsky has him referring to himself during their years of
forced exile as 'Mister Micawber, and [herself] as Mrs
Micawber,'[15] which must have been a frequent allusion because
Dostoevsky later writes to A. N. Maikov that 'I am positively in a
terrible situation now (Mr Micawber). Not a kopek of money'
(*Pis'ma* II, 262). His daughter Liubov recalls that 'he, who forgot
his wife's name and the face of his mistress, could remember all
the English names of the characters of Dickens and Scott which
had fired his youthful imagination, and spoke of them as if they
were his intimate friends.'[16]
Nor is it fanciful to suppose that Dostoevsky's intimate
knowledge of and love for Dickens would lead him to think in
Dickensian terms when he penned his own works. In fact, the
number of Dickensian touches in his works suggests that he was
not loath to make use of another writer's successful ideas and
devices. Dostoevsky's novels contain many oblique references

which indicate that Dickens' peculiar ways of viewing both situations and characters were assimilated and to some extent transformed by the Russian writer's imagination. I offer only a few of the more prominent of these references which have not, to my knowledge, been noted by previous critics.[17]

Crime and Punishment, often said to have a Dickensian cast to it, reflects a critical reading of *Hard Times* in particular. Indeed, Leonid Grossman asserts, of Dostoevsky's reading of English 'Chartist novels', that 'there is every reason to suppose that Dostoevsky, with his huge interest in reading Russian magazines in Semipalatinsk (that is, from 1854) knew *Hard Times* and read Nekrasov's review in *The Contemporary* (August 1855), acknowledging this book as one of the best among Dickens' novels, notwithstanding the absence in it of a single political idea.'[18] Dostoevsky's reading of *Hard Times* would seem to show up in *Crime and Punishment* when Marmeladov (often acclaimed brother to Mr Micawber) speaks to Raskolnikov at the tavern, saying: 'Mr Lebeziatnikov who keeps up with modern ideas explained the other day that compassion is forbidden nowadays by science itself, and that that's what is done now in England, where there is political economy' (*CP* 14). Mr Gradgrind, girded with Benthamism, leaps to mind. It is difficult to believe that Dostoevsky, writing with Dickens in mind when he introduced Marmeladov, was not also thinking of him in this comment of Marmeladov's. A little further on in the same novel, Raskolnikov thinks of Sonia's prostitution and says: 'A certain percentage, they tell us, must every year go ... [sic] that way ... [sic] to the devil, I suppose, so that the rest may remain chaste, and not be interfered with. A percentage! What splendid words they have; they are so scientific, so consolatory ... [sic]. Once you've said "percentage" there's nothing more to worry about' (*CP* 52). Tom Gradgrind is one of the percentage who go wrong as proof of Mr Gradgrind's teachings, and Raskolnikov's comment appears to reflect Dostoevsky's close reading of *Hard Times*.

Two other major Dickensian touches occur in Dostoevsky's novels. The mention in *Crime and Punishment* of 'spontaneous combustion of a shop-keeper from alcohol' (*CP* 157) probably echoes Dostoevsky's reading of *Bleak House*. Later, in *The Possessed*, Dostoevsky tells us that Stavrogin treated Maria Timofeevna 'as though she were a marquise' (*P* 188), thus aiding her to become more rational and normal. We know that Dostoevsky read *The Old Curiosity Shop*, and this seems to be a direct reference to the Dick Swiveller-Marchioness relationship in which Dick treats the ragamuffin as a high-born lady, and perhaps, as Dostoevsky knew *David Copperfield*, also reflects Emily's willing delusion that through Steerforth she would rise above her station. In such scenes as these we find Dostoevsky converting to his own uses those 'fantastic and wonderful' ideas that formed the essence of reality for him.

Finally, it must be noted that Dostoevsky's admiration of Dickens and other writers was not that of a passive reader, but rather of a voracious creative artist eager for food for his own imagination. Of course, no exclusive claim as to Dickens' influence is intended here; others influenced Dostoevsky in important ways. In addition to Dickens he read, with sometimes equal enthusiasm, Balzac, George Sand, Hugo, Paul de Kock, Walter Scott, Thackeray, Pushkin, Lermontov, Gogol, and a host of others, all of whom acted to shape his writings. From these influential sources he incorporated the ideas and techniques he found valuable: Kirillov's 'Now, now, now ...' repeated ten times just before his suicide echoes Lear's 'Never, never, never, never, never' (V, 3) as the old King dies, just as the case of spontaneous combustion in *Crime and Punishment* doubtless derives from Dickens. In regard to such adaptions, Dostoevsky wrote to his brother Michael on 24 March 1845, that 'something I read long ago I read through anew, and it is as if I exert myself with new powers. I look into everything, understand it clearly, and elicit from myself an ability to create' (*Pis'ma* I, 76). Dostoevsky believed in his own power to select the parts of a work that could be of use to him and then to use them to rethink his original ideas.

It is such talent which makes possible this study of Dostoevsky's borrowings from Dickens as they reflect a Dickens often unseen by the critical eye alone. Such a viewpoint is not new; Mark Spilka in *Dickens and Kafka* presents 'a comparative reading of *Great Expectations*, using appropriate parallels from Kafka's life and works to clarify its comic form' and reads '*Copperfield* in the light of Kafka's "imitations".'[19] The result of such readings is a new appreciation of some of Dickens' less visible techniques and concerns as they were developed by Kafka. Interestingly, Spilka also discusses Dostoevsky's influence on Kafka, suggesting yet another parallel between the English author and the Russian: their cumulative influence on later writers. The difference Spilka notes between Dickens' influence and Dostoevsky's is one of the major shapers of Dostoevsky's peculiar translation of Dickens: for Kafka 'the appeal of Dostoevsky was chiefly formal';[20] in other words, Dostoevsky's handling of techniques and themes offered Kafka a formal means to explore the unconscious. Dostoevsky's development of form thus allows for an advance in understanding—much what my work will claim for Dostoevsky's re-interpretation of Dickens.

Unlike Spilka, however, I do not need to break ground to show the similarities between Dickens and Dostoevsky and the reasons for my belief in the validity of Dostoevsky's interpretations of Dickens. That work has been done extraordinarily well in the works of Donald Fanger (*Dostoevsky and Romantic Realism*) and N. M. Lary (*Dickens and Dostoevsky*). Starting from a theoretical base, Dostoevsky commits himself critically, in *Diary of a Writer*, to an investigation of Dickens' 'ideal' and the ways that ideal could be achieved in Russian literature; for Dostoevsky was always aware of the difference between his own tormented conception of the Russian soul and Dickens' (relatively) calm portrayal of what was often for Dostoevsky the infuriating evenness of English complacency. But how to incorporate such differences into a consistent theory of the novel? This was Dostoevsky's self-appointed task, and for its completion he consciously set out to rework ideals—Dickens' ideal as one among many—through his own artistic vision. Like Shakespeare, Dostoevsky did not hesitate to borrow. Originality lay in transmutation, in nationalization of what he perceived as universal ideas and truths.

And so Dostoevsky borrowed from Dickens, reworked
Dickens' ideals into a uniquely Dostoevskian re-vision of what he
considered the essence of the master. In this study I explore in
detail two such borrowings: Nellie Valkovsky as a paraphrase of
Little Nell in *The Old Curiosity Shop*, and Steerforth's rebirth in
Stavrogin of *The Possessed*. The technique of reverse influence in
both instances draws a new portrait which, when superimposed
upon Dickens' originals, adds a new dimension of critical
appraisal, a dimension created by, and available only through,
artistic re-vision. Dostoevsky offers a new lens for focusing on
Dickens. I have chosen *The Old Curiosity Shop* and *David
Copperfield* for this study because both present problems in
criticism. No single effort can, or should, be used to 'explain' any
work of literature; however, reverse influence in these two cases
is particularly useful in presenting new possibilities for two
novels that have resisted more conventional critical probings.
This work is intended not to solve the problems inherent in
Dickens' works but instead to introduce and exemplify a
potentially useful method of literary criticism. It is practical rather
than theoretical, specific rather than general; it attempts to serve
as an *exemplum* of and an introduction to the possibilities of
reverse influence. As Spilka has noted:

A comparison which leads to mutual readings of specific texts,
and to the illumination of related worlds, is critically
rewarding. A fund of insights becomes available which might
escape direct approach; and, through mutual reinforcement, a
common vision emerges which supports the continuity of art
and culture.[21]

In this study I hope to provide one framework for such a vision.

To do so, however, I shall have to pull two of Dickens' novels
quite out of shape in the following pages. The effect will be as if
you dropped a balancing weight upon an unbalanced scale. First
the scale will swing wildly in the direction the weight was
dropped and the eye will perceive an even grosser unbalance. But
as you watch, the gyrations will slow, falter, and before you have

blinked the scale will have stopped, in much better balance than before.

Thus do I ask my reader to wait a moment, to read to the end. The weight I drop is potentially a heavy one, and it causes an initial distortion that unbalances the novels. But, like the scale weight, the point of view I bring to bear upon Dickens is ultimately a balancing one.

PART ONE

The Old Curiosity Shop

G. K. Chesterton is right. 'There is plenty to carp at in [Dickens] if
you are inclined to carp; you may easily find him vulgar if you
cannot see that he is divine; and if you cannot laugh with
Dickens, undoubtedly you can laugh at him.'[6] Indeed, as James
Joyce seems to be saying when he refers in *Finnegans Wake* to
'the old cupiosity shape',[7] Dickens is not always what he seems.
And Joyce merely continues a tradition of controversy that has
raged over *The Old Curiosity Shop* since its publication in 1841. It
has been called a tear-jerking piece of sentiment and a realistic
appraisal of the life of a poor city child. Response to it has ranged
from the pure physical relief of tears of pathos to an intellectual
refusal to submit to the enticements of Dickens' sentimental pen.
The basic critical question seems to be one of the extent of the
book's commitment to realism versus its tendency to romanticize
life and values in peculiarly Dickensian ways. As a conscious
realist, Dickens sought to reproduce 'familiar things' and to
represent contemporaneity.[8] Among other things, these two
tendencies result in what Dostoevsky called 'genre', a distillation
of the ideas for which he most valued Dickens. At the same time
Dickens consciously dwelt on 'the romantic side' of those familiar
things and believed in a 'light of Fancy' that controls 'the manner
of stating the truth' of contemporaneity. The two were for him
united by what Forster called 'fantastic fidelity', a juncture of the
possible real and the fiction within which it exists.[9] It was with
such a definition in mind that Dickens could argue the truth of
Nancy, the reality of Krook's spontaneous combustion, or the
validity of Little Nell. This fantastic fidelity allows for the
emergence of Dickens' characteristic juxtaposition, apparently
haphazard and uncontrolled, of realism and romance, or of what
some would call the truth and wishful thinking.

Nowhere does this conjunction seem to cause more trouble
than in *The Old Curiosity Shop* in general and in Little Nell in
particular. And so in this section I want to consider what some
would call a relatively minor critical problem: what to do with
Little Nell in *The Old Curiosity Shop*. Edward FitzGerald
collected the chapters about Nell and produced a 'Nelly-ad'
devoid of connection with the novel's world; other critics such as

Aldous Huxley or A. O. J. Cockshut have found it impossible to consider seriously a novel which contains such a 'vulgar' and 'sentimental' child, and they therefore eliminate her before dealing with the world Dickens created.[10] Little Nell is indeed 'minor' in that she does not bear the full burden of the meaning of the book, and certainly it can be discussed apart from her role in it. Yet such a discussion is clearly limited, for it prevents consideration of the book as a whole and makes impossible any conclusions about what Dickens might have either intended or achieved in it. This distortion results in criticism at best partial. So, while I in no way wish to overemphasize Little Nell's function or to confuse analysis of her role with analysis of the novel as a whole, it seems self-evident that no treatment of *The Old Curiosity Shop* can be complete without an understanding of that role and that function. If we fail to find a way to fit her into the world of the novel (a world of which she is so obviously a major representative), or worse yet, if we dismiss her, we miss the novel's full power. My reason for focusing on Little Nell is thus twofold: first, any successful attempt to show that she is an artistic as well as a functional part of her world is both critically and artistically satisfying; and second, our overall appreciation of the magnitude of Dickens' literary achievement is increased to just the extent that individual works more fully support and represent that achievement. To this end it seems appropriate to bring to bear upon a critical evaluation of Little Nell the resource of Dostoevsky's artistic recreation of her in the light of his own ideas about the typicality of the human soul.

And Little Nell is in rather sore need of reappraisal. She raises critical problems quite distinct from the novel itself. Virtually a cult of Nell-criticism has grown up around her, as the mixed bag of quotations at the beginning of this chapter attests. Both her life and her death have spawned a number of critical approaches. The most commonly mined vein is biographical: as the embodiment of Mary Hogarth, the virgin sister-in-law who died in Dickens' arms at the age of seventeen and whom he idolized to his death, Nell functions as a key to her creator's psychosexual problems.[11] As a social creature she represents a general Victorian desire for female innocence—particularly female child innocence. Spiritually she is the ultimate consolation for the untimely death of children, all too frequent and never well enough justified by nineteenth-century rhetoric. Allegorically she stands for the forces of good in a world Dickens and his readers saw as all too full of evil.[12]

Even Dickens' own critique tends to depersonalize her. He saw Nell as exemplary, and her death in particular he intended as a lesson, both about suffering and about its causes. He thought the ending 'very cheerful, or intended to be so.'[13] His intent was to be realistic and, based upon his own grief at the death of Mary Hogarth not quite four years earlier, to comfort his readers. In his Edinburgh speech of 25 June 1841, he said of the novel's ending:

When I first conceived the idea of conducting that simple story to its termination, I determined rigidly to adhere to it, and never to forsake the end I had in view. Not untried in the school of affliction, in the death of those we love, I thought what a good thing it would be if in my little work of pleasant amusement I could substitute a garland of fresh flowers for the sculptured horrors which disgrace the tomb. If I have put into my book anything which can fill the young mind with better thoughts of death, or soften the grief of older hearts; if I have written one word which can afford pleasure or consolation to old or young in time of trial, I shall consider it as something achieved—something which I shall be glad to look back upon in after life.[14]

To soften grief, to ease the way toward an acceptance of the inevitable disasters of life: Dickens was thinking of the desires and the needs of his readers. His constant sensitivity to reader reaction is well illustrated by his alteration of the ending of *Great Expectations*. Likewise, the ending of *The Old Curiosity Shop* was affected, so John Forster tells us, by Forster's own suggestion that Nell die,[15] a thought which he says Dickens had not previously entertained. However, Dickens' later assertion that he 'never had the design and purpose of a story so distinctly marked in [his] mind, from its commencement'[16] may indicate his subconscious adherence to his own and his readers' deeply felt but consciously inadmissable artistic truth (which Dostoevsky was later to plumb).

Any random sampling of reviews of and reactions to *The Old Curiosity Shop* gives an idea of just how Dickens' readers responded. The description of Nell's death scene as 'a tragedy of the true sort'[17] in 1847 but as 'a savoury dainty' in 1855[18] suggests that readers were looking for acceptable (if differing) treatments of death, especially the death of a child. Children often died young, and very real grief over such deaths sought release. For some, such as Dickens' friend Macready, whose own daughter had died during publication of *The Old Curiosity Shop*, the intent by Dickens to provide comfort was fully realized. Others, who sought perhaps forgetfulness rather than assuagement, objected to 'luscious deathbed scenes'.[19] Sales figures for *The Old Curiosity Shop* (100,000 copies, the largest selling of all Dickens' novels) suggest that while critics may have taken a generally unsentimental stand against the depiction of that common phenomenon the death of a child, the average reader found in it the consolation Dickens sought to convey.

Such consolation was, however, not often to be found in material as widely dispersed as the novel. Kathleen Tillotson says in *Novels of the 1840s* that 'to put a child at the centre of a novel for adults was virtually unknown when Dickens wrote *Oliver Twist* and *The Old Curiosity Shop*';[20] and George Gissing noted that 'in 1840 Little Nell struck readers not only as pathetic but as fresh and original, which indeed she was.'[21] This originality of presentation, coupled with the existence of an emotion nearly universally experienced but lending itself at that time only to intellectual and moral consolations and so remaining without any solely emotional outlet, made Nell's death all the more poignant to the Victorian reading public.

This rather simple reader response is complicated by an inadmissible corollary: innocence is inevitably corrupted by its mere accession to adulthood. It would have been difficult for either Dickens or his readers to fail to recognize Nell's potential

sexuality, while at the same time mere human fellow-feeling
would wish her to remain a happy child, and virgin, forever.
Innocent heroines would best be, and remain, children. Nell, as
Dickens' archetype of female innocence, had to remain in the
world of perpetual childhood; but, as Mark Spilka has said, 'since
there is no perpetual childhood, she must die rather than risk the
taint of sexual experience.'[22] Had Nell lived, she would have had
to marry and bear children. *Every single one* of Dickens'
important female characters marries. Adulthood without
marriage was inconceivable; later Trollope would create a
sympathetic Lily Dale, Meredith a charming Clara Middleton
(willing at least to risk spinsterhood); but Dickens could see only
Miss Tox, Miss Flite or Miss LaCreevy. The happy family is
central to his personal ethos, central to the Victorian ideal. The
determinant of success is marriage; this is true for Barbara in *The
Old Curiosity Shop*, for Kate Nickleby, for Florence Dombey, for
both Dora and Agnes in *David Copperfield*, for Esther
Summerson in *Bleak House*, for Biddy as well as Estella in *Great
Expectations*, for Amy Dorrit, and for Bella Wilfer in *Our Mutual
Friend*. But Dickens did not want Nell to marry. As a
representation of innocence and as the image of Mary Hogarth,
whom he could himself neither violate nor surrender to another,
Nell could not marry.

Nor was Dickens' response to Nell's dilemma of innocence
unusual. The list of weepers around Nell's tomb included, in the
novel itself, Grandfather Trent, his equally aged and unmarried
brother, the old sexton, and Mr Garland. Nell's death and burial
are entirely masculine scenes; Mrs Garland, the sole woman
accompanying the men who seek Nell, is inexplicably absent both
when Nell dies and when she is buried. These fictional death-
watchers seem to feast on death as much as did the living readers
K. J. Fielding mentions in *Charles Dickens*: Lord Jeffrey, John
Forster, Walter Savage Landor, Washington Irving, and Edward
FitzGerald, who 'were all quasi-bachelors, sick-at-heart, and
denied the love of children. ... She appealed to a strain of self-pity
and the lack of something in these men.'[23] The fear of sexuality
seems only a warping of an inadmissible fascination with

virginity which could more safely be expressed through identification, or identity, with Grandfather Trent, who drove as well as pursued Nell to her grave. The possibility of indulging in fantasy under cover of the most respectable of emotions drew many nineteenth-century readers to Nell and allowed public expression of inadmissible feelings.

If such release, however valuable, were Nell's only function in the novel, most readers who did not succumb to the fantasy would dismiss her as deliberately flawed, while those who could not see beyond their own lascivious needs would certainly not be considered reliable critics. But Nell is not so easily dismissable, nor are those who have objected to her.

The question of whether Nell was shaped from the 'curious and even rather repellent secretions' of Dickens' heart, as Aldous Huxley has said,[24] or from the equally curious drives of the reading public to whom he was so preternaturally responsive, does not help solve the problem of the *Old Curiosity Shop*. What Dickens thought he was doing with Nell, or what he subconsciously wished her to represent, even coupled with what his readers desired on various levels, is insufficient to explain the dynamic of Nell's function in the novel. Aldous Huxley has said of Dickens' treatment of Nell:

> He wanted to be unaware himself and he wanted his readers to be unaware of everything except Little Nell's sufferings on the one hand and her goodness and innocence on the other. But goodness and innocence and the undeservedness of suffering and even, to some extent, suffering itself are only significant in relation to the actual realities of human life. Isolated, they cease to mean anything, perhaps to exist.... Nell's virtues are marooned, as it were, in the midst of a boundless waste of unreality; isolated, they fade and die. Even her sufferings and death lack significance because of this isolation.[25]

The result of such a dichotomy between goodness and reality—the result, Huxley would say, of Dickens' vulgarity—is a critical tendency to turn away from the novel rather than to attempt to deal with its apparent conflicts. George Santayana turns away:

though the fault is mine and not his ... sometimes his
absoluteness is too much for me. When I come to the death of
Little Nell ... I skip. I can't take my liquour neat in such
draughts, and my inner man says to Dickens, Please don't. But
then I am a coward in so many ways! There are so many
things in this world that I skip, as I skip the undiluted
Dickens.[26]

Even that most broad of critics, G. K. Chesterton, turns away: 'It
is not the death of Little Nell, but the life of Little Nell, that I
object to.'[27] Obviously, any attempt at comprehensive criticism
must go beyond contemplation of the novel through the
intentional fallacy (or, one might say, through the unintentional
fallacy), for the treatment of Nell as an expression of Dickens'
subconscious desires or of the subconscious desires of his readers
offers no satisfying explanation of why she retains such force
within the novel and why her journey, her self-concept, and her
actions remain, even for the reader of today, so vital a part of the
structure of The Old Curiosity Shop.

Consequently, modern criticism has moved on to 'larger views'
of the novel. Such views rest on allegorical, mythic, fabulous, or
fairy-tale interpretations: Nell's journey parallels Christian's;
Quilp personifies evil, Nell good; the myth of rural England is
presented through Nell's rejection of the Wolverhampton
foundry in favour of the quiet churchyard of Tong; the fairy-tale
flight to rescue Nell, the fairy-tale marriage of Kit and Barbara,
both feed the public need for a modification of the observed
course of nature to account for human desires. Certainly the
novel attempts to recapture that bygone rural England where
things were simpler and purer, just as it sees a regeneration of city
folk in Kit's fecund marriage to Barbara. I refer the reader to
George Ford's Dickens and His Readers: Apects of Novel-
Criticism Since 1836 for a full view of The Old Curiosity Shop's
critical vicissitudes.[28] The fact remains that none of these analyses
is fully satisfactory in appraising both the book and Nell's role in
it. One might even call this a structural problem in the sense that
two different structures—Nell herself and the world of the

book—seem to be forced into coexistence. In her life and in her death, Nell is too idealized to fit into the realistic *world* of the novel and so seems to stand outside it. But at the same time she is an integral figure in the *idea* of the book; indeed, it is Nell's flight and death that give body to the struggle between good and evil. As a result *The Old Curiosity Shop* has been called a realistic novel (and Nell filleted out) by some and a romance (and Nell its central figure) by others. Consequently, a critic who chooses to view the novel primarily as realism, as romance, as an allegory, as a myth, as a fairy tale, as a fable, as a valuable piece of biographical information about Dickens, is forced to let a good portion of the novel slip between his fingers. It is broader than any category under which it could be subsumed.

More recent criticism tends to view Nell—usefully for the most part, although limitedly—as the representative of a concern rather than as an individual. In 1962 Gabriel Pearson, in the single most important piece of work to emerge on *The Old Curiosity Shop*, divided the novel into three 'force groups', with Quilp initiating evil and Nell good, and Dick Swiveller exhibiting the most human sort of vitality by his union of the two.[29] In 1971 James Kincaid, acknowledging Pearson's origination of the idea of force groups, expanded it by adding the idea of motion as Quilp and Nell, representing good and evil, slowly revolve around the developing Swiveller-Marchioness relationship through which most of the novel's positive action takes place. Both good and evil alone lead to death, observes Kincaid; it is the comic force—Dick Swiveller, Mrs Jarley—which opposes death.[30]

Such approaches, however valuable, still view Little Nell as largely a representative of good and cannot explain in what way she differs from the Garlands and why the particular child More weeps over and Wilde laughs at seemed to Dickens appropriate to the expression of his ideas and to Dostoevsky worth recreating. Nell and her story still do not coalesce. It is the contrast between good and evil that is important, not the individual struggle of Nell to free herself from the symbolic influence of Quilp.

It was therefore a great triumph for Dickens criticism when in 1965 Donald Fanger saw in Dickens the fusion of sentiment and

reality that he defines as 'romantic realism'. The lurid gleam of
Quilp, the bathos of Nell's death, become means of highlighting[31]
rather than mere expressions of disgust or desire, and the fabric of
Dickens can be seen more as a unit than as a patchwork. Yet even
here Nell is tacitly fingered: Dickens' 'failure to allow for the ...
monstrosity of his angels [as he allows for the monstrosity of his
devils] ... makes them ... scarcely tolerable.'[32] Even under the
umbrella of romantic realism, Nell doesn't fare very well. She's
an agent of Dickens' concerns, but she remains unredeemably
outside his techniques, and the question of her appeal or lack of it
is still merely one of taste (or lack of it, as Huxley would doubtless
interpose here). Indeed, to this day it is possible to use Nell as a
touchstone of bad taste: Mark Spilka, writing in *The Journal of
Popular Culture* (a journal which, had it existed in 1841, would
surely have reviewed *The Old Curiosity Shop* favourably and with
relish), says that '*Love Story* is *The Old Curiosity Shop* of our time
and Erich Segal its Little Nell.'[33] Obviously *The Old Curiosity
Shop* has not yet found its place in Dickens' canon of
masterpieces.

And just as obviously, Little Nell is *there*. She continues to live
beyond our poor power to interpret, as one of those characters
who, according to Georg Lukacs, 'once conceived in the vision of
their creator, live an independent life of their own; their comings
and goings, their development, their destiny is dictated by the
inner dialectic of their social and individual existence.'[34] The fact
that readers still respond to Nell and her situation attests to her
vitality.

For Dostoevsky, Little Nell evidently had that inner dialectic,
for he reinterpreted her story in the sub-plot of *The Insulted and
Injured*. As an artist rather than a critic, Dostoevsky often
attempted to find the meaning, the 'story' in everyday events. His
own works often take off from the reality of newspaper accounts
and, through what may seem the fantastic opposite of realism,
discover truths about the human soul. Dostoevsky said of himself,
'They call me a psychologist; this is not true. I am merely a realist
in a higher sense, i.e. I depict all the depths of the human soul.'[35]
Nellie Valkovsky, sister to Little Nell, emerges from Dostoevsky's

higher realism. While such imitation may be the highest form of flattery, it must be based, however, on genuine understanding before we can draw valid conclusions from it. Dostoevsky's understanding of Dickens arises from his unique interpretation of Dickens' art, which he saw as the highest form of realism and from which he drew many of his own techniques.[36] He believed that art was a direct outgrowth of contemporary existence; it 'is not only always true to reality but it cannot possibly be untrue to contemporary reality. Otherwise it is not true art.'[37] Such artistic reality must be seen and heard in everyday life; it must be *real*. During his exile in Switzerland, he complained to his brother Michael that he could no longer write realistically because he was no longer in daily contact with Russian life: 'I must be at home, where I can hear everything with my own ears and see it with my own eyes' (*Pis'ma* I, 44). For Dostoevsky the eye was singularly important, both literally and figuratively, for it opened reality to the artist and enabled him to perceive its essence:

> Not the subject but the eye is the main thing. If one has an eye one will always find a subject. If, in you, the eye is missing, if one is blind, one will find nothing in any subject. Oh, the eye is all-important; what to one eye appears to be a poem, to another one will be merely a heap. (*DW* 465)

Dostoevsky felt he had that eye, that ability to perceive what others—non-artists—could not. He found in Dickens the same ability. Although Dickens had never seen Pickwick with his own eyes, he nonetheless '[perceived] him in the diversity of the reality observed by him ... [and] thus, this character is as real as an actually existing one' (*DW* 82–83). Dickens too possessed the artistic eye.

This sort of realism Dostoevsky found missing in much of what was called contemporary realistic art. Gué's 'The Last Supper', for instance, portrayed Christ's last meal with a fidelity to real meals yet failed to show the overriding idea of the picture which was the momentousness of the outcome of Christ's death—in fact, the whole of Christianity. In such an instance, mere realism uninformed by an idea becomes no more than deceit. It is the idea, the ideal, the essence of reality that must transcend the mere literal presentation of faces and postures. True realism must be informed by an ideal and must create a 'type' whose existence in some way stands for actual reality. This familiar nineteenth-century critical term has been described by Lukacs:

> What makes a type a type is not its average quality, not its mere individual being, however profoundly conceived; what makes it a type is that in it all the humanly and socially essential determinants are present on their highest level of development, in the ultimate unfolding of the possibilities latent in them, in extreme presentation of their extremes, rendering concrete the peaks and limits of men and epochs. ... The live portrayal of the complete human personality is possible only if the writer attempts to create types.[38]

Type, so defined, 'constitutes the bridge between the present and the future, the real and the social ideal,' according to René Wellek.[39] Hugo says, 'Un type n'abrége pas, il condense.'[40] Dostoevsky himself consciously attempted to create such types in his novels. In describing his use of the Nechaev murder in *The Possessed*, Dostoevsky maintains:

> Neither Nechaev, nor Ivanov, nor the circumstances of the murder are known to me, except through the newspapers. But even if I knew it all, I wouldn't copy it. I am only taking the actual fact. My imagination may very well differ in the highest degree from the event which occurred, and my Petr Verkhovensky may not at all resemble Nechaev; but it seems to me that, once my imagination was stimulated, it created the character, the type that corresponds to this crime. (*Pis'ma*, II, 288)

For Dostoevsky, Little Nell and her grandfather represented 'type' or 'genre' (two terms he sometimes used interchangeably). He has described Nell and her grandfather as 'ideal', 'splendid', 'typical', 'fine'. He saw them as types that Russian literature had not yet been able to achieve. Nor did their ideality detract from the absolute realism of their presentation; for Dostoevsky 'idealism is as realistic as realism' (*DW* 387). Perfect realism, then, not only can but must represent the perfect ideal.

This seems a promising theoretical combination for appraising Little Nell, for it allows for Dickens' obvious realism of depiction while maintaining the ideality that he sought to express through that reality. The very fantasy and 'unreality' which critics find in Little Nell are for Dostoevsky the means of evaluating the extent of her reality. To him 'fantastic incidents are *facts*, and he is capable of understanding why they have come into existence. He does not only register the data for which the [newspaper] columns have already been prepared. His mind is open to see and understand life as it is.'[41] Part of this understanding, according to Dostoevsky himself, was an ability to balance simultaneous opposites and to create the most highly and fully realistic ideal out of the fantastic events that made up everyday life. Like Dickens' 'fantastic side of familiar things', Dostoevsky's realism transcends mere reality and fuses with the ideal, the type. And for him Little Nell was one such ideal, one such type.

It is clear that Dickens intended Nell to be both real and representative, a figure of 'romantic realism' moving within the structures of his romantically realistic world: the city, industrialization, popular art, religion. If she can be seen as at once a romanticization representing what might be and also a realistic response to the situations Dickens chooses to present in *The Old Curiosity Shop* and which he clearly intends to be taken at face value as indictments of wrong and celebrations of the possibilities of good, we will have a clearer view of Dickens' art, of his paradoxical kind of realism and how it works. This is particularly important for early novels such as *The Old Curiosity Shop*, because it is evident that Dickens' concerns with the nature of the human soul and the existence and nature of evil are present throughout his works, not mere excrescences and not limited to his later, 'greater' novels. It is important to be able to appraise *The Old Curiosity Shop* in the light of Dickens' development as an artist; and to do so we must approach it on Dickens' own terms, from the point of view of his paradoxical realism.

Dostoevsky's Nellie Valkovsky in *The Insulted and Injured* is patterned after Little Nell. Her tortured existence is an outward expression of what Dostoevsky found in Little Nell. In her Dostoevsky shows his vision of the depths that Dickens' child could not reveal and that Dickens himself perhaps wished to hide or disregard. Dostoevsky recognized that even artists were capable of closing themselves off from the truth beneath reality:

> Nearly always we perceive reality as we *wish* to perceive it, as we wish to interpret it to ourselves, *biased as we are*. ... At times, I swear, we would rather believe in a miracle and in an impossibility than in reality, in a truth *which we do not wish to see*. (*DW* 697 [emphasis Dostoevsky's])

But of course this does not mean that the truth is not there. In Nellie Valkovsky Dostoevsky recreated a truth he found in Little Nell, a truth independent of its creator's intent and its critics' limitations. In no way do I wish to suggest that we will find Little Nell herself in Dostoevsky's lines and pictures; as Fanger has amply shown, Dostoevsky transmuted Dickens' romantic realism into something uniquely his:

> In approaching Dostoevsky, who drew on Dickens as on Balzac, we must consider a writer who is utterly without the Dickensian Victorian ballast and who, sharing many elements of Dickens' vision and using many of the same techniques, realizes their extremer potentialities, leaving behind 'normalcy', community, and proportion.[42]

And yet he seeks the same truth.

If, unlike Gide's hero in *Les Faux-Monnayeurs*, Dickens seems to accommodate the facts to his ideas, at the level of meaning the ideas are validated by their accommodation to the facts. It is these 'higher facts', this 'higher realism', that Dostoevsky sought in Dickens.

CHAPTER II

Dostoevsky and *The Old Curiosity Shop*: Nellie Valkovsky

To climb from evil to a high spiritual level one must denounce the evil in oneself and suffer terribly, and these sufferings Dostoevsky depicted.

NICHOLAS BERDAIEV

The Insulted and Injured is an early and not entirely successful work. In the main plot, Natasha Nikolaevna Ikhmenev goes to live with Alyosha Valkovsky, her girlhood lover and son of the completely amoral Prince Valkovsky, who has maliciously ruined Natasha's father, once overseer of the Prince's estate. The story follows Alyosha's defection from Natasha and her father's gradual awakening of forgiveness for what he feels is her immoral behaviour toward him. The sub-plot parallels and highlights this story. In it 13-year-old Nellie, an orphan adopted by default almost by the story's narrator Vanya (who is, in a typically Dostoevskian complication, hopelessly in love with Natasha), vacillates between her desire to ally herself with Vanya emotionally, thus achieving goodness and love, and her compulsion to demonstrate that she does not need others' love, thus achieving independence. Nellie's history is the catalyst for the resolution of Natasha's situation; through revelation of Nellie's own history of forgiveness refused and forgiveness too late, Ikhmenev learns to forgive his daughter for wronging him. In the end Natasha and Ikhmenev are united through forgiveness, while Nellie, who has refused to forgive her father (Prince Valkovsky, as it turns out) for his brutal treatment of her mother, dies embittered.

In its details the story of Nellie Valkovsky in *The Insulted and Injured* is so similar to Little Nell's story in *The Old Curiosity Shop* that Viacheslav Kirpotin notes as a matter of course in his introduction to a reprinting of the novel (Moscow 1964) how strongly 'the plot line of Nellie in Dostoevsky's novel [recalls] the plot line in Dickens' novel.'[1] Nellie's only living relative appears to be her grandfather, an Englishman with the specifically English name of Jeremy Smith. Smith's only daughter is Nellie's mother; although adored by her father, she elopes with a rogue and bears Nellie, who resembles her in feature and temperament. After her money is exhausted, her husband leaves her and she returns to St Petersburg to seek her father's forgiveness. Smith refuses reconciliation with his daughter but conceives a fondness for his granddaughter, to whom he gives lessons; in return, she begs a few kopeks for food for him. When her mother dies unforgiven soon after their return to St Petersburg, Nellie remains under her grandfather's protection for a few more months until he too dies. Cared for thereafter by the novel's narrator, Vanya, Nellie finally achieves a sort of happiness, of which she promptly dies amid flowers and sunshine in the first happy home she has known, a haven never to be enjoyed on earth.

In addition to a similarity of background, Little Nell and Nellie appear to be alike in the effects of their brief lives. Nell's flight and pursuit reconcile Trent and his brother as no other event could; Nellie, witness to her mother's unhappiness and her grandfather's distress because of his refusal to forgive his daughter until her death obviates all forgiveness, effects a reconciliation between Ikhmenev, in whose home her final days are spent, and his daughter Natasha.

Seen thus in outline, Nellie Valkovsky could well have been patterned, in character and partially in role, directly after Little Nell. Both are children of a forbidden liaison. Both girls are helped by their grandfathers after their mothers die, and both beg to get money for their own and their grandfathers' survival. Each effects a family reconciliation, and each feels completely cherished only after death becomes inevitable. It is these general similarities which elicit comparisons such as Kirpotin's between the two novels.

There are of course other similarities between the two novels. The major one is their authors' early and continuing fascination with mystery. Both Dickens and Dostoevsky were from the beginning interested in 'detective fiction', in the solving of mysteries, and both began their investigation of the nature of mystery with the mystery of identity. Little Nell develops personally from an unsavoury hidden episode of love, a theme Dickens is to carry to its fullest in *Bleak House*, where he works out the complex plot of Esther Summerson's identity and heritage and the effect of that heritage on the interrelation of all that is human. Dostoevsky too carries out the idea of the mystery of character development through Myshkin's inherited instability in *The Idiot* and later in *The Brothers Karamazov*, where all are responsible for human interrelation and the mystery of unknown identity becomes a symbol for the human condition. And although both authors turned in later works to genuine mysteries—the murder in *Bleak House*, the death of Fyodor Karamazov, the tantalizingly unresolved mystery of *Edwin Drood*—neither ceased to view mystery in terms of identity (and, of course, identity in terms of mystery).

Both Dickens and Dostoevsky also tended toward melodramatization of mystery. The cloak of secrecy was carefully woven and embellished with many a cryptic embroidery precisely in an effort to stir a curiosity in the reader and therefore a response in the reader. And both authors became masters at melodramatic suspense; indeed, Dickens has been criticized for this very mastery. Particularly in the early novels of both writers, the tendency to overdramatize events led to a constant danger of overwriting, especially in the area of characterization. Little Nell and Nellie have been seen as victims of such overwriting. These similarities of viewpoint and technique make *The Insulted and*

Injured and *The Old Curiosity Shop* comparable in theory as well as plot and suggest a similarity of artistic development often claimed for the two authors but less often specified through detailed comparison. In the next two chapters I hope to show the extent of such similarity as it can be brought to bear on a fresh approach to Dickens.

Having detailed the likenesses between Little Nell and her namesake in *The Insulted and Injured*, however, one must immediately acknowledge extensive differences between the two girls. Most obvious is the fact that Little Nell's grandfather cares for her, while Nellie's seems torn between love and rejection; even his love can only be expressed through harshness. Although both girls are figures of innocence threatened, Nell appears to seek escape while Nellie cautiously tests the effects of sexual submission. While both girls suffer from the world's mistreatments, only Nellie overtly believes that she deserves her sufferings. Although both must repay obligations and refuse the benevolence of others, Nellie alone seems conscious of the possibility of paying for kindness with self-inflicted suffering. N. A. Dobroliubov, analysing *The Insulted and Injured* as an example of Dostoevsky's 'cruel talent', likened her to other of Dostoevsky's children; he believed Dostoevsky dwelt upon the 'type, early developed, of the sick, proud child—and he returns to it in Netochka [Nezvanovna], and in the Little Hero, and now in Nellie.'[2] She is one of the 'insulted and injured' whom Dostoevsky describes throughout his career. She combines the natural innocence of childhood* with an understanding of human nature which comes to her as a result of her sufferings and her observations of the sufferings of others. The author's major interest in her seems to lie in the causes and results of her sufferings rather than in their mere description.

* Like Nell, Nellie appears of uncertain age, somewhere around thirteen, although Dostoevsky, like Dickens, sometimes emphasizes her childlikeness by making her appear smaller, younger, or more vulnerable than her years. One character in Dostoevsky's novel estimates her age at ten or eleven, although she turns out to be thirteen; likewise Little Nell is always shown in short dresses and loose hair in Cattermole and Browne's illustrations, although she is nearly fourteen.

In spite of the apparent psychic differences between the two girls—in fact, *because* of them—it is necessary to ask why Dostoevsky bothered to pattern Nellie after Little Nell. He might have chosen that model in order to prove its invalidity; he might have wished to show that the Little Nell Dickens conceived was foolish, maudlin, sentimental, impossible. But these possibilities are not likely in view of Dostoevsky's constant reiteration of Dickens' ability to capture the essence of character. It is more likely that Dostoevsky was attempting to *develop* Dickens' idea of Little Nell just as, later, he was consciously to develop Pickwick into Myshkin of *The Idiot*. We have no examples of Dostoevsky writing out of hatred, with a desire to destroy; instead, we see him plumbing the depths of human nature in an attempt to understand and to convey that understanding.

Therefore the similarities between Little Nell and Nellie become less important than the apparent differences, for it is through these differences that Dostoevsky dissects what *he* saw in Little Nell and anatomizes it for the reader. Apparently unlike Little Nell, Nellie chooses to suffer and to sacrifice herself in order to gain independence. She seems to attract and approve punishment. Vanya's first acquaintance with her comes when she appears at his flat, which was formerly her grandfather's, to get her books. She flees; he follows her home and there witnesses a remarkable scene in which she is fiercely beaten for being late. She stoically accepts the punishment, almost as if she welcomed it as an opportunity to demonstrate her ability to bear it.

Her landlady next attempts to sell her into prostitution, and Nellie acquiesces in the attempt because her innocence is one of the few saleable items with which she can pay back her obligations. (Little Nell fled unequivocally from Quilp's suggested sexual violation; Nellie seeks to flee even more fiercely from obligation.) Even her helplessness seems to her reason to seek punishment. And so she does not resist the landlady's attempt to sell her sexually; once rescued from that degradation, she rises from her sickbed to clean house for her rescuer (Vanya). When a kind family offer to adopt her, she refuses, saying that she will seek menial work instead. Of her employers she says: 'They'd scold me, but I'd say nothing on purpose. They'd beat me, but I wouldn't speak, I wouldn't speak. Let them beat me—I wouldn't cry for anything. That would annoy them even more if I didn't cry' (*II* 158). From her state of weakness and inability Nellie seeks to create an independent self who, even at the expense of her dignity and health, would never need to feel entirely inferior. Bestowing on others the right to scold or hurt her is the only way she can hold or exercise power. Dostoevsky gives no indication that such behaviour springs from conscious self-analysis; indeed, he presents Nellie as specifically unconscious of the motives of her actions in order to trace those motives to their deepest and most real sources—to find the ideal, the type, of such suffering.

Ironically, Nellie's constant, almost frantic self-sacrifice is beneficial to everyone. Vanya lives better because she does his housework; he in turn is able to buy her decent clothing, which she could never have done for herself. Were Dostoevsky to leave Nellie at that, he would have given us the typical child who learns to be useful and receives the respect and blessing of all who know her—indeed, she would have been quite the sort of child Dickens' readers found in Little Nell.

But this is only the most superficial view of Nellie's character. Dostoevsky creates in her a sufferer, bearing the mistreatment of the world because she feels she deserves it. Her sufferings—their causes and their effects—create a parallel with the novel's main plot, in which Prince Valkovsky is the Manichaean force that threatens the possibility of ordinary human relationships. Soviet criticism has emphasized his anti-idealistic behaviouralism within a context of Dostoevsky's 'social protest' writings, but in fact the novel deals primarily with the nature of love and its battle with the *culpa*—not necessarily *felix*—that drives most of Dostoevsky's characters to seek suffering of one sort or another. Nellie's story becomes the archetype, showing what the outcome of the other characters' struggles will be if they are unleavened by the love that seeks and gives forgiveness. Nellie's story is thus instructive in the most profound sense, for it can teach how to live.

It is not fortuitous that the disclosure of Nellie's history, her confession of love for Vanya, and her discovery of Ikhmenev's casting off of his daughter occur simultaneously. Nellie overhears Ikhmenev declare that he will never forgive his daughter. She explains her immediate agitation by telling Vanya (in outline only) the story of her grandfather's unforgiving pride, which doomed her mother to die alone and unloved. This revelation of her history is a necessary preliminary to her unexpected confession of love to Vanya. Following as it does Ikhmenev's cursing of his daughter, Nellie's sudden recognition of the need to love requires some visible causation, and this Dostoevsky supplies by inserting at this point in his novel the Dickensian story of love, betrayal, and non-forgiveness which makes Nellie appear so like Little Nell. 'It was', Vanya tells the reader,

> the story of a woman abandoned and living on after the wreck of her happiness, sick, worn out and forsaken by every one, rejected by the last creature to whom she could look—her father, once wronged by her and crazed by intolerable sufferings and humiliations.... It was a strange story of the mysterious, hardly comprehensible relations of the crazy old man with the little grandchild who already understood him, who already, child as she was, understood many things that some men do not attain to in long years of their smooth and carefully guarded lives. (*II* 163)

When we hear of her grandfather's refusal to forgive his daughter until he reaches her deathbed too late to say the words that would heal both her wounds and his, we begin to understand not only Nellie's reaction to the novel's world but also her significance to the other characters in the novel.

Nellie's knowledge of the horror of dying unforgiven, awakened by Ikhmenev's re-creation of the very situation that doomed her grandfather, is connected in her own mind (and Dostoevsky's) with her desire to love and be loved, a desire that she had submerged beneath her need to remain free of obligation so that she could control her own life. In a flash of openness she confesses that she loves Vanya because he is the only person other

than her mother who has cared for her. Dostoevsky places this
unexpected softening in conjunction with Nellie's absorption
with forgiveness because it is her fear of being unforgiven that
causes her to seek, and give, love. She is finally able to see the
need for forgiveness, a vital facet of the individual's accession to
full humanity. Part of Dostoevsky's ethic of expiation involves
forgiveness of others for the sufferings they have caused and
acceptance of the forgiveness of others for the sufferings one has
caused them. Stretched on the rack between her impulses toward
retribution and those toward reconciliation, Nellie struggles to
understand her own nature, which needs to forgive.

But it is not enough to forgive and be forgiven by others.
Above all one must be able to forgive oneself. Such self-
forgiveness is tantamount to acceptance of the evil within, an
acceptance that requires suffering. A part of Nellie desires to
punish others for the hurts she gives herself—a part she is never
able to subdue. Thus, although she can recognize her need for
forgiveness of and by others and can even seek to effect
reconciliation between others, she is never able to love and
forgive what is evil in herself.

Nellie's ultimate inability to forgive herself is bound up with
her desperate need to be in command of her own life and
destiny—to be independent. Because so much of her life is in the
hands of others, she feels that she has no character to assert and
therefore no way to establish her personal worth. At the same
time, because she is not often able to love her imperfect human
self, she withdraws from the love of others in order to avoid the
obligations love places upon her. Nellie prefers to retain the
power to forgive by loving others more than they can love her or
more than they deserve, or by exercising control over them (even
through the voluntary increase of her sufferings on others' behalf)
whereby she can confer the benefits.

With the revelation of Nellie's history the major
correspondence with *The Old Curiosity Shop* is drawn. We know
as much about Nellie as we know about Nell. Yet Dostoevsky
does not end his book here. At the end of *The Insulted and
Injured* Nellie dies, as does Nell; but between the revelation of

history and the inevitable outcome of her suffering Dostoevsky shows the reader very clearly *why* Nellie behaves as she does. It is here that he expands upon Dickens' plot, exploring what Dickens seems to have evaded. How would a child in Little Nell's circumstances really feel?

In Part III of *The Insulted and Injured*, which covers less than two days, Dostoevsky presents the concrete roots of Nellie's sufferings. When she first meets the novel's ostensible central character, Prince Valkovsky, she immediately recognizes him as the father who had deserted her. Her hasty embrace followed by flight indicates instinctive love and forgiveness coupled with rejection of one who has caused her to suffer. By exploring Prince Valkovsky's character in Part III, Dostoevsky depicts the society that creates suffering. The Prince dismisses his responsibility for Nellie's mother by observing, in Dostoevsky's best Machiavellian manner, that if he had returned the money he took from her: 'I should have deprived her of the enjoyment of being miserable entirely owing to me, and of cursing me for it all her life' (*II* 248–49). He is convinced that people derive pleasure from contemplating their unjustified sufferings and remarks: 'there is positively a lofty ecstasy in unhappiness of that kind, in feeling oneself magnanimous and absolutely in the right, and in having every right to call one's opponent a scoundrel' (*II* 249). And so by being a scoundrel he argues that he is actually a benefactor to those he has abused. This sophistry allows him to use others without acknowledging the vileness of his behaviour. It is the existence of such people that makes Nellie's victimization inevitable, for good people will always be such a man's prey and will always suffer from his treatment of them. Prince Valkovsky thus represents the theoretical root of Nellie's sufferings.

In spite of the repugnance of Valkovsky's philosophy, however, there is for Dostoevsky truth in what he says. Nellie illustrates how enjoyment and self-justification can sometimes be found only in suffering. Nellie's mother too must have found gratification in being able to blame her poverty and wretchedness upon the meanness of another, for then her own foolishness in choosing him as her husband could conveniently be ignored.

In the first three parts of the novel, then, Dostoevsky presents all aspects of the basic themes of love and forgiveness. Ikhmenev loved his daughter and was therefore vulnerable to her rejection of him; Nellie's mother loved the Prince and could not forgive him for deserting her; Grandfather Smith's forgiveness comes too late; Nellie is the fruit of unjustified suffering coupled with ultimate non-forgiveness. Love is vulnerability; the right to forgive is power. Forgiveness itself, however, is both ultimate love and ultimate surrender of power. These ideas employ Nellie as focal point and resolution.

In Part IV we learn that Nellie is dying. In her final days she continues to act out her four basic ambivalences (innocence versus sex, desert of sufferings, obligations versus independence, and repayment through reciprocal suffering or forgiveness), but Dostoevsky provides a common focus: control. Forgiveness and love require the surrender of control; evil and suffering are attractive because they allow retention of control.

Following her experience in the whorehouse, Nellie consciously uses her sexual self as a means of gaining control over others. Her first attempt is with the doctor who treats her fever. Her experience with men is limited enough to suggest to her that a sexual relationship is the most likely sort to be formed with men, and so quite naturally she moves the relationship in that direction, if only in order to see what effect it will have on the doctor (who is an elderly man and not a usual or suitable love object for a thirteen-year-old girl).* Nellie therefore promises to take her medicines if the doctor will kiss her and will promise to marry her when she grows up. He in turn puts conditions on his willingness to relate to Nellie; he says he will maintain a relationship with her, 'if you turn out a good, well-brought-up young lady, and will be obedient and will. ...' Such a relationship

---

* It is worth pointing out that Nellie finds or creates a sexual aspect in any heterosexual relationship she forms; in fact, it seems to be an inevitable concomitant of any extended relationship between an unattached man and an unattached woman, of whatever age, in Dostoevsky's works.

is for Nellie more secure than one in which love is freely and unconditionally given, for with the doctor she knows what she must give in order to obtain his regard. Tentative control is established.

Nellie's pseudo-courtship with the doctor points to her approaching sexual maturity, a problem which Little Nell too faced but was forced to retreat from. But what if a child were not to retreat? One solution might be the benevolent protection of a father figure. A more reasonable solution for Nellie, of course, would have been Vanya. Indeed, Vanya seems almost constantly aware of Nellie's physical presence, her femaleness and dependence. When he is sick and she falls asleep tending him, he says, 'very softly I kissed that thin little arm.' Later, when she confesses she has been reading his novel he says, 'I don't know what I would have given to have kissed her at that moment.'

Although Vanya himself seems unaware of 'the little romance', as Albert Guérard calls it,[3] Nellie sees and responds to it as any sensitive adolescent would. To inspire love is to control. When she discovers Vanya's love for Natasha, she must seek another means of controlling him. So she withdraws, forcing him to approach and soothe, to seek conciliation: 'Her strange ways, her caprices, at times almost hatred for me, continued up to the day when she ceased to live with me, till the catastrophe which was the end of our romance.' The Russian word 'roman' [POMAH] means both 'romance' and 'novel'. Vanya uses the word here largely in the latter sense, meaning until the end of the story in which he is participating and which he, as the author, is also writing. But the second meaning of 'roman' cannot be dismissed, as Garnett indicates by translating it as 'romance' rather than merely 'novel'. Vanya's choice of the word shows that he too senses a sexual side to the relationship, and his coupling of it with Nellie's peevish behaviour toward him indicates that he is aware of the connection between his implicit rejection of her in favour of Natasha and Nellie's apparent hatred of him for it. It is therefore not surprising that at the same time Nellie is rejecting Vanya for his failure to love her, she is attaching herself to the doctor, whose unfailing patience has won her over:

Nellie was very fond of him and always greeted him with a good-humoured smile however sad she had been before he came. For his part the old man began coming to us every day and sometimes even twice a day even when Nellie had begun to get up and had quite recovered, and she seemed to have so bewitched him that he could not spend a day without hearing her laugh and make fun of him, sometimes very amusingly. He began bringing her picture-books, always of an edifying character. One of them he brought on purpose for her. Then he began bringing her dainties, sweetmeats in pretty boxes. On such occasions he would come in with an air of triumph, as though it were his birthday, and Nellie guessed at once that he had come with a present. But he did not display the presents, but only laughed slyly, seated himself beside Nellie, hinting that if a certain young lady knew how to behave herself and had been deserving of commendation in his absence the young lady in question would merit a handsome reward. And all the while he looked at her so simply and good-naturedly that though Nellie laughed at him in the frankest way, at the same time there was a glow of sincere and affectionate devotion in her beaming eyes at that moment. At last the old man solemnly got up from his chair, took out a box of sweets and as he handed it to Nellie invariably added: 'To my future amiable spouse.' At that moment he was certainly even happier than Nellie. (*II* 263)

This is obviously a courtship scene. One is reminded of Svidrigailov's courting of his fifteen-year-old bride-to-be in *Crime and Punishment*, or Stavrogin's early feelings for the child he later ravishes in *The Possessed*. There is a persistent longing, in Dostoevsky's works, of an older man for a young girl, even for a child. The doctor feels this longing for Nellie; and Nellie, whether she reciprocates his feelings or not, plays upon his longing, urging him to further gallantries by her pleasure in his treats and games. She can control her relationship with him by behaving in certain pre-specified ways, and for the first time in her life she is certain of the rewards elicited by her behaviour. The safest relationship is one bound by conditions whose fulfilment assures acceptability.

The parallels with the Natasha-Ikhmenev plot are obvious. Ikhmenev requires that Natasha fulfil certain conditions before he will forgive her. Natasha, on the other hand, refuses to set such conditions for the errant Alyosha, thus requiring of him perfect love which he is unable to give. The pressure of her failure to make demands drives Alyosha away, and Natasha is left alone and ruined. Nellie sees Natasha's plight; in her fury she urges that Natasha refuse to allow her father to forgive her. The failure of the surrender of control is no less painful than the failure of the refusal to surrender control. There seems to be no solution to the problem Dostoevsky poses in *The Insulted and Injured*.

Nellie's need for control arises from her acute sense of suffering. She feels simultaneously that she is innocent and that she has brought her sufferings upon herself. In both roles, as we have seen, she maintains independence—and therefore control. As victim of an incurable heart disease, she is innocent of causing her own suffering and therefore calls forth others' pity, but as a member of a society whose other members seem able to love one another freely, she cannot but see herself as intrinsically evil and therefore as the cause of her own sufferings. Others' love puts her in their debt, increasing her dependence and therefore her sense of unworthiness. And so she has to resist love in order to have an opportunity to show that she is not dependent. At the same time, she believes that if she can define the love relationship herself and control its intensity and movement, perhaps that power will prove her goodness. Yet by attempting to overcome her evil by her own efforts, she becomes, like the Underground Man, the main cause of her own suffering; but Nellie cannot know this and so must continue to act on a self-created plan which makes control of others the highest aim.

Control implies independence, but in fact it carries obligations. Because Vanya has given her a comfortable home, she must care for him. Because she fears Vanya will marry Natasha, she offers to become Natasha's servant so that the humiliation of not being chosen as Vanya's marriage partner could be transferred from his act of repudiation to her own act of subjection. One cannot maintain control and also act independently, for all acts must be chosen or rejected based upon the amount of control they offer. As people become kinder, Nellie must become more severe. Thus, when Ikhmenev repeats his offer of a permanent home, she refuses categorically:

> I am wicked, we're all wicked, but you're more wicked than anyone.... Yes, more wicked than I am, because you won't forgive your daughter. You want to forget her altogether and take another child. How can you forget your own child? How can you love me? Whenever you look at me you'll remember I'm a stranger and that you had a daughter of your own whom you'd forgotten, for you're a cruel man. And I don't want to live with cruel people. (*II* 270)

She denies obligation to Ikhmenev by condemning his motives. She denies obligation to Vanya by saying she will become a beggar:

> 'It's not shameful to beg. I beg of all, and that's not the same as begging from one. To beg of one is shameful, but it's not shameful to beg of all'; that's what one beggar-girl said to me. I'm little, I've no means of earning money. I'll ask from all. I won't! I won't! I'm wicked, I'm wickeder than anyone. See how wicked I am! (*II* 271)

She proves this statement by throwing one of Vanya's teacups to the floor. Independence is control but dooms the individual to self-exacerbating suffering.

Repayment of obligation restores control but sacrifices independence. Ashamed of her violent rejection of Vanya, Nellie turns compulsively from hate to love and wishes to replace the broken cup; but just as compulsively she humiliates herself by begging for the money to buy a new cup. Vanya analyses her rapid shifts of mood:

> It was as though she wanted to shock or alarm some one by her

exploits, as though she were showing off before some one. ...
She seemed purposely trying to aggravate her wound by this
mysterious behaviour, this mistrustfulness of us all; as though
she enjoyed her own pain by this *egoism of suffering* if I may so
express it. This aggravation of suffering and this revelling in it I
could understand; it is the enjoyment of many of the insulted
and injured, oppressed by destiny, and smarting under the
sense of its injustice. ... She seemed trying to astonish and
alarm us by her exploits, her caprices and wild pranks, as
though she really were asserting herself against us. (*II* 273)

Only through such self-assertion can Nellie resist the pull to
succumb to a dependence on the love of others, a dependence
which she could not bear. In none of the ways which Nellie
apparently differs from Little Nell can she find satisfaction, for
Dostoevsky sees them as mutually exclusive. Independence
precludes love; forgiveness surrenders forever the power to
withhold forgiveness.

At this point Dostoevsky appears to have effectively disconnected
himself from *The Old Curiosity Shop*. Similarities of situation
have been submerged in differences of philosophy as Nellie works
toward a relief of her sufferings through a framework which
clearly includes forgiveness. If Dostoevsky continued to veer
away from Little Nell's story we would be fully justified in
maintaining that he had merely chosen a clever plot device for
initiating his own story.

However, it is at the point of Nellie's final illness that
Dostoevsky's story *returns* to Dickens, indicating a distinct
consciousness on Dostoevsky's part of parallel development. As
Nellie lies on her deathbed, her history is told in full, filling in the
sketchy outline Nellie furnished Vanya. And this history is the
impetus for a family reunification, a blossoming of love reflected
by the flowers on Nellie's grave no less than by the winter fruits
on Little Nell's. And it is this re-establishment of parallelism that
allows us to suggest that Little Nell was more than a mechanical
model for Nellie.

Let us now look at Nellie's revelation of her history. By telling Ikhmenev the story of her grandfather's lack of forgiveness, Nellie can soften his heart toward his own daughter; she can reconcile the two. For Nellie this is an opportunity to give back what she has received from others: love that seeks no repayment. Nellie is given a second chance to start anew and to eschew her assertive and independent self. Yet she does not do so. Rather than rejoicing in her selflessness, she has a fatal epileptic fit. She dreams of her grandfather scolding her; she dreams of begging money for him only to have him reject her because he believes she has kept some of the money for herself. In her dream of her grandfather, self-sacrifice gains no rewards and she is thrown back into suffering that others (her grandfather) impose upon her. In spite of the love and attention showered on her, she cannot respond.

Only in the final half-dozen pages of the novel does Dostoevsky fully reveal the deeply hidden springs that had formed and nourished Nellie's character. Masloboev's detective work discloses that Prince Valkovsky is not only Nellie's father, but in all probability her legal father, and that Nellie's mother retained proof of the marriage in order to be able 'to crush her seducer by her spiritual grandeur' in refusing to take back either him or the money he stole. 'She fed on evil dreams instead of bread,' says Masloboev; and the insult of the Prince's rejection embittered her soul so deeply that, as the Prince himself had predicted, she cursed him on her deathbed, refusing him the forgiveness she had herself sought so fruitlessly from her father. Her bitterness and her curses never ceased to echo in Nellie's childish heart. The girl's three weeks with Vanya and six weeks with the Ikhmenevs were enough to show her how to accept love, and she learned to forgive the innocent so that she might in turn seek their forgiveness for her own evil acts. She forgives Ikhmenev for his mistakenly severe treatment of his daughter; she forgives Vanya for loving Natasha and not her; she even forgives Natasha for not loving Vanya. Yet her mother's curses are never forgotten.

Three days before her death Nellie confesses to Vanya that she carries a letter from her mother to the Prince. Her mother's dying instructions to her were to go to her father and reveal her identity; if he did not repulse her, perhaps her mother might be able to forgive him as her own father had finally forgiven her, although that forgiveness came too late for either to be cleansed by it. 'But Nellie had not done her mother's bidding. She knew all, but she had not gone to the Prince, and had died unforgiving' (*II* 345). Nellie herself says: 'I've been reading the Gospel lately. There it says we must forgive all our enemies. Well, I've read that, but I've not forgiven *him* all the same. ... And so I curse him, not on my own account but on mother's' (*II* 344).

In spite of her experience with the corrosive power of non-forgiveness, and in spite of her life-giving reconciliation of Ikhmenev and Natasha, Nellie is in the end unable to forgive her father. From the nature of her dreams, the reader can surmise that she could not forgive her grandfather either and so suffered the mental pangs of this dual torment. Nellie's soul is so corroded by the bitter events of her childhood that she cannot recapture the innocence which comes with pure love and forgiveness. As pure love relinquishes control, so does forgiveness. To forgive is to open oneself fully to the invasion of human demands and desires. Nellie's final tragedy is that she cannot do this; she cannot give up her pride to the unscrupulous Prince (and I think Dostoevsky creates for Nellie a situation in which the one she must forgive is unworthy of it, showing, if not solving, the problem of undeserved forgiveness). Nellie's own sufferings should have enabled her to forgive, but they did not. Instead, they created a need for control over others that made forgiveness impossible.

Vanya says of Nellie that 'she did not understand her own feelings and could not express them,' but in fact she expresses them very well through her contradictory personality. She cannot hate, but she cannot completely love either. Both good and evil are mixed in Nellie, and she is helpless to suppress either. In all of Dostoevsky's characters the holy and the profane co-exist (even Sonia, who alone can lead Raskolnikov to salvation, is a prostitute). Dostoevsky sees that man, try as he will, cannot divest himself of evil. He must instead admit it, subdue it, and suffer for it, thus turning it into beneficial channels. Nellie, young and

inexperienced as she is, does not know how to do this. She tries
alternately to suppress first one side of herself and then another,
and as a result her behaviour is in constant vacillation. The more
successful her efforts to integrate herself into Vanya's world, the
less she is in contact with her whole self. Her ultimate inability to
forgive saps her vitality.

Because she cannot forgive but continues to need love, Nellie
must die. 'Even now Nellie held out for a long time; for a long
time she intentionally concealed from us her tears of
reconciliation and only at last surrendered completely. ... And,
strange to say, the more the disease gained upon her, the softer,
sweeter and more open she became with us' (*II* 328). Indeed so;
for only the promise of rescue through death could shift the
burden of dependence enough to allow Nellie to accept love.
Death is the ultimate repayment. Once assured of imminent
death—and *only* then—Nellie can allow herself a happiness
dependent upon others. For her, death becomes the ultimate
means of self-control.

Dobroliubov thought the ending of *The Insulted and Injured*
pessimistic in the extreme, expressing Dostoevsky's belief that
human beings are doomed to remain ever unfulfilled.

Man's search to preserve his individuality, to remain himself,
never succeeds, and whichever of the searchers does not
succeed in dying early of consumption or another wasting
disease comes as a result only to bitterness, unsociability,
madness, or simply quiet torpor, suppressing in himself all
human nature, or a sincere acknowledgement of himself as
something lower than a person.[4]

Polzinsky takes a more optimistic view:

In her short life Nellie felt and suffered so much and expended
so much spiritual energy that nothing more was left her, and
the poor little one paid with her life for prematurely tasting of
the tree of knowledge of good and what, failing death, would
have been evil.[5]

Polzinsky suggests Nellie's fate, a fate Dickens denied Little Nell: sexual maturity. Dostoevsky shows very clearly the helplessness of women within sexual liaisons: Mrs Ikhmenev is powerless even to suggest to her husband that he forgive their daughter; Natasha is totally dependent on Alyosha's whim for the maintenance of her reputation, and the Prince even suggests that her audacity in living with Alyosha is punishable by imprisonment. To marry would be to sell once and for all her innocence, receiving in exchange benevolent imprisonment. Sexual maturity was as useless and destructive to Nellie as to Little Nell, and far less emotionally satisfying than death.

Having closed off all usual paths of development, focusing on Nellie's inability to forgive and her continuing need to control those who might hurt her, Dostoevsky closes *The Insulted and Injured* at the same point at which Dickens closes *The Old Curiosity Shop*. Dostoevsky's solution to the problems raised by Little Nell is complete.

What does this solution suggest about Little Nell? We must remember that Dostoevsky pictured her as 'a soul full of wonder as though before some mystery', in Trishatov's words in *A Raw Youth*. When Dostoevsky thought of Little Nell he chose to remember not only the mystery of God but also the mystery of the 'thought of man'—both the church through which man worships God and the existence through which he lives his worship. Her existence seemed to Dostoevsky, as we have seen, an ideal, a type, a mystery of identity which he sought to plumb. And in Nellie he retains enough of the ideal that we can recognize Little Nell in her: the childhood innocence threatened, the mystical purity at the core which, although in Nellie not finally predominant, is never completely lost. Dostoevsky's awareness that the ideality of reality, as achieved by Dickens in such a creation as Nell, had not yet been achieved in Russian literature may have spurred him on to try to do what he saw the English author doing so superbly. Yet if Little Nell represented an ideal for Dostoevsky, it would have to encompass all of her character; Dostoevsky realized that the saint was not human and could never be an object of the sort of realism he wrote and saw

Dickens writing. Little Nell could not have been either ideal or real to him had she been merely the perfection of innocence. Rather her innocence is poignant and mysterious to Dostoevsky because he senses in her an undescribed conflict. When Trishatov says, 'I don't know what there is in [her], but it's fine,' he points the way for Dostoevsky's exploration of just what it is that makes Little Nell typical and ideal for him. Dostoevsky's analysis of Dickens' techniques and ideas in *A Raw Youth* and elsewhere has led critics to believe he interprets more deeply, borrowing the innocence Dickens presents and disclosing the obverse of innocence; this is surely true of most critical comparisons of Pickwick and Myshkin. Of *The Old Curiosity Shop*, Igor Katarsky, the leading Soviet critic of Dickens, has said:

> It is possible to speak about the great artistic impact of Nell on Dostoevsky, about the deeper and finer comprehension of the psychology of the child deprived of childhood. Dostoevsky's depiction of the character of Nellie emphasizes deep, torturous truth, whereas the vitally true traits of Dickens' Nell are often supplanted by the 'heavenly'. The image of the Dickensian Nell Trent certainly touches the reader: to this fragile girl's lot fell a hard burden—to be the 'elder', to be guardian to the old man who was retreating into childhood again. The figure of Dostoevsky's Nelly Valkovsky not only touches, but also stuns, life has so hardened this girl, completely bereaved of the joys of childhood. Dostoevsky consequently set as his task as an artist-realist to show to what degree the cruelty of life can cripple the nature of a child, can traumatize its soul.[6]

From this analysis Katarsky concludes that 'the figure of Nelly Valkovsky is not only much deeper, but also richer, more many-sided, than Dickens', whose Nell is ' "monotoned", presented only in a pathetic-sentimental plot with tinges of the heroic.'[7] Because such criticism has never been supported by a close reading of *The Old Curiosity Shop* in direct comparison to *The Insulted and Injured*, it seems to relegate Dickens to the status of an 'influence'. In fact, such criticism is almost always offered by critics of Dostoevsky rather than of Dickens. Critics of Dickens have gone so far as to note, as does Angus Wilson in 'Dickens and Dostoevsky', that 'the death of children is used in a way as a kind of atonement'[8] by both authors and that *both* are conscious of the susceptibility of the child to the infectious loneliness and degradation of the adult world. N. M. Lary even suggests:

> Perhaps then we should say that Dostoevsky valued Dickens' ideal and villainous characters while recognizing that human psychology was a bit more intricate? To anyone who looks at what Dostoevsky makes of Little Nell in *The Insulted and Injured*, this would seem an obvious suggestion to make.[9]

Katarsky speaks of the 'vitally true traits' of Little Nell and Lary sees that Dostoevsky's view is a 'bit more intricate'. If the established critical relationship between Dostoevsky and Dickens does indeed exist to the extent to which these critics believe, then Dostoevsky's reinterpretation of Little Nell in Nellie Valkovsky suggests that a critical re-reading of Little Nell is possible. I wish now to look back at *The Old Curiosity Shop*.

CHAPTER III

Little Nell and the Cupiosity Shape

> *Of course, to suggest taking Little Nell seriously would be absurd: There's nothing there. She doesn't derive from any perception of the real; she's a contrived unreality, the function of which is to facilitate in the reader a gross and virtuous self-indulgence.*
>
> F.R. LEAVIS

It has often been stated that Little Nell is really nothing at all like Nellie. Her mawkish goodness and tiresome assumption of responsibility have caused many readers to rejoice at her death. Dostoevsky's more 'realistic' treatment of Nellie has, in fact, been alleged to 'prove' his superiority over Dickens as a realist and as a psychologist. Nellie suffers from causes she cannot understand, causes which fill her youth with hatred and a desire for retribution. Growing up with a concept of her own unworthiness, compounded by her sordid life in St Petersburg, she learns to satisfy her sense of unworthiness by insisting on exercising control over the events of her life. By accepting others' mistreatment of her when she considers herself worthy of better, she can justifiably feel sorry for herself. And when she finally meets people who can love her, she is unwilling to love in return because love obligates her to forgive and seek forgiveness, and she believes that she cannot be in control of her life if she is at the mercy of forgiveness by others. Nellie's eventual realization of her inability to maintain such absolute independence leads, psychologically if not physically, to her death at the age of fourteen, unable to forgive because forgiveness would require sacrifice of the sense of self she had so painfully acquired.

Little Nell, on the other hand, is a good girl pursued by evil, both actually and allegorically. She appears to be arrayed with the Garlands as one of the forces of good in the novel, opposing Quilp, the epitome of all evil, against whose encroachments she struggles with all her childish strength. Her journey seems more a self-sacrificing search for a good and safe life for herself and her grandfather than a flight from a feared self. Rather than seeking to control others, she appears to desire only to evade the forces of evil which seek to control her. She does not seem to want independence for its own sake, but merely to avoid the contamination of a lecherously threatening Quilp; and no one has suggested that Nell uses forgiveness as a weapon to make others love her. Certainly English-speaking readers and critics of *The Old Curiosity Shop* seem to have found no traces of human sin or evil in Nell, and wilfulness is not one of her recognized characteristics. Yet direct comparison of Nellie and Nell yields several significant resemblances in situation and behaviour. Both girls beg; both are unusually insistent on working to pay their way; both show a need to assert their ability and therewith their independence; finally, they are both pubescent beings whose threatened innocence speaks of their creators' views of a society which exalts innocence yet feasts on its destruction.

Both girls beg alms:

Nellie	Nell
She begs for her grandfather's sustenance: 'I used to beg in the streets' ... 'And he let you! Nellie! Nellie' (*II* 161).	When Trent remonstrates that they will be reduced to beggary if they leave the shop, Nell replies: ' "What if we are?" said the child boldly. "Let us be beggars, and be happy" ' (*OCS* 71).
She breaks Vanya's cup: ' "There, now it's broken," she added, looking at me with a sort of defiant triumph'	'Hear me pray that we may beg,

(*II* 271), and begs for money to replace it.

work in open roads or fields, to earn a scanty living' (*OCS* 71).

'She had evidently been begging since the morning. [She] laid the money on the counter and was handed a cup, a plain teacup very much like the one she had broken that morning' (*II* 274).

'I will go and beg for both' (*OCS* 71).

She actually begs 'a morsel of bread' at the wayside hovel outside Wolverhampton (*OCS* 337).

Rather than live with non-forgiving Ikhmenev, 'I'd better go into the street and beg. ... I'm little, I've no means of earning money. I'll ask from all' (*II* 271).

Nell is willing to beg rather than be obligated to others for support. Quilp could discomfit but not attack her while her grandfather was independent; presumably he would have been similarly powerless over her were she to live with the Nubbleses. Yet she chooses to beg rather than accept the help of others, however well-intentioned.

In addition to willingness to beg in order to be independent of others, Nell is ever willing to do menial tasks for those who are kind to her. In this too she is similar to Nellie:

Nellie
She wants to 'work' at Mme Bubnov's 'and pay her back' for her mother's burial expenses (*II* 141).

Nell
In the shop, 'everything was done by the child, and ... there appeared to be no other persons but ourselves in the house' (*OCS* 6).

Still delirious, Nellie 'was doing the housework' for Vanya two days after her rescue from Mme Bubnov's (*II* 142).

'I used to sweep the floor here for grandfather too' (*II* 143). Vanya says: 'It seemed to me that she felt oppressed by my hospitality and that she wanted in every possible way to show me that she was doing something for her living' (*II* 143).

Perhaps one reason Kit's home is unacceptable to Nell is that as Kit says, 'You'd have [Mrs Nubbles] to wait upon you both, and me to run of errands' (*OCS* 89).

Meeting Codlin and Short on their journey, Nell 'was soon busily engaged in her task [of mending

To Nellie Vanya says: 'It's disagreeable to you to take the smallest present from me' (*II* 146). When the Ikhmenevs offer to take her in she says, 'No, I'd better get a place as a servant' (*II* 158).

When she learns Vanya is in love with Natasha she says, 'I'll be her servant. I'll do everything for her and not take any wages' (*II* 265).

Immediately following Vanya's refusal she goes to the doctor for refuge, saying 'she would behave well and learn her lessons that she would learn "to wash and get up his shirtfront" ' (*II* 267); next to Masloboev's where 'she begged to be taken if only as a housemaid or a cook, said she would sweep the floors and learn to do the washing' (*II* 268).

All this, Vanya says, was strange and unnatural, for 'she was not begging through need; she was not forsaken, not abandoned by some one to the caprices of destiny. She was not escaping from cruel oppressors, but from friends who loved and cherished her' (*II* 273).

Judy's clothes] and accomplishing it to a miracle' (*OCS* 124), even though there was no need for such kindness.

In return for a night's lodging, Nell 'bestirred herself' to make the schoolmaster's house 'neat and comfortable' (*OCS* 186), and 'asked his leave to prepare breakfast for him.' As payment for a further night's stay Nell 'was happy to show her gratitude to the kind schoolmaster by busying herself in the performance of such household duties as his little cottage stood in need of' (*OCS* 187).

She responds to the schoolmaster's kindness to her on the road thus: 'It makes me very unhappy even in the midst of all this kindness ... to think that we should be a burden upon you' (*OCS* 343).

In the village where she soon will die Nell clears neglected graves and shows the church to visitors, as if in payment of her keep. (*OCS* 408).

Nell, like Nellie, is unwilling to remain obligated to anyone for her welfare. Her approaching maturity is probably at least partially responsible for much of this; the child is ordinarily unaware of his obligations to those who rear and support him, but the onset of responsibility for self marks the onset of a desire to control one's own life, to be independent. This is what Nell seeks when she offers to help in the menial feminine ways she has learned. Such independence can be admirable, especially in a case like Nell's where she makes a graceful exchange without Nellie's oppugnant sense of obligation. Dostoevsky, if he took this attribute from Nell, hardened and sharpened it into a seemingly non-Dickensian feature—but a feature which Nell exhibits nonetheless, although in a much softened, perhaps even deliberately masked form.

The sense of obligation felt by both Nell and Nellie leads to a boldness or defiance which is very Nellie-like but unexpected in Little Nell.

Nellie	Nell
Nellie is constantly defiant. When Vanya, in their first conversation, suggests that lack of shoes and stockings will cause an early death, she says, 'Let me die' (*II* 109) in the most matter-of-fact manner.	When Nell suggests leaving the shop, she brushes aside the suggestion that she and her grandfather will be reduced to beggary. ' "What if we are?" said the child *boldly*. "Let us be beggars, and be happy" ' (*OCS* 71; emphasis mine).
To the beating Mme Bubnov will give her when she returns, Nellie says, ' "Let her beat me!" she answered, and her eyes flashed' (*II* 110).	Later we hear an element of pride when she says to Kit, 'We shall be very poor. We shall scarcely have bread to eat' (*OCS* 88)—a pride which rejects even the kindness of Kit and his mother, who would have given her a safe home.
Breaking Vanya's cup: 'I'm wicked, I'm wickeder than anyone. See how wicked I am!' (*II* 271).	To the foundryman: ' "We are here and must go on," said the child *boldly*' (*OCS* 333; emphasis mine).
	' "I must have that dream I told you of, no more," said the child, with a momentary firmness' (*OCS* 327), as she commands her grandfather to flight from Mrs Jarley's.

In *The Old Curiosity Shop* we hear Nell speak boldly only when she is defying the conventions of her world for something she wants personally: to her grandfather she as much as says that she would rather be a beggar than submit to Quilpism and acknowledge any indebtedness to it; to the foundryman, that his foundry is too threatening for her to remain longer. Nell's journey itself is so defiant of the established social order—a young girl leading her helplessly senile grandfather into an unknown exile from friends and help—that in itself it becomes a symbol of Nell's defiance of a world which threatens her existence. Her independence is a proof of self; therefore she seeks (and enjoys) independence, albeit in the charming, helpful way which has made her so attractive to generations of Dickens' readers.

A fourth and common comparison between Nell and Nellie is that both are looked upon, either directly or obliquely, as sexual beings. The innocence of the child belongs to each.

Nellie	Nell
She is 'small for her age' and, although probably thirteen, could be passed off by Mme Bubnov as 'eleven, and another time [as] fifteen' (*II* 131).	Dick Swiveller calls Nell a 'fine girl of her age, but small,' although her brother Fred asserts that 'Nell is nearly fourteen' (*OCS* 55).
The attempted rape at Mme Bubnov's shocks Nellie; she cries 'a terrible, piercing shriek,' rushes into the room 'with a white face and dazed eyes ... and her hair, which had been carefully arranged, dishevelled as though by a struggle' (*II* 134).	Quilp is the most obvious threat to Nell. His overt sexuality in spite of his ugliness is attested to by his wife when she says, 'The best-looking woman here couldn't refuse him if I was dead, and she was free, and he chose to make love to her' (*OCS* 32).
When Vanya takes her to the safety of his flat she becomes 'feverish and delirious.' When she hears the name of Mme Bubnov 'her cheeks suddenly flushed fiery red probably at the recollection of the past' (*II* 138).	Quilp asks Nell if she would 'like to be my number two' (*OCS* 45) and remarks, 'smacking his lips ... "what a nice kiss that was" ' that Nell had given Trent, as he follows her retreating figure with 'an admiring leer' (*OCS* 72).
Nellie is sexually as well as emotionally attracted to Vanya. 'She's in love with you,' Natasha tells Vanya. 'It's the beginning of love, real grown-up love' (*II* 275), a	Quilp appropriates Nell's bedroom—with obvious sexual suggestiveness—and is the last object presented to her eyes as she flees the shop, he 'gasping and growling with his mouth wide open' (*OCS* 96) as if to devour in this way

love for which Nellie had been practicing with the doctor, asking him, 'When I am big and grown up will you marry me?' (*II* 257).

We have also seen the thinly-veiled sexual overtones in the episodes with the doctor (*II* 258–63).

what he could not devour in any other.

Other threats to Nell include Dick Swiveller, to whom Fred Trent intends to 'give' his sister as a rich and 'beautiful young wife' (*OCS* 57); and Kit, who offers Nell his house and tacitly admits his love of her to his mother (*OCS* 79).

At the Valiant Soldier Nell is awakened from dreams by a figure who creeps into her room and takes her money. The dream preceding her awakening is of 'falling from high towers' (*OCS* 228), which in Freudian dream language symbolizes a male or phallic source.

Nell's dream of falling from a high tower epitomizes both her and Dickens' subconscious awareness of her sexual nature. Although it is unlikely that Dickens intended any sexual imagery, the underlying symbolism of Nell's dream would certainly seem to indicate a fear of loss of innocence connected with the unidentified figure who steals into her room at night. As it turns out, the figure is her grandfather; but Nell is nonetheless subconsciously sensible of a continuing threat and shows a symbolic and perhaps even conscious understanding of what is threatened. In comparison with Dickens' Nell, Nellie Valkovsky's sexual encounters are altogether more threatening to her innocence than Nell's, for they are overt. Had Vanya not rescued her from Mme Bubnov's, she would clearly have become a prostitute. The threat of prostitution in Nell's case is oblique, but Dickens' readers would sense it even more than modern readers because of the strict guards that customs of the times set up to protect its 'respectable' girls and women; specifics were not necessary. In fact, Dickens' intention in showing Nell as innocence threatened was undoubtedly as conscious as his readers' perception of it. Certainly the more sophisticated among them could have had little need to question what became of penniless young girls on the streets of Mayhew's 'impersonal wen of London', of whom Blake wrote that 'the harlot's cry from street to street/Will weave Old England's winding sheet' [*Auguries of Innocence*].

The girls differ, however, in their own awareness of awakening sexual feelings. As Mark Spilka has said in *Dickens and Kafka*, Dostoevsky treats explicitly the theme of sexuality in young girls which, according to Spilka, he found implicit in Dickens: Dostoevsky's 'recognition that little girls can appeal to innocent love and furtive lust, and, more appallingly, can *respond* to both appeals, reflects insightfully on the little-girl theme in Dickens, Eliot, Carroll, Dowson, Barrie, Spyri and others.'[1] If we are to view Nell as in any way a symbol of sexual innocence (as many critics unreservedly do) then she must flee any suggestion of violation. There is no question that Nell wishes to evade the power of evil as exemplified by Quilp. But Kit's proffered haven, even apart from the insuperable class distinctions which would in any event prevent Nell from accepting it, suggests the possibility of violation.

The 'little-girl theme' of which Spilka speaks conveys to reader and critic alike all the unspoken sexuality which the novel's imagery and movement confirm. The very depiction of sexual innocence implies the possibility of its opposite. Yet Spilka is the only critic to suggest that a Dickensian Nell might be capable of a Nellie-like response to her sexual nature.

We can see how valid his suggestion is by positing Nell's future were she *merely* a symbol of sexual innocence. In that case Kit's offer would provide her the perfect escape from Quilp. In marrying Kit, Nell could lose innocence to maturity and fulfilment, for there is nothing in the Kit Dickens depicts to suggest his involvement in other than a normal Victorian marriage. Indeed Dickens shows us, in Kit's union with Barbara, what would have happened to Nell had she accepted Kit's hospitality and love. Their union, described so cheerfully by Dickens, is as normative and idyllic as those of Agnes and David, Amy and Arthur, and Bella and John.

But Nell is another matter. Dickens equates innocence with purity, whereas Dostoevsky draws a distinction between physical purity, i.e. clinical retention of chastity, and emotional or mental innocence which for him includes an awareness of sexual forces as a part of the human makeup. The retention of purity does not guarantee the preservation of innocence, as we see with Nellie. She is aware of and fosters sexually-based relationships as she develops a consciousness of the intrinsically sexual nature of the world in which Dostoevsky places her. Little Nell, on the other hand, is never allowed a visible lapse from sexual innocence. It is important to Dickens and to his readers that at the same time as her innocence is obviously threatened by sexually-motivated forces of evil, she herself should stand in opposition to those forces at least partially through unconsciousness of them—and, by extension, mitigation of their power through refusal to see that it exists. But we must not be too ready to accept whole Nell's, or even Dickens', evaluation of her motives.

While Nellie seems to escape the natural fulfilment of sexuality only through death, Dickens offers Nell another path. Once outside London, in her quiet Gothic cottage—a curiosity shop of peace and retirement—she might be able to live in some attenuated capacity, like a Miss LaCreevy or Miss Tox, unsullied because time could weave around her its protective cocoon. Death was inevitable for Nellie; but for Nell? Could it have been avoided? If Forster can be believed, Dickens did not intend to have Nell die until Forster suggested it. Her death might not therefore have been a thematic necessity from the start. On the other hand, Dickens himself said in a letter to Thomas Latimer of 13 March 1841: 'I never had the design and purpose of a story so distinctly marked in my mind, from its commencement. All its quietness arose out of a deliberate purpose; the notion being to stamp upon it from the first, the shadow of that early death.'[2] If this is to be taken literally, there must have been more involved in Nell's death than a mere evasion of sexuality, for that alone could have been solved happily by mere flight and seclusion for the rest of Nell's life. It was not an impossible solution for Dickens to come to.

It is useful here to examine such a possibility, to look at Nell in relation to the novel's other forces of good. In *The Old Curiosity Shop* the Garlands seem to fill the same function as those Pickwick, Mr Brownlow, the Cheeryble brothers filled in earlier novels. They invariably act to elicit behaviour of which they can approve, expending both time and money in their pursuit of goodness as they define it and in their encouragement of such goodness in others.

However, as J. Hillis Miller has pointed out, such 'communities of good' are not without fault. They seem, he says, 'rather to engulf and absorb the personalities of their members than to sustain them, and to transform everyone into a copy of a standard pattern swallowing up all uniqueness.'[3] This is the very real threat such goodness as the Garlands' poses, for by moulding and forming individuals, goodness can be an insidious and self-perpetuating controller. Indeed, as Leonard Manheim has said, 'if we dwell on some of the elements of Abel's upbringing, which the author seems to hold up as a model, the Garlands may fill us with a horror such as only Quilp could otherwise inspire.'[4]

The Garlands first appear in the novel at Mr Witherden's office to apprentice their son Abel to the Notary. Abel's very name is significant of weakness and submission. He has not a brother to kill him, but he does come complete with parents to control him. Although he is a full-grown man, he has spent only two nights away from his parents, an excursion which gave him 'quite a dissipation' and made him ill. 'He was not used to it, you know,' his mother informs the world. 'He had no comfort in being there without us, and had nobody to talk to or enjoy himself with.' 'That was it, you know,' Abel confirms, corroborating perfectly his mother's reiterations of his dutiful, affectionate nature toward his parents. When Mr Garland says that 'no son had ever been a greater comfort to his parents than Abel Garland had been to his,' the velvet glove only partially covers his iron control over his son. The Garlands have convinced Abel that he feels ill away from them, and so he does. Such power of suggestion is well known and is in fact a recommended method of behaviour alteration in naughty children. Baldly seen, however, it is no less an iron grip than that in which Quilp holds Mrs Quilp. The result of such control is that Abel looks and acts as old as his father and is a Garland down to his club foot.[5] Dickens makes no use of Abel in the book because there is nothing Abel can do; he is a captive of the Garland goodness and has thus no identity or capacity for real action.

It is not fanciful to see this sort of controlling goodness in Mr Garland's treatment of Abel, for he treats everyone and everything else in the same way. His house and garden 'behave' perfectly—'everything within the house and without, seemed to be the perfection of neatness and order. In the garden there was not a weed to be seen!' Nor are Mr Garland's associates allowed to be weedy. When he cannot find a sixpence for Kit's horse-holding fee, he gives the lad a shilling: ' "There," he said jokingly, "I'm coming here again next Monday at the same time, and mind you're here, my lad, to work it out." ' His tone may be jocular, but his intent is not. Kit merely happens to be in an auspicious position for the inculcation of a little Garland goodness. The method is clear. It is also clear that it would not work on Sampson Brass nor on Dick Swiveller. It would not work on Brass because he so delights in the evil in his nature that he has no desire to get rid of it. Nor would it work on Dick, for Dick's commitment to a glass of 'the rosy'—in other words, as fine a portion of life as one can create out of whole cloth and cheer—evidences a practical relish for life itself that Mr Garland's curtailment could never contain as it does Abel's. It works on Kit, however, because Kit is so anxious to please others and thereby win affection for himself, and so unsure of his ability to please, that he is easily suggestible. In seeking to avoid the controlling force of evil he overreacts and succumbs, instead, to the controlling force of good, which stifles the individual's awareness of the natural evil within himself and thereby cripples him by robbing him of half of himself.

The humorous antics of the Garlands' pony give us an example of behaviour unaltered by the control of goodness. No matter how kind Mr Garland is to his pony, the pony persists in doing what it will. It is not really a bad pony, for it gets where it is supposed to go eventually; it merely persists in proclaiming its right to get there in its own way according to its own nature. That nature happens to contain a substantial allotment of perversity, and the pony, by its behaviour, insists upon its right to be perverse in the face of goodness. Not even Mrs Garland's exhortation—'Oh, dear, such a naughty Whisker! ... I am quite ashamed of him'—can keep the pony in line, although it has worked remarkably well with Abel and Kit. The pony maintains its independence throughout the novel; even when it becomes docile for Kit it retains its self-will with the Garlands. It represents the natural state of free animal behaviour, a state which the human beings in the novel often seem unable to attain.

Unlike the recalcitrant pony, Kit is completely in the control of the Garlands. They tell him what a good lad and a good son he is, and this reinforces his desire to be a good lad and a good son. There is nothing to be said against good behaviour: Dickens, and his readers too, certainly wish the forces of good to prevail. But the Garlandian kind of good desires not only to prevail but to control. Kit is so good that he does nothing but work and in fact becomes something of a moral snob about it. He fails to engage the reader as Dick Swiveller does because, as Chesterton points out:

> Dick Swiveller is not only a much funnier fellow than Kit, he is also a much more genuine fellow, being free from that slight stain of 'meekness', or the snobbishness of the respectable poor, which the wise and perfect Chuckster wisely and perfectly perceived in Kit.[6]

The observation is apt, for Kit has a horror of associating himself with anything which would besmirch his character. His snobbery might also have been apparent to Victorian readers in his aspirations for Nell, just as Nicholas Nickleby's love for Madeline seemed even to that worthy young man an overreaching. Finally, Kit is capable of blinking at evil if it brings him material gain. He justifies the taking of shillings from Sampson Brass as payment for bringing messages by the fact that he uses the money to buy gifts for his mother. Actually, however, he accepts the money because he wants it, but rejects Brass and all he represents because he feels himself better than Brass. As Edmund Wilson has said, Kit is 'even a little disgusting'.[7]

Because Kit is attempting to suppress the part of himself he considers undesirable, the Garlands are able to control him with their moral-baiting rhetoric. Unlike the self-willed pony, Kit loses his freedom of action by falling victim to the flattery that only what the Garlands define as the good in him is of any importance. The question for him is not even whether the bad is truly bad (one thinks of the Marchioness); it is different from the Garlandian good and therefore to be suppressed.

As the same time Kit is a loving son and a faithful and generous friend to Nell, offering her the resources of his home and family when she is in distress. He is also genuinely comic, and the Cattermole and Browne illustrations of him retain from beginning to end a large-headed, alarm-faced young man who struggles through life in an endearing way. Any reader meeting him on a London street would like him. The fact that he is corruptible makes him human and lovable at the same time that it leads him into questionable or snobbish behaviour. He is a superlative illustration of Dickens' attempt to deal with moral imperfection without damning the human being.

If, in opposition to Kit, we accept Dick Swiveller as the hero-figure in the novel and the representative of its moral balance (as his name would suggest),[8] a brief look at him and his friends can illustrate the harm inherent in a goodness that controls or is controlled. The wine-drinking in which Dick and Fred Trent engage is perhaps the scene of the most unalloyed fun to be found in the novel. Dick is quite aware of the moral as well as the physical ramifications of his financial antics and yet feels no need to condemn either self or society. And not least, the Marchioness, who saves Dick's life and eventually solves the mystery of Kit's apparent crime, would never have been seen outside the Brass basement had not Dick befriended her. Certainly the Garlands would have been unable to redeem her, as is evident when Abel is brought to Dick's flat by the Marchioness to obtain evidence of Kit's innocence. Even knowing the good intent of his errand,

> Mr Abel, who was one of the simplest and most retiring
> creatures in existence, and naturally timid withal, hesitated; for
> he had heard of people being decoyed into strange places to be
> robbed and murdered, under circumstances very like the
> present, and, for anything he knew to the contrary, by guides
> very like the Marchioness. (*OCS* 487)

Abel has been made so good that he is nearly paralyzed, almost
unable to act to bring about a good result. Only Dick—that
glorious mixture of good and evil, love and hate, generosity and
plotting all thrown together with no attempt on his part to quash
the supposedly morally undesirable—can recognize, nurture, and
bring to bloom the real Marchioness. The Garlands can recognize
only their own brand of goodness, and not even the appearance of
difference is to be tolerated.

To ignore the Marchioness à la Garland would have resulted in
a catastrophe for true morality. Dickens seems to suggest that
only the existence of the non-good can insure the existence of the
good, an age-old idea central to many religious and philosophical
systems.[9] This is not to say, of course, that Quilp must be
celebrated as a force for good; he is definitely evil and must be
combatted. We need not go into Quilp's attempts to control others
by encouraging their own evil dispositions; these attempts are
more heinous than those of the Garlands, but the latter are
certainly no less morally manipulative. B. S. Rurikov's statement
about Dostoevsky can be applied equally well to the Dickens
Dostoevsky read:

> He considered that evil was hidden in the very nature of man
> and ... that in man's soul the eternal struggle between good and
> evil, light and gloom, beauty and ugliness, goes on.[10]

Both Kit and Dick Swiveller show that Dickens knows this
struggle too.

Given Dickens' qualified portrayal of the sort of good exercised
by the Garlands, his desire to keep Nell from contact with them
would quite naturally result in her perhaps overly convulsive

flight from London and from her friends. Thus far a comparison of Little Nell with Nellie Valkovsky has made possible a clearer understanding of Nell's actions within the book's moral framework.

I would like now to go one step further, to move more deeply—and for some, more uncomfortably Freudianly—into Nell's characterization and draw parallels between Nellie's struggle with the evil she knows is within her and Little Nell's flight and behaviour toward her grandfather.

Nellie Valkovsky lives in a Dostoevskian world in which all good is co-mingled with evil. Wherever Dostoevsky might have transplanted her, even into Myshkin's domain, she would have been subject to the evil forces rolling through a universe attuned to the satanic as well as to the divine in the human struggle to survive. We have seen Nellie fly from Vanya's sincere desire to love her as if that desire were as harmful as Ikhmenev's unfeeling use of her as a replacement for his banished daughter. Even the good she accepts she turns to a value exchange. Dostoevsky makes clear that her always equivocal reception of the good reveals the seeds of evil within her. Without condemning Nellie herself as a figure of evil, Dostoevsky manages to show both the lights and the shadows in her behaviour and motives. She is capable of measuring the benefits of others' kindnesses and of rejecting those kindnesses when they threaten her sense of independence and control. In this she is, surprisingly perhaps, comparable to Little Nell.

Nellie	Nell
She is willing to return to Mme Bubnov in spite of Vanya's offer to care for her.	Nell rejects Kit's offer of a home, with its implicit romantic connections.
She refuses to allow the Ikhmenevs to adopt her.	She flees Mrs Jarley's under the greater compulsion of her grandfather's gambling mania.
Following the terrifying scene with Ikhmenev, Nellie escapes to the	She rejects the foundryman's offer

doctor's and thence to Masloboev's, seeking a refuge from Vanya's continued care.

of a home amid the fire and noise of the foundry.

She accepts Vanya and Ikhmenev only when she is doomed to die.

Nell accepts the schoolmaster's help only when her illness is irreversible.

Nell's apparent rejection of aid is never necessitated by clearly expounded, rational forces. Her refusal of Kit's offer of a home, of course, is largely controlled by Dickens' desire to maintain her innocence. Nor does Dickens allow her within the Garlands' purview. Likewise, she has reasons for moving beyond both Mrs Jarley and the foundryman.

The help offered Nell by Mrs Jarley is of particular interest, for Mrs Jarley, like Dick Swiveller, has been seen by critics to be an agent of the life force in *The Old Curiosity Shop* (as James Kincaid says, both show a 'small but powerful glimpse of immortality'[11]). Nell works for her as she has worked for others, but she gets paid a salary and so there can be no possibility of indebtedness (and therefore control) on either side. It is a matter of exchange of value given for value received, which binds neither side when fairly done.

Mrs Jarley is a comic figure who offers Nell the possibility of acceptance of the fullness of human nature without judgment. But Nell is impervious to comedy. Dickens himself says that 'Nell's anxieties ... were of a deeper kind [than could be routed by laughter], and the checks they imposed upon her cheerfulness were not so easily removed' (*OCS* 239–40). In fact, Nell laughs but once in the book, less than halfway through the first chapter, at Kit's antics. The release of comedy is not for Nell. If it were, she might have been able to confess to Mrs Jarley her concern for her grandfather and seek help. But, as with Kit's offer of refuge, she is driven by forces beyond the mere need for shelter and help with her overt problems. And so she uses her grandfather's gambling mania as a further reason for escaping an environment—this time comic—that does not answer her needs. Not friendliness, nor good, nor comedy offers Nell refuge.

In her flight away from the controls of others, Nell descends into hell itself, in the shape of the Wolverhampton foundry, and makes the startling discovery that good can live in the very bowels of evil. The foundry itself is hellishly imaged. 'Unearthly', 'demons', 'giants', 'the black vault above', 'the eyes of savage beasts'—Dickens paints a picture of an inhuman industrialization which reduces people to demonic cogs in a giant machine. Yet within this hell lives the foundryman, who extends to Nell the only haven a city such as Wolverhampton has to offer. Says the foundryman of his fire:

> It's like a book to me ... the only book I ever learned to read; and many an old story it tells me. It's music, for I should know its voice among a thousand, and there are other voices in its roar. It has its pictures too. You don't know how many strange faces and different scenes I trace in the red-hot coals. It's my memory, that fire, and shows me all my life. (*OCS* 331)

Amid the tumult Nell 'yielded to the drowsiness that came upon her, and, in the dark strange place and on the heap of ashes, slept as peacefully as if the room had been a palace chamber, and the bed, a bed of down' (*OCS* 383). Yet when she awakens to reality she recoils both from its satanic implications and from the genuine peace it could offer her. She moves on, only vaguely aware of 'the danger that we shun!' (*OCS* 383) The visible presence of evil in the foundryman's fire, in the noise, in the blackness, is sufficient to move Nell instinctively away from the foundry. True, she fears it for the obvious physical reasons; but she fears too its power and the enforced nature of the foundryman's submission to that power.

Let me emphasize here that I do not wish to minimize the very real threats Quilp, Trent's gambling mania, and the foundry pose. Dickens creates an England which offers no safety, no warmth, no succour for a child. No reader would suggest that the threats to Nell are not representative or that she herself overestimates their power. When we examine the havens Nell is offered, however, it becomes obvious that Quilp can be circumvented in several ways, that there is help for Trent's gambling fever, and that worlds hospitable to the values Nell represents and seeks to preserve exist within the framework of the novel. Yet Dickens moves her away from these worlds. Therefore, while not underestimating the perniciousness of the forces driving Nell from London, we must also look at the choices she makes—for they *are* choices—and attempt to understand them in terms of Nell herself.

On the outskirts of Wolverhampton Nell again meets the schoolmaster. First and last, he offers Nell something Kit, Mrs Jarley, and the foundryman cannot: he shows Nell the power a child can exercise. He says of his dying pupil: ' "That I should love him is no wonder, but that he should love me—" and there the schoolmaster stopped, and took off his spectacles to wipe them, as though they had grown dim.' This is the sort of devotion each person in the world seeks, a blind commitment uncontaminated by personal drives. Nell desires it from her grandfather; Dickens desired it, and no doubt felt he had found it in Mary Hogarth; the dying pupil also has achieved it. Little wonder that Dickens was attracted enough to the example to allow Nell to interrupt her flight and spend two days absorbing it, or that the schoolmaster should be the only character she encounters twice, and also the one who offers her her final, acceptable refuge.

On their second meeting Nell agrees, albeit reluctantly, to accept the schoolmaster's continued generosity. It is he who takes her to her final home, a home she can accept as safe. On the surface there seems to be no reason why Dickens should only now allow Trent to relinquish his desire to gamble so that Nell, instinctively recoiling from the aid of all others, could accept the schoolmaster's. In fact, however, the schoolmaster offers Nell what Vanya eventually offers Nellie: an opportunity for what could be called 'creative death', through which 'Dickens protects Nell from sexuality by early sounding the mortuary note that is to keep her forever a child', in Gabriel Pearson's words.[12]

Nellie	Nell
She refuses to take proper care of herself or accept the care of others. 'Let me die' (*II* 109), for want of	Nell tells Mrs Quilp of her grandfather's stories about her dead mother: 'He used to take me on his

stockings; 'she would not eat' (*II* 138).

'She has epileptic fits' (*II* 215), which Freud would maintain were neurotic in nature.

'The patient has an organic defect of the heart, and at the slightest unfavourable circumstance she'll be laid up again. ... She'll be ill again and at last she'll die' (*II* 256).

Refusal to take her medicines (*II* 257–58; 268). Epileptic fit after telling Ikhmenev her story and reuniting him with Natasha—as if she had to punish herself for her good deed (*II* 320).

'The more the disease gained on her, the softer, sweeter, and more open she became with us' (*II* 329).

Ikhmenev 'filled her room with flowers. ... I remember how the old man decked her little coffin with flowers, and gazed in despair at her wasted, little face, smiling in death, and at her hands crossed on her breast' (*II* 344–45).

knee, and try to make me understand that she was not lying in her grave, but had flown to a beautiful country beyond the sky, where nothing died or ever grew old—we were very happy once!' (*OCS* 49).

The old wife teaches her how to find the secret of peace in contemplation of her dead husband's grave (*OCS* 129–30).

The schoolmaster's favourite maintains an eternal hold over the schoolmaster by dying from the mental and physical overexertion required to please his master (*OCS* 191–95).

Mrs Jarley's wax-work is like death; the figures can be defined, contained, controlled precisely because they are life-like and yet unreal, giving them an immortality untouched by human attempts at control (*OCS* 203).

Nell's final home is 'a place to live and learn to die!' (*OCS* 386).

Nell loves the church both in spite of and because of the fact that 'the spot awakened thoughts of Death' (*OCS* 398).

Nell clears and tends graves (*OCS* 408).

'She was dead. ... Her couch was dressed with here and there some

winter berries and green leaves,
gathered in a spot she had been used
to favour' (*OCS* 538–39).

'She turned to the old man with a
lovely smile upon her face ... and
clung with both her arms about his
neck. They did not know that she
was dead, at first' (*OCS* 540).

It is taking too naïve a view of Nell simply to say, as Patrick
Braybrooke does in *Great Children in Literature*, that 'it is only
when Little Nell gets to the end of her wanderings that she begins
to have an idea that she is also getting to the end of her life.'[13]
Nell's (and Dickens') preoccupation with death begins in the
curiosity shop itself, that original home of 'fantastic carvings
brought from monkish stalls' in which, for Nell, it is death to
remain. Her journey leads from this shop, through several actual
and symbolic graveyards, to a final 'shop' which, like its
predecessor, is a 'pile of fragments of rich carving from old
monkish stalls.' Nell's earliest life is filled with beautiful, if
unrealistic, thoughts about death. Her grandfather's version of
Nell's mother's death establishes her belief that death is a release
into a perfect life. But Nell also associates this perfect life with the
happiness of the past: 'We were very happy once!' Even before
her journey from the curiosity shop, Nell sees death as a restorer
of past joys that have fled.

Nell's life is a circle trod through graveyards. On the second
afternoon of their journey she and Trent walk through a
graveyard because 'the ground was soft, and easy to their tired
feet,' just as it was for those buried there; here they meet Codlin
and Short and find the possibility, if not the realization, of
succour. The next morning Nell walks again in the graveyard:
'She felt a curious kind of pleasure in lingering among these
houses of the dead, and read the inscriptions on the tombs of the
good people (a great number of good people were buried there),
passing on from one to another with increasing interest.' The
graveyards Nell visits seem to be peopled only by the good, as if

good people were uniquely destined for the grave, whose sanctuary alone could contain such an amount of goodness. His use of the word 'good' twice in a single sentence shows a preoccupation with death in connection with the eternal preservation of goodness. As if to justify this preoccupation, Dickens introduces Nell to the old wife, who tells her how her pain and grief were assuaged by her visits to the grave of her husband, as were the memories of all hard and bad things that life had laid upon her. Her familiarity with the grave had turned to fondness, and she could think 'of herself in connexion with [her husband], as she used to be and not as she was now'—a true recapturing of the past and of the goodness and beauty accompanying it. Nell '*thoughtfully* retraced her steps' (emphasis mine), pondering the possibility of her own return to a purer past.

Nell's subsequent visit to the schoolmaster also impresses her with the power death has to attach the affections permanently. She hears the boy's grandmother tell the schoolmaster: 'If he hadn't been poring over his books out of fear of you, he would have been well and merry now, I know he would.' In death the boy will become master. His mentor, who had loved him because he had seen his own image in the boy, is made to feel responsible for the boy's illness and approaching death. In trying to mould his pupil's mind and future, he fears he will have killed him. Yet the child's death brings Nell comfort as well as sadness:

And though she thought as a child herself, and did not perhaps sufficiently consider to what a bright and happy existence those who die young are borne, and how in death they lose the pain of seeing others die around them, bearing to the tomb some strong affection of their hearts (which makes the old die many times in one long life), still she thought wisely enough, to draw a plain and easy moral from what she had seen that night, and to store it, deep in her mind. Her dreams were of the little scholar: not confined and covered up, but mingling with angels, and smiling happily. (*OCS* 194)

Here Dickens is describing one of the more common

philosophical stances toward the death of a child (not necessarily his own stance, it should be noted). And, in applying this general statement to Nell's own thoughts about this particular death and its relevance to her, he goes on to say that Nell does not consider the general sentiment so much as she considers her own special case. The moral inherent in the boy's death, although unspecified by Dickens, can be related to Nell's own sentiments about the power of death. 'The dead boy had been a grandchild, and left but one aged relative to mourn his premature decay,' a situation so close to Nell's own that she decides not to tell her grandfather about it, yet Dickens says that she drew 'a plain and easy moral from what she had seen' and stored it 'deep in her mind' for later examination. Such an observation by the author supports his contention that he had Nell's death in mind from the beginning; the element of mystery in her secret preservation of the lesson of the schoolmaster's favourite would seem to show Dickens' intention, however vague at this juncture, to seek through Nell some sort of positive justification of death, especially the death of a child.

Dickens' view of Jarley's wax-work delineates Nell's confusion over death, for the wax-work purports to present life-like figures, and yet, says Mrs Jarley, 'I won't go so far as to say, that, as it is, I've seen wax-work quite like life, but I've certainly seen some life that was exactly like wax-work.' Steven Marcus says of these lines that 'art is in fact a parody of life only in so far as life contains the possibility of becoming its own parody,' so that 'the immortality of art ... comes to be regarded as an immortality of death' which in turn creates a fear that perhaps the opposite may be the truth: 'a belief in the possibility of stasis, of rest and permanence, may be as factitious as the idea of an eternity of waxen peace.'[14]

I would suggest that Dickens' preoccupation with Nell's death—'spiritual necrophilia', as Marcus calls it, or 'necrophiliac brooding' in the words of Laurence Senelick'[15]—shows both a horror of death and a curiosity about it which produce a strange attraction that Dickens cannot help but probe. The ultimate underlying question is whether Dickens feared death to be not ideal and final, but as uncertain as life (the life of the young Mary dying in his arms, for example), and used Nell's wanderings to help him find out. Surely the novel's logic points from the very beginning toward death as both fearsome and desirable, and Nell's attraction to it amounts almost to a death-wish. Leonard Manheim expresses, within a sexual critique of the novel, Dickens' fascination with Nell's death:

> In the light of the violence of the unconscious drive which led to her creation, it is obvious that Nell could never be permitted to attain an age at which the coarseness of the gross world of reality might sully her. She could not long remain as the custodian and exhibitor of the old church without growing up, and then either marrying or become an odd old spinster. Either course was repugnant to the author; hence she had to perish.[16]

We have seen that the alternatives Manheim mentions were indeed closed to Nell because of her author's inability to confront either of them. As Rex Warner has said,

> The fantastic company in which the two find themselves in their wanderings, even the sentimentality and strain of some of the scenes between the girl and the old man suggest that in this part of the book Dickens is describing forces which are bigger than the characters themselves, and is embodying in his people and scenery the cruelties and delusions which he observes in a wider society.[17]

Warner's analysis suggests that there is a depth of which Dickens was not conscious and a force which guided his artistry but escaped his understanding. It is this force that remains to be delineated.

The logic of the plot of *The Old Curiosity Shop* dictates that Nell meet the schoolmaster a second time, for his was the only shelter that did not threaten her. When Dickens creates the churchyard of Tong (whose edifice dwarfs Nell in Cattermole's illustration) the two small houses 'hard by these gravestones' draw her eye.

Her new home is, she tells the schoolmaster, 'a place to live and learn to die in!' Nell holds the same office in her new residence as she did in Mrs Jarley's—she shows the premises to strangers. From showing lifelike death, Nell turns to showing deathlike life and becomes a part of the latter. She communes with the 'dreamless sleepers' who lie beneath the churchyard soil and dreams of them, 'a sweet and happy dream' in which no reader would fail to note the element of wish fulfilment which lies so heavily over this closing portion of Nell's life. Within the church, she reads the Bible amid 'awakened thoughts of death' and muses: 'Die who would, it would still remain the same; these sights and sounds would still go on, as happily as ever. It would be no pain to sleep amidst them.'

It is at this point that critics such as Swinburne and Huxley turn away from the story, for Nell's sweet thoughts about death become ever sweeter until the culmination of the schoolmaster's peroration on the benefits of dying:

'There is nothing ... innocent or good, that dies and is forgotten.... An infant, a prattling child, dying in its cradle, will live again in the better thoughts of those who loved it, and play its part, through them, in the redeeming actions of the world, though its body be burnt to ashes or drowned in the deepest sea. There is not an angel added to the Host of Heaven but does its blessed work on earth in those that loved it here. Forgotten! Oh, if the good deeds of human creatures could be traced to their source, how beautifully would even death appear; for how much charity, mercy, and purified affection, would be seen to have their growth in dusty graves!' (*OCS* 406)

In one sense this is Dickens' message to his readers, a consolation for the loss of his own Mary and for all children who die before their time. It is immaterial that this may be cheap consolation for loss; any consolation is cheap in the face of the dearness of death. In another sense this is superficial justification for Nell's own drive toward death. It is not sentimental, however, in that it is *necessary* for Nell to justify her death. This particular sentimentalized picture is aesthetically and psychologically desirable within the context Dickens has set up. Her role in her own death results from the often stated complaint that Dickens created her out of his desires and illusions rather than out of the exigencies of the world of *The Old Curiosity Shop*. But his careful preparation for her death in part obviates such criticism; a comparison of Nell with Nellie Valkovsky shows Dickens' pattern in moving Nell through a world that has no answers to her needs. Now I wish to examine those needs more closely, again in comparison with Dostoevsky's Nellie, to discern how Dostoevsky saw Dickens develop Little Nell as a response to her world.

Nellie's relationship with her father and her father-figure grandfather leads to an examination of Nell's relationship with Trent (on which, it will be recalled, Nellie's relationship with her own grandfather was based) in the light of the theme of forgiveness, of which Nellie's story is such a superb illustration. It is in Nell's relationship with her grandfather that her character is most clearly displayed. That relationship contains, from the first, undercurrents of emotions other than pure love. Master Humphrey notices Trent's preoccupation with something besides the welfare of his granddaughter and, in his recollection of their conversations, hints by omission at other emotions than pure love even in the child's breast:

'Do I love thee, Nell?' said he. 'Say; do I love thee, Nell, or no?'

The child only answered by her caresses, and laid her head upon his breast.

'Why dost thou sob?' said the grandfather, pressing her closer to him and glancing toward me. 'Is it because thou know'st I love thee, and dost not like that I should seem to doubt it by my question? Well, well—then let us say I love thee dearly.'

'Indeed, indeed you do,' replied the child with great earnestness, 'Kit knows you do.' (*OCS* 8)

Not, we note, 'I know you do.' Nell allows gestures and external witness to say for her what she herself will not say. Something holds her back from telling him she loves him or from directly acknowledging his love. A part of her cannot understand his preoccupation nor her own role in it and so must feel, as the child Dickens felt when denied schooling and placed instead in his personal hell-hole of Warren's Blacking, a resentment at a situation she can neither comprehend nor change. Dickens may not have been consciously writing into Nell's story his own feelings about his childhood sense of neglect and misery, but we know this experience never left him through all his life, and its reality echoes through his imaginative creations, Oliver Twist and young Smike as well as the better-known David and Pip. Nell, being a girl, would not be sent out to work; but, like Oliver and Smike and David and Pip and Charles himself, she cannot understand why her happy childhood should so soon fade and why the parent-figure who professes love for her should wilfully fail now to provide the simple happiness of the calm past. The reader cannot know whether that past is a creation of the child's ignorance of the workings of the world (in either Dickens' or Nell's case), but he does know that Dickens felt deprived of his natural child rights and resentful of the deprivation, as perhaps does Nell. That she does not articulate her feelings is no more surprising than that Dickens did not until he confided them to Forster (never to his wife or family) late in life.

Added to the author's inescapable sense of deprivation, which emerges in Nell, is Nell's feeling of responsibility for her situation. The past which she mourns was one in which Trent told her stories of how her mother had died and 'that she was not lying in her grave, but had flown to a beautiful country beyond the sky, where nothing died or ever grew old'—the very paradise Nell seeks. This past, when one was happy, merges in her imagination with the ultimate future in which all will be happy, and death would be the bridge between the two. From her earliest childhood Nell's thoughts of death had always been eager, happy ones until undercut by her grandfather's overheard admission that 'if it was not for the child, he would wish to die.' Nell in her childish innocence begins to feel responsible, recognizing that she may be depriving her grandfather—by her very existence, which must be provided for—of that pleasant, happy place called Death. Regardless of the irrationality of such ideas, they are plausible to the mind of a child. Nell's love for her grandfather may not have diminished, but such a sense of guilt would qualify it in ways only dimly understood by, or even totally incomprehensible to, a child.

Little suspecting Nell's thoughts, Trent 'went on, content to read the book of her heart from the page first presented to him, little dreaming of the story that lay hidden in its other leaves, and murmuring within himself that at least the child was happy.' But on the very page on which we find Trent thinking this consoling thought, Nell daydreams about his death:

> If he were to die—if sudden illness had happened to him, and he were never to come home again, alive—if one night, he should come home, and kiss and bless her as usual, and after she had gone to bed and had fallen asleep and was perhaps dreaming pleasantly, and smiling in her sleep, he should kill himself, and his blood come creeping, creeping, on the ground to her own bedroom door! These thoughts were too terrible to dwell upon. (*OCS* 69–70)

Joseph Gold's suggestion that 'part, however small, of this terror is the element of wish-fulfilment in such a thought, a wish that reflects perhaps the author's barely disguised anger and dislike for her grandfather,'[18] is partially correct, surely, mirroring as it does Dickens' lifelong anger at his father's responsibility for his sufferings in the blacking factory, coupled with John Dickens' chronic financial recklessness which may have made even the successful author's support of him seem but an extension of the boy's six-shilling contribution to his impoverished family.[19]

All autobiographical speculation aside, however, the wish-fulfilment in the daydream is Nell's, and its bearing on the thematic intent of the novel must be examined. She rehearses in her mind (accompanied by visions of her own perfect innocence in sleep, as shown by her 'pleasant dreams') the various ways he might die, dwelling upon the most horrible of them. That Nell might harbour such a wish is not unreasonable, for the alterations in her grandfather's behaviour have not only made her life unhappy but have burdened her with a sense of guilt as the cause for the changes. Nell has matured from the child she was when she first came to live with Trent to a young lady of thirteen who is only just becoming aware of life's hard realities. Her fear of an unknown future rapidly approaching through her own growth from girlhood into incipient womanhood would make her eager to retain as much of her secure past as possible, and her grandfather's apparent changes, threatening to destroy the continuity of the past, would be natural catalysts to bad dreams and a wish for destruction of the forces for change, one of which is her grandfather himself.

Now, Nell's thoughts are in the form of a daydream, in which the mind wanders much as in sleep and produces a form of dream less powerful than, but nonetheless related to, the sleeping dream. Freud has said that 'the dream can be recognized as a wish-fulfillment'[20] which is not necessarily straightforward: 'in every human being there exist, as the primary cause of dream formation, two psychic forces (tendencies or systems), one of which forms the wish expressed by the dream, while the other exercises a censorship over this dream-wish, thereby enforcing on it a distortion.'[21] The idea that Trent might kill himself is a necessary distortion to mask Nell's own subconscious desire for his death, which psychoanalysis would say amounts to a desire to kill him. But because it is he and his changed behaviour which have caused her to wish his removal from her life, his death becomes suicide in Nell's waking dream.

In Freudian terms such an intent is well supported by the events immediately preceding Nell's daydream. Freud says that 'the dream may select its material from any period of life, provided only that a chain of thought leads back from the experiences of the day of the dream (the "recent" impressions) to that earlier period.' Just prior to Nell's daydreams, Dickens describes a scene in which she watches a coffin pass in the street, thus loosing the chain of reverie leading directly, both in her mind and on the page, to her daydream. This daydream is the first visible sign of a level in Nell's unconsciousness which permits her to harbour evil thoughts. The frequent use of dreams by Dickens for the revelation of personal, internal evil has been pointed out by M. Elizarova in the 1935 edition of the *Bol'shaia Sovetskaia Entsiklopediia*: 'Often the *evil*, unhappiness, and suffering of his heroes appear only as nightmares, dreams, or the fruit of some character's imagination.'[22] Nell's dream parallels Nellie's of her grandfather, which expresses Nellie's fear of rejection by the figure she must depend upon for ultimate acceptance of forgiveness. Because her grandfather refused to forgive his daughter, Nellie fears he may withhold forgiveness from her too, denying her the ultimate exercise of goodness. The elements of fear and wish-fulfilment present in Nellie's dream can be seen in embryo in Nell's dream.

Three inchoate emotions—a longing for the carefree past, a fear of the future, and an unformed sense of guilt—inspire Nell from the very beginning of her story. Like most children, she seeks to escape from what threatens her rather than to deal with it, although she is unable to say exactly what the threat is. To her grandfather she says, 'Do not let me see such change and *not know why*, or I shall break my heart and die' (emphasis mine). Knowledge gives power, but Nell seeks knowledge from without rather than from within.

But the source of the changes causing the child's guilt is not left unspecified to the reader. Trent is a gambler. The wastrel nature of John Dickens appears, perhaps in its truest form, in Trent. The gambler attempts to best fate by winning. His omnipotence will be rewarded by prosperity, and this prosperity will bring control. Just as Nell wishes to control her grandfather, so too he wishes to control her, to maintain his position of father and authority-figure. Only a mania such as gambling would be of sufficient strength to create a genuine conflict between the compelling force of the child's goodness and the equally compelling force of the man's possession. Dickens' knowledge of the mentality of the gambler is of a depth that suggests first-hand experience, for Trent's mania is described with a fullness and accuracy that look forward to Dostoevsky's *The Gambler*, whose protagonist, although known to be a devastating self-portrait, yet shows a remarkable resemblance to Trent. Nell, then, has good reason for her intuitive fear of a 'greater love' drawing her grandfather from her. Her battle is, all unconsciously, early set against the most formidable of obstacles, a mania stronger than duty and more compelling than love.[23]

The crisis for Nell's latent emotional conflict between good and evil comes when her grandfather does in fact become dangerously ill. Her terrible wish for his death seems about to be fulfilled, a fulfilment which may well have seemed to Nell like an only-too-well-deserved punishment. If Trent, her guardian and only parent-figure, has been brought near death by her selfish, if unconscious and unwilled, desire for that death, she must now, in retribution, become his guardian and herself die in his service. This is not to suggest that Dickens had Nell plan her journey and its conclusion in any such clear-sighted, deliberative way; yet a subconscious need to atone for a consciously unacceptable wish for his death makes it possible to see Nell's journey as an entirely necessary means of expiation for the wrong she believes she has done him and makes plausible her rejection of all outside help.

When they are actually to leave the curiosity shop, Trent asks Nell's forgiveness for the hardships he has caused her, but she does not actually say she forgives him, just as earlier she did not say she loved him. If Nell is literary parent to Dostoevsky's Nellie, this small scene must have impressed the Russian author. Nell's subconscious feeling of resentment against her grandfather, culminating in a wish for his death, would create a need of forgiveness for her sin against love. She thus desperately needs her grandfather's forgiveness of her thoughts; but as she can never confess those thoughts to him, his forgiveness must be sought in other ways. And just as Nell cannot ask forgiveness, she cannot afford to forgive.

'Forgive you—what?' said Nell, interposing to prevent his purpose. 'Oh, grandfather, what should *I* forgive?'

'All that is past, all that has come upon thee, Nell, all that was done in that uneasy dream,' returned the old man.

'Do not talk so,' said the child. 'Pray do not. Let us speak of something else.' (*OCS* 93)

The reference to an 'uneasy dream', which to Trent means his night of gambling, must have affected Nell strongly as she remembered her own uneasy dream of the old man's death and sought by dismissal to evade further recollection.

Nell's refusal to forgive is the ultimate source of her control over her grandfather. Just as Nellie withheld forgiveness, so too does Nell. She is drawn at this juncture not toward an erasure of the past, which mutual forgiveness would bring, but toward a future in which there would be no need for forgiveness because circumstances would not evoke evil dreams and disguised evil wishes. If she can forget her crime against her grandfather, she will be able to blot out the part of her that was capable of dreaming of his death and become whole again—wholly good.

In her attitude toward forgiveness Nell is remarkably like Nellie. Nellie refuses to forgive her grandfather for his cursing of her mother, or Valkovsky for his desertion of her. Forgiving and being forgiven erase the score and put one back where one began. Nellie cannot return to where she began, and she has a fairly clear idea of what she wishes to retain by not forgiving, i.e. her independence and her pride. Pride—that greatest of Christian sins—becomes Nell's companion as well, as she leads her grandmother away from the lesser sins that London represents. In her search for perfect goodness Nell must make unholy alliance with evil itself. From this point she is doomed, for such wilful evil can achieve eventual atonement only in death. For Nell, however, the past is well lost, especially that part of it involving her dream; and to return to the same past, in the same place and with the same circumstances that elicited the dream, would provoke an endless cycle of acts demanding her forgiveness and evoking endless guilt over her inability to forgive. Nell's wish for her grandfather's death and her refusal to forgive him, both slight incidents in themselves, show a seed of evil in Nell of which

Dickens himself may not have been conscious. Yet this was for Dostoevsky a universal and inescapable theme, and one which he could hardly have helped seeing in the story of Dickens' Nell.

The night her grandfather steals from her, Nell dreams about death again, but this time it is her own death, not his, that she dreams of. Thoughts not consciously connected in her mind are nonetheless connected in her dreams, and Dickens shows us in Nell's dream of 'falling from high towers' the beginning of her subconscious death-wish as a way of transferring her guilt to her grandfather.

In his study of the death instinct in Dickens' novels, Leonard Manheim describes how Karl A. Menninger, the noted physician, divides the death-urge

> into three components: a wish to kill, a wish to be killed, and a wish to die. The first of these is present in all forms of psychological aggression, whether sublimated or 'raw'; the second is found in all guilt-and-propitiation mechanisms. The third element, the true death-wish, is the most difficult to comprehend; yet its presence can be shown by a deep penetration into the motives inherent in life and in literature.[24]

Nell exhibits the wish to kill in her vision of her grandfather's death. Her efforts to atone to him are evidence of the wish to be killed, according to Menninger's classification. The death-wish itself is more difficult to determine; Manheim does not think Nell exhibits it, and Menninger himself feels that it is to be found not in verbal or psychological desires for death (these show the wish to be killed rather than the genuine wish to die), but rather in daredevil activities such as car racing and Houdini exploits. However, Manheim overlooks the fact that Nell's journey away from safety and into the unknown qualifies as a daredevil exploit for a child who is in sole charge of a penniless, senile old man. When she presses on in spite of her failing strength she is, in part, making inevitable her own death. Such an analysis is supported by her early thoughts on the value of death and her preternatural preoccupation with graveyards and churches. Her dream about her own death shows both despair and hope: despair at her grandfather's mania, which tears him from her; and hope that perhaps death will bring her the peace it brought her mother.

At this point it becomes clear why Dickens endowed Trent with a mania which engulfs all finer feelings: anything less would lessen the significance of his struggle against Nell's flight in search of peace and the preservation of innocence, and the true pathos of her death would be undercut. Nell's genuine terror at the thought of her grandfather as a gambler and a thief compels her to seek the only permanent happiness she has been taught—that of her mother and of all those in the graveyards she had visited, namely death. Her own death will be at once the supreme controller and the supreme atonement for her subconscious desire for the death of her grandfather.

It is at this point in the novel, when the two seek the oblivion of unknown countryside, that Nell's pride becomes her major support. It is also here that her death finally becomes inevitable, as if her creator were unable to deflect the ultimate punishment for what has been seen, from the Bible to Bunyan, as the cardinal sin. In succumbing to a sense of pride in her ability to control her grandfather, Nell joins the Garlands as a force against humaneness. What Nell effects is beneficial, just as the Garlands' manipulations of Kit have a favourable outcome. But both Nell and the Garlands seek to define their world by controlling all its inhabitants. This is perhaps why Dickens could not allow the child to meet those benevolent despots. The collision might result in the destruction of one kind of goodness—probably Nell's, for marriage to Kit would be a logical outcome of any imaginable Garlandian protective scheme. The parallels between Nell's need to control her grandfather and the Garlands' need to control Kit and Abel thus set up a mutual exclusivity which at once prevents the subsuming of either kind of goodness by the other and emphasizes the factor of control present in even the most benevolent of human relationships, that between parent and child.

While still in Wolverhampton, Nell exclaims: 'Oh! if we live to reach the country once again, if we get clear of these dreadful places, though it is only to lie down and die, with what a grateful heart I shall thank God for so much mercy!' (*OCS* 334) Once she reaches the countryside, her words are nowhere directed toward a resumption of life, but only toward a welcoming of death. Her dreams show this most clearly. On her way to Tong she has 'pleasant dreams of the little scholar all night long' (*OCS* 337)— the same little scholar whose death impressed upon her the final control offered by death. Once established in her antique house in Tong, she again dreams 'a sweet and happy dream' of 'the little scholar' (*OCS* 389). The conjunction between Nell's thoughts of death and her sweet dreams about the scholar shows her growing intentness upon the connection between death and goodness. She can work the ultimate good by dying and can evade forever any further knowledge of that evil from which she flies. Her grandfather will benefit because the memory of her will keep him from gambling (indeed, it inadvertently keeps him from sanity as well, as if Dickens sensed that pure sacrifice to another destroys the self). At the same time she will have been able to do the ultimate good for herself, for she will no longer have to flee from an unknown pursuer which neither she nor her creator can name but which has penetrated the deepest recesses of her heart. Only death will achieve for her and for her grandfather all she has been seeking, for her search has been for the superhuman, the angelic ideal, which can never be realized in life, much as Dickens might have longed for it, or might even think he had found it in Mary Hogarth. This personal battle was not to be resolved in *The Old Curiosity Shop*; indeed, as Angus Wilson remarks, 'the struggle between some idea of an innate evil in the world from which children cannot be wholly immune and the belief in a pre-Adamite childhood innocence is not resolved until *Great Expectations*'[25]—if then, some would add. But the mere existence of Nell's sexuality and Quilp's response to it indicates the reality of evil, however unconscious.

Dostoevsky appears to have taken from the closing pages of *The Old Curiosity Shop* the idea of a revelation of his heroine's history in *The Insulted and Injured*, for we have seen that Nellie's disclosure of her history is delayed until it is of use in uniting

Ikhmenev and his daughter. Nell's history too is only sketchily alluded to during the progress of the novel; on his anxious trip to save her the single gentleman reveals her background of love unworthily given, of anguish and death, with love unable to heal and Nell as the sole fruit of both love and loss. Nell's death, representing the extinction of the family's good qualities (only Fred Trent remains to carry on old Trent's lineage), coincides with Trent's reconciliation with his brother. Dickens makes it seem as if the reconciliation were a direct result of the effect of Nell's death on her grandfather, and in the pared-down version of the novel that Dostoevsky read in 1843 the single gentleman's motivations were omitted, leaving only Trent's newfound meekness and receptivity to his estranged brother for Dostoevsky to ponder. Dostoevsky's emphasis in telling his story is altogether more sombre and sinister than Dickens', but his final fidelity to Dickens' model brings us back to the point at which we began: the reader's use of Dostoevsky's recreated vision of Little Nell as a means of access to the springs of the English author's genius.

Of course any such Freudian excursion into the possibilities behind Nell's relationship to her grandfather unbalances the book; and I emphasize such an interpretation beyond its actual magnitude in the novel because it was through just such tiny chinks that Dostoevsky saw new light. Beneath the essentially comic exterior of Pickwick he sensed the saintly fool and through him developed Myshkin, a character expressive of the tragic depths of comic saintliness. Dostoevsky saw this sort of Nell as a real child, haunted by dreams rooted in the pain of her experiences and responding to that pain the best way she knew; it is this Nell I emphasize here, not to the exclusion of the Nell readers have wept over but as an expansion of the limited characterization Dickens could present within the covers of a novel and the context of his reading public. If one of the aims of criticism is to look beneath the surface of a work, we cannot rely alone on what we believe an author thought. Georg Lukacs has said of writers that if

in the process of creation their conscious world-view comes

into conflict with the world seen in their vision, what really
emerges is that their true conception of the world is only
superficially formulated in the consciously held world-view
and the real depth of their *Weltanschauung* ... can find
adequate expression only in the being and fate of their
characters.[26]

If this is so, then it is valid to look to Nell's own imperative of
development rather than to Dickens' conscious desires or choices
as he fashioned her.

The mutual exclusivity between Nell's search for inner
goodness and the Garlands' exteriorizing of it leads to Nell's
death. The concrete situation in which she is placed of course
controls the timing and direction of her flight, but Dickens gives
no convincing rationale for its power outside of Nell's own
compulsion to flee—not just from London, from Quilp, from the
licking flames of the foundry, from her grandfather's gambling,
but also from Kit and from the Garlands, either of whom could
have sheltered her and 'saved' her. And so, while I would not
suggest that Nell's economic and physical situations did not
prompt flight, I do suggest that they are not the sole determinants
of that flight. If we limit ourselves to seeing them so, we are
forced to consider Nell a martyr and saint (an unusual figure in
Dickens' works, to say the least) or to overlook the implications of
what Dostoevsky suggests about her: that real (and realistic)
emotions combine with circumstances to create a fictionalized and
particularized response to life.

Glimpsing the sources of Nell's choices in no way lessens the
magnitude of her struggle for self-definition against huge odds. A
close comparison of Nell with Dostoevsky's Nellie makes it
possible to discover sources of motivation in both: a discovery
which gives Nell greater stature within *The Old Curiosity Shop*
and makes not only more plausible but also more significant both
her journey and her death. The meaning of her death, apart from
its pathos, is the novel's ultimate concern and is carried through
thematically (consciously and unconsciously) in the imagery, the
pattern of Nell's journey, her dreams, her relationship with her

grandfather, the endowment of Trent with as severe a disease as gambling fever, and, most of all, in the equivocal nature of good as shown through its primary agents, the Garlands. The overall theme is the depiction of a human soul in its struggle against its own duality. In such a Nell, who strives to be perfectly good, the evil she finds in herself, or fears to find, must be denied. Yet as Dickens has perhaps all unwittingly shown in Nell, whom he tried to make as perfectly good as she would have had herself be, no one can escape being human. The death which translates Nell into final and total perfection also denies her further life, further humanity, since to be alive is to be imperfect.

I refer the reader back to F. R. Leavis's quotation at the beginning of this chapter. Little Nell's apparent unreality derives, for Leavis, from the fact that Dickens did not perceive her as real. But Dostoevsky did. His view of the reality underlying the actions we see as expressive of Nell's apparent goodness gives her a dimension, slight though it be in the context of the book as a whole, which allows for 'perception of the real' and therefore permits us to take her seriously as a real response to the sorts of encroachments Dickens saw threatening human beings. Thus, rather than isolating Nell from *The Old Curiosity Shop*, Dostoevsky's interpretation of her integrates her more convincingly into the novel. It is for this purpose that I have expanded a minor facet of Nell's motivation and explicated it within the framework of her actions. Only with the possibility of such depth and realism of character can Nell support the burden the book places on her, the burden of the human urge toward goodness compounded by human frailty.

Seen thus, *The Old Curiosity Shop* reveals the mind of the artist as it moves deeper and wider than his consciousness, bringing together truths ultimately available to the careful reader on the third, thirteenth, or thirtieth reading, even though they may have been unavailable to the author who created them. This is the supreme realism of which Dostoevsky found Dickens capable and which he himself tried to achieve—a truth which illuminates the hidden nature of experience and shines forth from the works of a great artist.

But, as Dickens himself says in *The Old Curiosity Shop*, the truth is not less true because it is seen through the filters of desire or imagination. One should not, he says, 'strip fair Truth of every little shadowy vestment in which time and teeming fancies love to array her' (*OCS* 400). And so Nell's death must not be viewed as exclusively prefiguring the evil in the human soul any more than we should accept it merely as an emotional recreation of Dickens' own ambivalent feelings about Mary Hogarth's life and death or his father's chronic insolvency, or as a pretty story designed to comfort the parents of dead children. Dickens' very ambiguity is part of his achievement as an artist, for little in his works can be reduced to a simple formula, a flat statement, an absolute—not even an absolute truth, and certainly not an absolute human good—however much his sentimental public could read him as offering them what they (and he) wanted to find.

The naming of Nellie Valkovsky after Little Nell is Dostoevsky's open and honest acknowledgement of his debt to the English author he had praised and was to praise until his death. A Nell of sufficient emotional complexity to serve as an example of the checkered birth of goodness among human beings is not only more satisfying to the reader, she is also more comprehensible within the scope of Dickens' development as a writer. Further insight into Little Nell helps place *The Old Curiosity Shop* within that development in much the same way that Dostoevsky's Nellie Valkovsky stands in the line of Dostoevskian sufferers.

CHAPTER IV

Whence Little Nell?

> *When two men and one woman are marooned on*
> *a desert island:*
> *If they are French, the woman marries one man*
> *and becomes the mistress of the other and they all*
> *live happily together.*
> *If they are English, nothing happens because*
> *there is no one to introduce them to each other.*
> *If they are Russian, the woman falls in love with*
> *Ivan and marries Georgii and suffers for the rest*
> *of her life.*
>
> *Russian joke*

From *Poor Folk* to *The Brothers Karamazov*, people suffer in
Dostoevsky's novels. He himself says, 'I think man will never
renounce real suffering, that is, destruction and chaos. Why,
suffering is the sole origin of consciousness' (*WN* 86). Since N. K.
Mikhailovski complained in 1881 that Dostoevsky enjoyed
creating wretched, unhappy creatures,[1] critics have believed that
one of his main concerns was the exploration of the reasons for
what appears to many to be undeserved suffering; M. Babovich
devotes an entire essay to the single idea that the struggle between
the forces of good and the forces of evil makes all weak people
suffer.[2] The connections between evil and suffering are subtle, but
without an understanding of them it is impossible to approach
Dostoevsky's ethic.

Suffering has been well defined in our own century by Mahatma Gandhi:

> Suffering is the mark of the human tribe. It is an eternal law. ... It is impossible to do away with the law of suffering which is one indispensable condition of our being. Progress is to be measured by the amount of suffering undergone ... [sic] the purer the suffering, the greater is the progress.[3]

These are universal sufferings, upon which life depends. Dostoevsky believed they arose out of evil, for to him it was human sinfulness that cursed mankind with the travail of birth. The fruit which gave the knowledge of good and evil doomed the human race to suffer for the evil it would both encounter and incur. Out of the primal curse came the need for suffering, for in gaining the freedom to know, we lost the ability to remain innocently happy. From that fatal moment man has struggled against the evil within him which causes him to suffer at the same time as it nourishes him, because it represents his freedom—even freedom to choose a path apart from the dictates of reason.

It is this problem Dostoevsky turns to in his writings. Freedom is good; evil is necessary for freedom; therefore evil is good because only through it can one approach an ultimate good. This central paradox in all human experience never left Dostoevsky's creative imagination.

Dostoevsky speaks at length about suffering as evidence of an expiation of evil. In a letter of 17 August 1870, to his niece Sofia Aleksandrovna, he writes: 'Without suffering, one does not comprehend joy. The ideal is purified by suffering, as gold is by fire' (*Pis'ma* II, 284). Anatomizing suffering in *The Diary of a Writer* in 1873, he recalls the Russian tradition of referring to convicts as 'sufferers' and giving them small gifts. The passages are worth quoting at length:

> There are unexpressed, unconscious ideas which are merely strongly felt. There are many such ideas and they are, as it were, fused with the soul of man. They also exist in a nation at

large, and in mankind taken as a whole. So long as these ideas dwell unconsciously in the people's life, they are but strongly and truthfully felt—up to that time only can the people pursue a vigorous and animated life. In the endeavours to interpret these concealed ideas consists the whole energy of the existence of the people. The more firmly the people cling to these ideas, the less they are capable of betraying the original feeling; the less they are inclined to submit to different misinterpretations of these ideas, the more powerful, solid and happy they are. Among these ideas concealed in the Russian people—ideas of the Russian people—is the denomination of crime as a misfortune, and of criminals—as sufferers. ... Briefly, by this word 'sufferers' the people, as it were, say to the 'sufferers': You have sinned, and you are suffering; but we, too, are sinful. If we had been in your place, possibly, we should have done even worse. If we ourselves had been better, perhaps, you would not be kept in jails. Together with the retaliation for your crimes you have also assumed the burden for general lawlessness. Pray for us, and we shall pray for you. Meanwhile, accept you 'sufferers', our pennies; we give them to you so that you may know that we remember you and that we did not sever our brotherly bonds with you. (*DW* 14–15)

However, the mere fact of suffering does not mitigate the criminal's guilt. He must expiate his crimes through his suffering, which, says Dostoevsky, is 'purifying and invigorating' (*DW* 16). Evil thus carries with it a personal responsibility for the guilt incurred by its expression; although the commission of evil can be expiated, evil's concomitant guilt remains. Man cannot refrain from being evil, and once he has actualized his evil into a specific anti-human act and thereby, in effect, released it from within himself, he must carry guilt with him ever afterward.

Suffering thus becomes the outward expression of generic evil and its unavoidable burden of guilt; it is through suffering that one admits one's evil and accepts it as natural and human. Atonement removes responsibility but not guilt; it is the desired end-result of creative suffering. It therefore seemed logical to

Dostoevsky that a willing assumption of suffering was one of mankind's basic responses to universal guilt. Such a response occurs in *Crime and Punishment*, when the painter Nikolai confesses to the murder of the old pawnbroker even though he knows, and we know, that he did not do it. Ironically, the chief of police, Porfiry Petrovich, expounds his theory about Nikolai's confession to the murderer himself, who is suffering from his failure to confess: 'Do you know, Rodion Romanovitch, the force of the word "suffering" among some of these people! It's not a question of suffering for some one's benefit, but simply, "one must suffer." If they suffer at the hands of the authorities, so much the better' (*CP* 441). Suffering 'at the hands of the authorities', of course, makes it all 'official'; a law has been broken, there is machinery to extract retribution, and one knows that one has something genuine to suffer for and that the debt can be paid. Such suffering, as with the convicts, is believed to gain the sufferer expiation. He knows he is guilty of evil (although in the case of a peasant like Nikolai the knowledge represents the unconscious mythic patterns of his nation's thinking rather than any conscious ratiocination), and he believes he can atone by receiving pain at the hands of those authorized to determine and account for the amount of atonement required. This makes him 'good' again, and he can then be happy—or so he believes.

When suffering becomes a conscious aim, however, it can deteriorate into an eternal quest in which the sufferer devotes himself to seeking degradation so that he can continue to suffer. Suffering becomes an end in itself to him; and because he has come to believe that nothing can be attained through suffering save the experience of suffering itself, he may seek to export it, to universalize it, to convince himself that everyone must suffer in order to gain an end which he is unable to define even to himself. Pushkin's poem *Gypsies* illustrates this sort of sufferer in Aleko, whom Dostoevsky analyses thus:

In Aleko, Pushkin had already discerned and ingeniously noted that unhappy wanderer in his native land, that traditional Russian sufferer detached from the people who appeared in our society as a historical necessity. And, of course, Pushkin found him not only in Byron. Aleko's is a true and unmistakably conceived character, a lasting character long since native to our Russian land. These homeless Russian ramblers are wandering still, and it seems it will be long before they disappear. If, in our day, they no longer visit Gypsy camps with their wild and odd mode of living in a quest for their universal ideals and in order to seek refuge in the bosom of nature from the confused and incongruous life of our Russian educated society—all the same they embrace socialism, which did not exist in Aleko's times, and with their new creed they journey to another field, eagerly tilling it, believing, even as Aleko, that through this fantastic labour they will attain their goal and happiness not for themselves alone but for all men. A Russian sufferer in order to find peace needs precisely universal happiness: with nothing less than that is he content. (*DW* 968)

This is a Byronic hero of the soil, seeking not physical satisfaction but a return to the Eden for whose loss he believes he suffers.

For a man who disclaimed any pretensions to being a psychologist, Dostoevsky is remarkably acute in perceiving the pleasure element which inevitably creeps into suffering such as Nikolai's and Aleko's. These are but simple instances, however, of the pleasure obtainable through suffering. One who considers himself worthy only of suffering, for instance the *débauché* or Dostoevsky's Underground Man, may provoke suffering to convince himself of his worthlessness and at the same time of his personal perspicacity.

Suffering can thus act in several ways: it can cleanse the guilty and make them truly happy; it can provide social expiation for those not sensitive or intelligent enough to realize why they must suffer; or it can reinforce self-conceptions of worthlessness by promoting a feeling of happiness which springs from the satisfaction of saying, 'I always knew I was worthy only of suffering.' The Slavic 'ability to rise spiritually in suffering' (*DW* 425) is only half the story. Raskolnikov's salvation through confession and suffering is countered by Golyadkin's creation of his own instrument of torture (his double) or by the Underground Man's conscious search for degradation.

Suffering, then, arises from the inescapable duality in human nature, which opposes evil to good and thus prevents the individual's full mental and emotional integration. We can attribute suffering, as Mikhailovski did, to a 'consciousness of sin',[4] or to the more modern idea of human propensity for rationalization, which often entices to pro-intellectual but anti-human actions; in either case it is a direct outgrowth of evil.

At the same time, suffering can itself lead to evil. When it is used for self-aggrandizement or to gain the pleasure of auto-flagellation, suffering becomes an evil in itself. A sufferer can also cause unhappiness to others because he is himself unhappy, and in this way generate new evil. It is this generative relationship between suffering and evil, where the two constantly recreate one another, that Dostoevsky most often explores. First of all, such a relationship is the more interesting; we prefer Satan to Christ in *Paradise Regained*, in spite of Milton's (and perhaps God's) intent. Second, and much more important, it is an authentic illustration of the direction in which Dostoevsky saw the world moving—toward an increase in evil. Finally, Dostoevsky believed that a study of the reciprocal generation of suffering and evil could lead the artist to an understanding which would allow him to break the chain and find similar generative ways to move away from, rather than toward, evil.

Such a progress through suffering in its positive form becomes to Dostoevsky one of the individual's most desirable states, since, in his view, only by suffering—for one's own crimes and for the sins inborn in mankind—can a human being find happiness. Such suffering, however, cannot be aimed solely toward expiation, for if that is its only motive it must fail because of its over-concern with self; much greater and more difficult is suffering with a full consciousness of the evil within and yet no expectation of reward.

Evil and the suffering inevitably arising from it are thus of great importance to an understanding of any of Dostoevsky's works. His preoccupation with such themes has caused many critics to bemoan what appears to be circular reasoning, in which the cause of suffering (evil) becomes its effect as well. This circularity is artistically depicted by the mythic representation of the snake eating its tail. The symbol stands for eternity: no beginning or end, birth or death; yet, because it is a serpent, it is also equated throughout mythology and Christian art with evil. Thus it suggests the Dostoevskian idea of the eternity of evil, which is, like the uroboric snake devouring its own tail, unavoidably circular. Yet it is possible to understand Dostoevsky's idea of the circular nature of evil if we accept his basic premise that the evil in mankind which causes suffering also causes individuals to seek self-punishment or to punish others, thus creating new evil which in turn causes more suffering.

There is a perceptible evolution in Dostoevsky's novels of his theories about the relationship between evil and suffering. He begins with the idea of the double as a visible externalization of the coexistence of good and evil. After observing how duality destroys, he moves toward modes of integration. In this second phase he turns to confession as a technique whereby the existence of evil can be acknowledged and the individual can atone through suffering for the evil of which he is guilty. This leads to a desire for expiation. Finally, passive expiation must be followed by action (always, for Dostoevsky, a journey), at the end of which the human sinner has repaid mankind and exorcized evil—not all of it, for that is never possible, but some important part of it.

In *Poor Folk* (1846), which Belinsky hailed as the height of realism and humaneness, society oppresses the individual, who is helpless against its evaluation of him as without value. Those who differ from the social ideal are destroyed. Makar Devushkin, a poor clerk in a faceless bureaucracy, deprives himself of necessities to buy luxuries for the woman he loves. She recognizes the value of his suffering on her behalf but, herself oppressed by the same society, marries a rich man she does not love. Devushkin holds her responsible for his sufferings (he did, after all, incur them initially in response to her need for love) and thus ignores his own responsibility. For him there are no solutions; indeed, he does not want any, for that would deprive him of the felicity of unjustified suffering. Thus arises the pathos Belinsky praised.

In his second published work, *The Double* (1846), which followed *Poor Folk* by only a few weeks, Dostoevsky explores explicitly the split he presented as implicit in Devushkin. The concept of the double is nearly as old as literature itself. Originally a device in Greek comedy, the double has come to serve the literature of the last two centuries as a particularly useful means of displaying the inherently ambiguous state of human nature which seeks simultaneous goodness and freedom.[5] According to Otto Rank, the hero must necessarily have a double nature. In the first place, he has inherited such from his two parents, who are opposites at least in gender. Many early heroes were twins or brothers (Romulus and Remus, Cain and Abel) or were in situations in which another child was required for sacrifice (Oedipus), indicating the necessity for an original duality which the hero would resolve in attaining to his heroism. Thus 'the idea of a doubled self ... is the essential characteristic of the genuine heroic type'[6] and is basic to the character of every person, each of whom is necessarily the hero of his own life.

Yakov Petrovich Golyadkin, the protagonist of *The Double*, has an autoscopic, or hallucinatory, double.[7] This simple double form often involves no more than a ghost or shadow, such as William Wilson's mirror image or Dr Jekyll's chemically-induced monster. The autoscopic double is almost always born from a character's attempt either to rid himself of undesirable traits or to take on desirable ones. William Wilson does not want to be confronted with the urgings of his conscience; Dr Jekyll needs to indulge his evil fantasies. Dostoevsky uses the autoscopic double to show how Golyadkin confronts his undesirable self.

Because he is unable to cope with the conflicting behavioural requirements of society, Golyadkin creates a new self that can conform. This superposition of appearance upon essence is at best an uneasy alliance, and for Golyadkin it ends, predictably, in insanity. In the attempt to deny part of his personality, Golyadkin loses the whole of it. Obviously Dostoevsky does not find the autoscopic double a useful one for the development of human wholeness.[8]

In *Notes From the Underground* (1864) Dostoevsky turns to a theoretical discussion of suffering, and it is here that we see clearly for the first time the deep and complex links between suffering, evil, and freedom which he was to explore in all his great works.

The Underground Man combines an insatiable desire to confirm his own superiority to the mass of mankind with a paradoxical sense of inferiority (rising, as did Makar Devushkin's, from his dissonance with social forms) which paralyses him professionally, socially, and almost physically. He finds meaning in suffering because suffering belongs to the individual alone and therefore is a means of creating and expressing free will. A man may choose to suffer, thereby asserting his individuality and thereby his existence. Existential suffering, 'condemning' man to be free, is a necessary concomitant of absolute freedom. The Underground Man perceives this and so constantly creates suffering for himself in order to reassure himself that he is free. His attempt to expiate through confession (his *Notes*) fails because he cannot relinquish his focus upon self as the centre of existence. And so he stays in his Underground, imprisoned by his insistence upon freedom.

Stavrogin in *The Possessed* (1871) is in many ways brother to the Underground Man. Stavrogin seeks perfect freedom because he believes it will give him control over his life. To be free, however, he must avoid all commitment and all values, for both require the acknowledgement of an existence of worth beyond the merely personal and require an allegiance which inhibits individual freedom. For both Stavrogin and the Underground Man, as Edward Wasiolek reminds us, 'the price of this freedom is necessarily to cut [oneself] off from humanity.[9] But even a complete dissociation from human values does not promise freedom, for both Stavrogin and the Underground Man are trapped by their forced lack of commitment and are in fact less free because they cannot but choose to suffer.

Immediately following *Notes From the Underground* Dostoevsky turned from the mere depiction of suffering to an analysis of the positive uses of suffering, gradually developing a theory of redemptive suffering through which the human being, victim of his own assertions of his freedom, learns to accept his sufferings and through them to love humanity. Only when he accepts his personal responsibility for evil can he begin to free himself from the human compulsion toward evil. As Dostoevsky saw when he created the Underground Man, redemption begins with confession. But the Underground Man's confession is tied to no specific 'crime' which requires social absolution, and therefore it can take no specific direction. It was necessary to devise a crime for which confession would be the first step toward a prescribed expiation.

In *Crime and Punishment* (1868), Raskolnikov commits such a crime. The theoretical basis for the crime is the assertion of his freedom, his superiority to the rest of mankind. He has expected to be free of remorse yet is driven to disclosure by inner compulsions he cannot explain. Intellectually convinced that he is free from the moral restraints confining the rest of the people in the world, he finds that physically and verbally he cannot refrain from placing himself under suspicion. Like Nikolai, who confesses to the murder in order to gain for himself the lawfully ordained punishment and expiation, Raskolnikov becomes desperate to right himself with society in order to right himself with God, as if the former assured the latter. His inevitable suffering for the moral evil of his act is intellectualized into an arithmetical proposition: crime plus payment equals cancellation of debt. This is attractive to him, as it was to Nikolai, because he believes it will obliterate all his unrecorded debts for his inborn evil, evil for which society has no prescribed expiation. By being caught, therefore, he stands to gain more than he loses.

Raskolnikov's confession, however, is blemished by his arrogant desire to take on suffering, as if through it he would gain superiority. Wasiolek has noted that he confesses only '*so that he can prove his strength by bearing the punishment.* ...It is not guilt or atonement that drives him to pursue his pursuers, but pride and self-will. He had committed the crime to prove his superiority; he pursues punishment and suffering to protect this superiority.'[10] Thus, although he gains a degree of freedom hitherto unattainable in Dostoevsky's fiction, it is marred by his continued insistence on his own virtue in assuming suffering. This fault is mitigated somewhat by his acceptance of punishment. The journey to Siberia is visible proof of his willingness to pay for his crime and begin anew. In spite of the fragility of his motives for confession, Raskolnikov's journey suggests that he may be able to work out his redemption.

The only possible freedom comes to those who are able to accept the strictures placed upon the individual by God and Society ('Thou Shalt Not Kill', for example). Real freedom is the freedom to eschew irrationality and evil. In choosing to suffer, man chooses to be free in the only way he can hope to be free— free from the ruling power of evil which seduces the Underground Man and Raskolnikov into believing in a freedom that is in fact the most constricting of bondages; for if a person can assert freedom only by flying in the face of rationality, law, or advantage, his forced choice becomes complete lack of freedom. Such freedom is obtained only in *The Brothers Karamazov*, in which Dostoevsky achieves a real resolution of man's dual nature and a synthesis of good and evil that allows constructive suffering.

The Brothers Karamazov is considered by many to be the culmination of all Dostoevsky's important themes and artistic techniques. Of all his novels, only this one does justice, in the words of Eliseo Vivas, to 'the breadth and depth of Dostoevsky's knowledge of the man that flourished in Europe and Russia in the nineteenth century and whose descendants have merely refined his neuroses.'[11] It is *The Brothers Karamazov* that most fully anticipates the Freudian filter which has so dominated our interpretation of the human being in the twentieth century. This is why modern readers respond so strongly to it, often with only the most shadowy notion why. The novel deals with the infinitely subtle and delicate problem of achieving both freedom and goodness in a world filled with men and women born to evil.

The Grand Inquisitor places the problem in its theoretical framework: the burden of freedom to choose God (good) is too great for man to bear, and so the Church or Society will designate, and thereby limit, the amount and quality of suffering necessary for a satisfactory life. In such a world evil can be expiated by a specific amount of suffering, whereupon the sufferer is decreed exonerated and guilt-free; but in such a world no redemption on Dostoevsky's terms is possible.

Opposing the Grand Inquisitor is Christ. He symbolizes a world in which freedom can be attained only through its renunciation; happiness can be found only through unhappiness; good can be achieved only through evil. The way is hard, and many are too weak to achieve the goal. For these the Inquisitor's pseudo-salvation offers temporal happiness and eternal damnation, which is at least preferable to temporal *un*happiness and the same eternal damnation. For those few who are strong enough for the struggle, however, the achievement of full humanness, equated in Dostoevsky's mind with Christianity, is possible.

Dmitri Karamazov is among the strong. His suffering arises from three sources: his love for Grushenka, his love for Katerina Ivanovna, and his desire to murder his father. The first energizes him but causes him to betray Katerina Ivanovna. The second leads him to a betrayal of himself, first by arousing Katerina Ivanovna's love through a false display of honour and later by stealing from her to go to Grushenka. For these acts Dmitri suffers spiritually. But it is only the third, his desire to murder old Karamazov, which brings physical punishment.

Through circumstantial evidence Dmitri is apprehended, tried, and sent into exile for a crime he did not commit. Yet in a larger sense he knows he *did* commit a crime. What one Karamazov does, the others are accountable for. Smerdyakov and Dmitri share the human condition, and so when Smerdyakov commits murder Dmitri becomes the murderer. For this he must suffer. Whether the suffering is self-inflicted or decreed by society, his conscious acceptance of it for a crime he did not physically commit acts as a means to expiation.

Once he recognizes his participation in guilt, Dmitri is able to seek forgiveness. He asks a bewildered peasant, 'for every one, for every one, you here alone, on the road, will you forgive me for every one?' (*BK* 433). Even those who have nothing to forgive must forgive, for it is only through such universal forgiveness, eternally sought, that Dmitri can be redeemed.

Dmitri's journey to Siberia for his official expiation is, like Raskolnikov's, a step toward actualizing his human good. He accepts his Siberian punishment and refuses to co-operate in Ivan's plan for his escape, feeling that a physical journey of expiation is necessary. It is as if a voyage to a new place would lead to the discovery of a new life, without the sins of the old. Both Raskolnikov and Dmitri seek such a new life, and Dostoevsky himself apparently accepted it as a way of evading the demands of established society with its Golyadkins and Smerdyakovs. His own journey to Siberia brought him into contact with the peasant faith which was later to nurture his Christian convictions, and so the idea of a journey to salvation must have held special interest. It is impossible to know whether, could he have returned with Dmitri to Siberia in 1880, he would have found what had awaited the young Dostoevsky there in 1849. But we do know he intended to send Alyosha on a long journey in subsequent volumes of his projected 'The Life of a Great Sinner', probably to determine whether such a journey could indeed offer new life or whether, as Dostoevsky no doubt suspected, one takes one's self wherever one goes. It is unfortunate that we will never know what ultimate use he might have made of the technique of the journey. It is certain, however, that in both *Crime and Punishment* and *The Brothers Karamazov* he saw it as a symbol of the infinite possibilities for re-creation of the individual.

Unlike Raskolnikov, however, Dmitri does not accept a just punishment brought on himself by his own illegal act. He accepts punishment for the existence of evil within himself, within his human brothers, within the murdered father, within all. He accepts his punishment because 'we are all responsible for all' (*BK* 625), and it is only through carrying the cross for all that the individual can be said truly to live. 'So he will perish an innocent victim!' Kolya Krassotkin exclaims. 'Though he is ruined he is happy!' (*BK* 812). And yet, Dostoevsky never allows us to forget that Dmitri's redemption comes about only because he continues to carry his evil within him. Perfection is never possible, and Dmitri's acceptance of his own responsibility for his evil would become meaningless if he could rid himself of that evil. Only through evil's eternal existence does redemption become possible, just as Adam's 'Happy Fall' earned Christ's redemptive death.

'In so far as the hero does return from the underworld of his being and is able to use his new knowledge for the benefit of his fellow men ... the Double novel reveals not a disintegration of the personality but a reintegration, a recognition of the necessary balance between order and freedom,' says Claire Rosenfield in her study of the doubles in literature.[12] It is this integration that Dostoevsky sought in Dmitri Karamazov. At the end of *The Brothers Karamazov* hope remains a possibility, but, as Eliseo Vivas observes, 'we are also left with the insight that so long as a man remains in the world that possibility cannot be fully realized.'[13]

Nellie Valkovsky is an early Dostoevskian sufferer, unable to comprehend the reason for her sufferings and unwilling to relinquish the sense of self she shares with the Underground Man. Her journey to the Ikhmenevs' is fruitless, for through it she seeks not forgiveness but independence of the need for forgiveness. Within Dostoevsky's theory of the interrelationship of evil and suffering, Nellie is doomed; yet through her sufferings she is able to light the way for others. She is part of the continuum of suffering Dostoevsky saw as the human inheritance, and she represents a distinct and important step in his development as a writer. She stands in relation to his exploration of human nature approximately where Little Nell stands in Dickens': at the beginning, where the personality lies exposed through actions but the soul remains hidden, impervious alike to its inner imperatives and to its responsibility to the rest of mankind.

Dickens has long been viewed primarily as a social novelist, and his works are most often explicated as social documents whose characters either represent or bear the burden of social policies and practices, inflict or stagger under social doctrines. And a developing sense of society as the embodiment of evil characterizes the progression of his personal politics. Within the web of contemporary criticism of Dickens, Little Nell's veiled complexities stand as part of the continuum of his developing social and moral sense.

The external world is for Dickens not so much the incentive or foil for human action, as it often is for Dostoevsky, as the cause. This difference is bound to result in very different approaches to character development, just as it elicits differing responses to social stimuli. Dickens would not have dreamed of creating a band of ruthless, deluded revolutionaries such as those in *The Possessed*, any more than Dostoevsky could really have reincarnated Pickwick. Yet in all Dickens' novels, society as antagonist opposes individuals who are themselves members of microcosmic societies impinging on yet other individuals in a strongly cyclic fashion. And ultimately, it is impossible to consider Dickens without considering his view of the nature and workings of evil among these moving cogs and wheels.

In the end society is for Dickens a conspiracy of individuals, a circumlocution office run by finite and countable Tite Barnacles, under an official mask as false as the brick front of Mrs Clennam's house. But this sort of evil usually remains faceless and moves on silent motorized rollers, while those who oppose it do so from a base of disorder called individuality. Such particularization of Dickens' overall concerns is fully consistent with his methods of realism. Truth is expressible only through an artistic ordering, and hence interpretation, of facts as they can be seen to exist within the observed life of England. If the artist's ordering does not express the whole historical truth, as Dostoevsky believed Gué's 'Last Supper' failed to show the uniqueness of Christ's communion as the future of all Christianity, then it is not realism and therefore in the truest sense not *real*. And so, while Dickens consciously addressed himself to social problems, these are expressed so fully through individual characters and plots that it is both necessary and reasonable to approach the expression of the great evil—corrupt society—through the individuals who create and suffer from it. Like Dostoevsky, Dickens saw suffering as the basis for understanding. And because, as Edmund Wilson has said, 'Dickens never really repeats himself,'[14] we can look for a progression of thought and an attempt to work through the questions his novels raise.

As early as *Pickwick Papers* Dickens shows an awareness of the fact and causes of suffering. Not only in the interpolated tales does he show suffering; Pickwick himself chooses to suffer in the Fleet rather than partake of the false, and therefore evil, judgment wangled by Dodson and Fogg. Pickwick's 'mind and sensibility' are 'made incandescent by poverty, injustice, suffering, and social oppression.'[15] Like Dostoevsky's *Poor Folk*, *Pickwick Papers* posits social origins for suffering and shows the futility of individual opposition: Pickwick is forced to concede in order to save Mrs Bardell, just as Makar Devushkin must relinquish Varvara Petrovna in order to save her. The individual is, at the outset of both writers' work, helpless against the power of society to control behaviour and belief. Early on, Pickwick's comic adventures take on the weight of suffering. The interpolated stories, often spoken of as the major conveyers of what small evil exists in the book, are actually merely a reinforcement of Pickwick's own growing sense of the difficulty of justice and benevolence. Thus it is possible for Monroe Engel to speak of 'the accretive weight of seriousness of this novel'[16] because of its acute awareness of the existence of evil and the powerlessness of the individual.

In *Oliver Twist* we get Dickens' initial attempt to polarize the forces with which Pickwick was unable to contend. Fagin is offset by Mr Brownlow, and society holds crime at bay only because crime itself stumbles. Oliver is something of a puppet, snatched from faction to faction. He is the *tabula rasa* to be imprinted, and only his genteel heritage saves him from the inscriptions that shaped Bill Sikes and Nancy. There is little sense of hope here. Dickens' purpose seems to be to make criminality unattractive, as he says in his preface to the novel; but at the same time, he can find nothing powerful enough to work against it. Only Nancy, who, he vehemently insists, 'IS TRUE', moves between both worlds and can really be said to partake of both. The twentieth century finds her willingness to help Oliver less unbelievable than did Dickens' original readers. It is possible to see in Nancy an early combining of the knowledge of evil with the possibility of good. Dickens' intent to polarize good and evil admittedly makes it more difficult to recognize, or accept, Nancy's bridging of the two, but even as early as *Oliver Twist* there is a noticeable tendency toward exploration of the nature of good and evil. It is easier, of course, to show the good lying within evil; far more heart-warming, far more likely to be believed by the reader who really does want it all to come out right in the end. But the seriousness that underlay *Pickwick Papers* is never absent from Dickens' subsequent works.

Nicholas Nickleby repeats the structure of *Oliver Twist* as it focuses on abuses in schooling. Here Dickens turns to an influence specifically child-orientated, and here he explores the ways in which a child can control and manipulate his surroundings. To some extent it is possible for Nicholas to choose how he will be influenced; but his choices are accompanied by specifically masculine and sometimes unfortunate actions, such as his tendency to lose his temper when opposed. He is angry, impotently so, over Ralph Nickleby's elaborate deception about Smike's ancestry; over Mr Bray's treatment of his daughter; even over the marrow-throwing suitor's advances to his mother. Dickens focuses here on the development of a moral sense that includes anger and a perception of human fallibility, but Nicholas is largely the ready-made ware of others, altered to suit. There is too much plot obscuring him, too little scope for his own imperative of development.

The Old Curiosity Shop comes next. In it Dickens focuses on Nell, attempting still to develop her within a polarized world. But that world is more highly developed; evil arises not solely from social abuses but also from individuals and seems to have a malign existence even apart from its human manifestations. Within such a world of irrational evil, a child develops her response. Again the response is finally unsatisfactory, for it leads to death rather than to an accommodation of life. But within Dickens' development of the idea of evil and its manifestations within the human world, *The Old Curiosity Shop* is a distinct advance both in theory and in execution.

Following *The Old Curiosity Shop* there is a change in Dickens' approach to social evil. Previous to this novel, and to a large extent within it as well, Dickens separated good from evil to allow for the victory of the good. But, as Engel notes,

Dickens' early novels are products of his period of relative optimism, when he could dissociate himself somewhat from the sufferings of his childhood because he did not yet understand that they were only an introduction to the sufferings of adulthood.[17]

This view changes when he moves from a depiction of children to an exploration of the young adult, and comes to full focus in *David Copperfield*. Little Nell is the last of his children to attempt a separation between good and evil. Her failure must have been for Dickens something of a revelation.

Nor is it fanciful to see Little Nell as the beginning of an exploration of the human struggle against innate evil, for in Dickens' next major novel, *Martin Chuzzlewit*, even the hero is tainted with evil. Dickens emphasizes his genealogy, his connection with original sin 'undoubtedly descended in a direct line from Adam and Eve.' This direct line includes suspicious old Martin as well as the murderer Jonas. It is perhaps true, as Hillis Miller says, that Martin's greatest sin is selfishness;[18] but even this opposes the society of love Dickens seeks in all these early novels. Selfishness as much as big business circumvents individual happiness; 'the vice of Pecksniff, Jonas and Young Martin penetrates into every corner of life, public and domestic, in mid-Victorian England.'[19] In *Martin Chuzzlewit* Dickens deals with adult sufferings; but the impossibility of a complete victory of good is everywhere evident after his development of Little Nell. And 'from this time forward he had the ability to show *repressed* feelings,'[20] an ability he was yet learning with Nell.

In *Oliver Twist* Dickens wants to rid the world of the causes of suffering. In *The Old Curiosity Shop* Nell wants to rid herself of suffering. But by *Martin Chuzzlewit* Dickens has acknowledged that suffering exists, cannot be avoided, and must be somehow dealt with. Thus it is appropriate that he begins again with children (following two novels about young adults), applying his conclusions about the universality of suffering and the inescapability of evil and guilt developed up through *Martin Chuzzlewit*. Most critics nowadays agree that *Dombey and Son* marks the turning point in Dickens' career. With this novel he stops trying to find facile answers and becomes increasingly pessimistic about the possibility for love or good. 'Immediate social ills are always set now in a larger context of possibility and limitation,' says Engel.[21] But Dickens has been toying with possibility and limitation for quite some time. In *Dombey* the forces opposing the child's development are clearly delineated; and, in keeping with the idea of direct descent from the Fall of Man, the child's major persecution comes from her father. Paul Dombey is significant as an example of the failure of Dombeyism, but Florence is even more important because she survives. It is survival that Dickens becomes increasingly concerned with. After the death of Paul, his major child characters all live to adulthood. Adaptive mechanisms that lead to death are ultimately not very useful. And so Florence survives. She mouths the same rhetoric as Nell did about that happy place called Death, to which her mother was called and where all will be reunited in joy. Too, she is rejected by her father without knowing why; and throughout the book she suspects some hidden fault which causes his rejection. Dickens desires to exonerate Florence: 'Florence will never, never, never, be a Dombey ... not if she lives to be a thousand years old'; but the fact remains that she *is* a Dombey, just as Nellie Valkovsky is the Prince's daughter and heir to his evil. Instead he gives Florence the memory of her mother's love and the reality of Paul's need for her.

These two offset her inheritance and seem to make it possible for her to accept Dombey's estimate of her without either changing her own view of herself or requiring that he change, neither of which Dickens any longer sees as possible. If she could elicit his love she would be able to control him, control her life; by refusing to love her, Dombey resists such control and she has to learn to live without it. But unlike Little Nell's attempts to control her grandfather, Florence's hopes are not disguised. She explicitly wants 'to be allowed to show him some affection, to be a consolation to him, to win him over to the endurance of some tenderness from her' (*D* 249). This is her aim throughout his courtship and early remarriage; it is only when she fully acknowledges that he will never allow her even so much that she finally runs away—not from him so much as toward something she can control, toward a life which will be hers to shape. Would he ... forgive her if she were to die? she wonders. Might death be the means of ultimate control? But she rejects this idea. This is the beginning of adult responsibility.

From here, of course, Florence is transported into another sort of happiness with Walter Gay, into which her chastened father enters when, like Florence at fourteen, all else is lost to him. When he comes back, she 'ask[s] forgiveness on [her] knees' and confesses, 'I know my fault. I know my duty better now.' Like Little Nell, Florence conceals the seeds of the knowledge of human evil. But Dickens allows unmotivated coincidence to solve her problem, and it is this that causes critics to complain about the lack of reality in Dombey's return and to find Florence's acceptance of him almost disgusting.[22] The book ultimately fails to deal with what happens after the destruction of the dream of ultimate goodness. But it points toward Dickens' next great discovery: individual responsibility for others. Florence chooses to remain responsible for her father even though she is able to renounce the need to make him responsible for her. The latter is a precondition of the former for Dostoevsky, as we have seen. Thus *Dombey and Son* is a great advance for Dickens, for in it he is able to renounce the need for perfect goodness that drove Little Nell to her grave. Goodness no longer strides; it limps to a less than satisfactory conclusion, but for the first time the conclusion is predominantly a real one.

I deal with *David Copperfield* in the second part of this book and so will not speak much about it here, except to note that Dickens showers David with facile successes that do not accord very well with the darkness of vision that permeates this as well as the earlier novels. Insofar as David is a re-creation of himself, Dickens must turn away from other considerations. It is one thing to imagine Florence Dombey accepting her failure to earn her father's love, quite another to see David/Dickens making such admissions.

In *Bleak House* Dickens returns to the development of a child's sense of responsibility. Esther Summerson and Jo have both long been seen as bearers of Adam's sin, themselves innocent and yet suffering from the sins of their mothers, a sort of 'tragedy of the irrevocable', as Hillis Miller calls it.[23] Death is one escape; Dickens gives it to Jo. Esther's escape is through acceptance of responsibility. One critic has noted that 'freedom lies in the recognition of [the] necessity [to do one's duty].[24] Esther achieves this freedom by acknowledging her 'sin' and attempting to make restitution. She feels 'guilty and yet innocent' about her mysterious heritage, asks 'why is it my fault?' Her aunt's declaration that she has forgiven Esther's mother rings false even to Esther's inexperienced ears; the stone-hard demeanour of the forgiver bespeaks a sense of righteousness that Esther must learn to abjure, through what Judith Wilt calls 'Confusion', that ability to hold 'the [critical] power [of Animus] just at the threshold of consciousness' so that she can act correctly without having quite to know why.[25]

Although I would not go so far as to attribute this quality to Dickens' conscious artistry, as Wilt does, it seems a good metaphor for what Esther must indeed do, that is acknowledge evil (responsibility) without condemning herself. She does this first through recognition of her connectedness with all of humanity, as shown in her dream of being a bead in the necklace of life and finding it 'such inexplicable agony and misery to be part of the dreadful thing'; then through forgiveness of her mother (although, to her credit, she never claims the right to stand in the position of forgiver); and finally, after her first revulsion at Lady Dedlock's disclosure causes her to feel 'as if the blame and the shame were all in me,' by acceptance of herself. But she comes to accept her innocence within guilt, to see that the blame is not hers, and at the same time to see that through her existence she is responsible for humanity: both the mass of mankind and its movement toward humaneness. To the novel's almost 'universal abnegation of responsibility,'[26] she replies, 'I am afraid everybody is obliged to be responsible.' And although Skimpole stoutly doesn't 'intend to be responsible', Esther does. Of course her moral responsibility takes, for Dickens, the form of social responsibility. Her housekeeping is God's housekeeping. Dickens cannot yet accept the full extent of human impotence in the face of social corruption. But *Bleak House* does fully posit individual responsibility as the key to social order.

Such responsibility cannot be achieved without forgiveness. Esther forgives her mother readily, something Little Nell could never do; she even forgives herself for her birth; and, when she first looks in the mirror following her disfiguration by smallpox and 'feels the clear imperative to find and fully forgive in advance that changed unchanged face,'[27] she forgives her own acquired shortcomings. Next she must make such forgiveness clear and acceptable to the reader. 'Surely it is impossible to address one's partly known, labyrinthine, undisciplined heart or the reader's without deciding in advance to forgive it, without desiring in advance its forgiveness.'[28] Thus does she come to terms with the evil which she, as bearer, is responsible for. There is no reason why it is her fault. Fault merely *is*. For that we all need forgiveness. Esther seeks, and gives, such forgiveness.

At the same time, however, she makes responsibility into a role and a self-justification. Like Raskolnikov, she half believes she can pay off her responsibilities. To the end she retains a vanity and a self-congratulatory tone that make her resolution of evil less than entirely satisfying. Dickens has, nonetheless, come quite a distance from Little Nell's inadmissible evil. And his little girls are growing to adulthood.

Little Dorrit has been seen as a quest for responsibility, both on the personal level and on the social level through Dickens' emphasis on limited liability companies, then emerging as a means to protect the public from unscrupulous investment advisors. Like Esther, Amy Dorrit is able to come to terms with this world and her place in it. She never questions the world; she merely seeks her place. She not only accepts responsibility, she does so naturally, not as a self-chosen suffering but as part of her birthright. In the prison world of the novel, 'no specific cause or explanation of any individual's suffering can be found,'[29] but that suffering exists; in fact, 'there is a great increase here over the earlier novels in the self-consciousness and articulateness of suffering or malice.'[30] Although *Little Dorrit* shows 'the seductive attractions of "contracting out", of cultivating the sort of insensibility to the world and its troubles that Mr Dorrit has selfishly cultivated in the Marshalsea,'[31] Amy herself never seeks this escape. She does not take on her suffering as a burden nor seek to control her father through forgiveness of him; she merely forgives him. Both suffering and forgiveness are a necessary part of Amy's existence. Dickens rewards her with marriage to Arthur; but in spite of the common tendency to scoff at the impotence of their alliance, it represents a journey outward from self, a tiny island of freedom within the responsibility for all that Amy Dorrit chooses as her self-definition.

As early as 1958 Hillis Miller recognized that in *Little Dorrit* 'Dickens approaches Dostoevsky's recognition of the complicated relations of good and evil in a world in which evil subtly corrupts and frustrates good and even the worst evil is qualified by a small measure of good.'[32] Amy Dorrit's willingness to accept and believe in both is what allows her to succeed, for she need not, like Nell, delude herself about her own nature. Like *Bleak House* before it, *Little Dorrit* insists 'that we are all involved with one another.'[33]

Pip in *Great Expectations* makes much the same choice as Amy Dorrit does. Once he becomes aware of his guilt and comes to see 'himself the source of all that has happened to him,'[34] he is tempered by his experiences and is able in the end to renounce his expectations, accept Estella's parentage, and love Magwitch. Thus does Pip earn, as does Amy Dorrit, 'the muted happiness that comes after acceptance.'[35] If, as Barnard says, the theme of *Great Expectations* is guilt—'guilt imposed, guilt assumed, guilt transcended'[36]—then Pip's acceptance of himself as flawed and with no expectations save himself is the first step toward forgiveness of others' guilt. And indeed, Pip forgives both Estella and Magwitch in the form of truly 'Christian forgiveness.'[37] Julian Moynahan sees Pip's sense of complicity with Orlick as parallel to Ivan Karamazov's recognition of intellectual guilt for his father's murder; Dorothy Van Ghent suggests that Pip's bowing down before Magwitch functions much the same as Zossima's prostration before Dmitri Karamazov in prediction of Dmitri's future role as overt bearer of human guilt.[38] The themes Dostoevsky explores are present as well in Dickens. It is moral guilt Pip assumes, for he is not physically guilty toward Magwitch; in fact, Magwitch is guilty toward Pip, just as old Karamazov was toward Dmitri, who was innocent of his actual murder. Moynahan sees Pip's regeneration as fuelled by the power motive, which 'involves the aggressive wish to push beyond the authoritarian figures who hold the child powerless'[39] just as Nell sought control over her grandfather. But in forgiving Magwitch, Pip renounces the power motive that Nell could not renounce because she could not specify it. Pip's acknowledgement of responsibility is 'a precondition of his regeneration.'[40] One believes in this regeneration as one cannot believe in Esther's, for it leads to no benefits for Pip, save, of course, the one overwhelming benefit of true and full responsibility to others. With Pip Dickens achieves what he was almost unconscious of desiring for Little Nell: full participation in humanity.

This full participation carries over into the far more sombre world of *Our Mutual Friend*. There is no Joe Gargery, no John Jarndyce, to help Eugene Wrayburn. Unlike Pip and Esther, he is fully grown into a studied irresponsibility which is the result of his rejection of socially defined responsibility. Eugene must learn to choose responsibility. *Our Mutual Friend* seems to go beyond good and evil. Good becomes at best neutral, and Eugene and Lizzie present the weakest resolution in all Dickens' novels. The journey Eugene must take is no longer a physical or emotional journey through death itself. John Harmon, Eugene, Riderhood, and Headstone cannot live except through baptism. Only death regenerates. Harmon 'dies' and creates a new existence, refusing inherited benefits and seeking instead his natural responsibilities. Eugene's second life requires a similar renunciation of the values of the first. Riderhood, given a second chance, continues in the old way and proves there is no third chance. Headstone is so tied to a belief in rights that duty kills him. Only through a death to the world and regeneration into a new life can one live. It is as if Dickens tries Pip's and Esther's solutions in a harsh forge to see whether they will work there. If life is truly a living hell, as Dickens seemed to believe toward the end of his writing career, then there is nothing to do but move forward, slowly and lamely. Good may be at best neutral; one must make the best of this neutrality. Dickens' reconciliations may be 'a part that will not stand for the whole', as Barbara Hardy says of the ending of *Bleak House*;[41] but at least there is that part; and for Dickens, in the later novels, it is at last genuine.

Throughout his works Dickens is preoccupied with the problems of suffering, guilt, responsibility, and forgiveness. It is not surprising that Dostoevsky, who was so strongly influenced by him, should treat the same problems. What is perhaps surprising is how parallel the two writers' ideas really were. Dostoevsky, of course, began with an advantage; he had read much of Dickens by the time he began writing, and he could see where Dickens' answers wouldn't work. The faint overtones of the existence of evil in *Pickwick Papers* becomes Myshkin's complicity in the murder of Natasha; Little Nell's inadmissible need for control becomes Nellie Valkovsky's manipulative pre-sexuality.

It is by now commonplace to say that Dickens and Dostoevsky were both concerned with the darker side of life. George Gissing saw 'spiritual kindred' between the two[42] and Angus Wilson finds this spiritual kindred in their belief 'in absolute evil ... a kind of innate evil. ... The picture of society ... that they both held was black.'[43] Edmund Wilson saw clearly that 'Dickens never really repeats himself' and that in *Edwin Drood* he had abandoned the purely social analysis of the early novels in favour of an investigation of 'the duality of good and evil' through portrayals of 'moral uncertainty, of evil'.[44] Such a moral progression is confirmed by many critics;[45] I quote largely from them in this brief overview in order to show how embedded in the contemporary estimate of Dickens a deeper, more complex picture of Little Nell really is. And although 'moral progression' takes the form of many different symbolic systems to 'explain' Dickens, there is general agreement over Dickens' gradual increase in concern for the individual in the struggle to find a meaningful place in the world. Dostoevsky clearly saw this concern—after all, it fitted so nicely with his own—and desired to understand the ways Dickens made it palpable in his writings. The Little Nell he re-created in Nellie Valkovsky is in the direct line of Dickens' children as they learn to grow up in a world that threatens them with the burdens of humanness.

There can be little doubt that Dostoevsky was the greater 'psychologist', but this does not mean that Dickens did not deal with many of the same problems. The 'theme of the growth of love and social sense ... may be more subtly explored by greater psychologists than Dickens, but [it] still shapes his moral categories.'[46] Little Nell is a part of that 'dark view that even at his most optimistic moments is just beneath the surface.'[47] Dostoevsky saw this; he reproduced in his Nellie the obverse of Little Nell, whom Dickens was not to examine closely until much later. The fact that Dickens returned again and again to the subject of the deprived child indicates that for him Nell's predicament was one of 'those recurrent configurations of experience to which an artist's imagination responds.'[48] When I say this I do not say anything new; critics have been writing as much for many decades now. As we slowly extend to Dickens' earlier works the same sort of serious consideration we are used now to giving the later, it will become obvious that the allusions to Dickens' continuity of ideas, to his increasingly sophisticated methods of shaping worlds, to his fidelity to human values can be substantiated in specific works, as I have tried to do here with Little Nell. Dostoevsky's is but another critical vision which can illuminate.

PART TWO

David Copperfield

CHAPTER V

The Hero of My Own Life

When reading, Dostoevsky was never satisfied with the manifest creations of the author he read and not even with the hidden intentions for which the manifest situation might be only a disguise or a symbol, but that he followed up other possible developments of a story in his imagination, discovering aspects which no ordinary reader might have seen in it.

GEORGE KATKOV

David Copperfield presents quite a different critical problem than does *The Old Curiosity Shop*. Dickens viewed Nell from without, and Dostoevsky provided a way to see within. But *David Copperfield* is an autobiography and a *bildungsroman*, and David presents himself directly. Here the problem is to see and evaluate the outside world more objectively than David can present it, so that we can untangle the forces shaping him. David lacks the breadth of vision to show us not only what he is but also, as Dickens himself must sorely have sought, why he is. His superlative delineation of Pip in *Great Expectations* has its roots in David's story, and I want here to explore those roots more fully than David himself allows us to.

'Whether I shall turn out to be the hero of my own life, or whether that station will be held by anybody else, these pages must show' (*DC* 1). David's credentials for telling us his story are immediately apparent and are not related to his heroism, such as it may prove to be: 'If it should appear from anything I may set down in this narrative that I was a child of close observation, or that as a man I have a strong memory of my childhood, I undoubtedly lay claim to both of these characteristics' (*DC* 14). David is, in short, a storyteller. Of his early observational talent, he says, 'I could observe, in little pieces, as it were; but as to making a net of a number of these pieces, and catching anybody in it, that was, as yet, beyond me' (*DC* 23). It is this very net, woven round the reader, that is the force and meaning of *David Copperfield*. Yet this same net obscures evaluation of David's growth because of the use of David as autobiographical narrator.

David's centrality poses several critical problems. 'Since the hero's life obviously constitutes the central pattern of the book,' says James R. Kincaid, 'it is vitally important that this pattern be the most interesting and the most fully developed. Very few critics, however, feel that this is the case.'[1] In fact, 'it seems to be essential that we recognize that David is, in many key ways, neither the voice of the author *nor the voice of the novel*.'[2] In fact, it has been questioned whether he actually exists at all. Stephen Leacock calls him 'the looking glass in which we see the other characters'[3]; E. M. Forster comdemned him as more like a bubble than a solid[4]; Percy Lubbock called him 'a pair of eyes and a memory'[5]; he is 'colourless, and impossible to visualize physically' for Q. D. Leavis[6]; even G. K. Chesterton bemoans the fact that David gradually 'gives up the exhausting habit' of living in the reader's mind.[7] The only way David can attain substance and reality is through clear causation for his character development. His apparent lack of colour and solidity arises from the critic's inability to comprehend intellectually the sources for the reality of such a character. In fact the book does provide such sources, but they are necessarily clouded by the autobiography's requirement that David see his life entirely subjectively; he cannot tell us what he does not see. Yet it is Dickens' shaping of David through opposing forces that creates what heroism the novel exhibits.

Primarily, David grows through contact with Steerforth, Heep, and Traddles, and much of what he becomes is a reflection of or revulsion from these three contemporaries. All three exhibit parallel development and 'are alike in that *they take the ways David might have taken*.'[8] They offer a panoply of choice and moral ambivalence: there is no intrinsic need for Steerforth to have been punished, since Heep is allowed to live; David learned from the first mistaken impulses of his undisciplined heart, but Emily was punished for the same impulses; David's colourless maturity contrasts unfavourably to Traddles' scenes of bliss with Sophy and the girls; and both David's love for Dora and Steerforth and Emily's passion make it doubtful that many readers could prefer a marriage like David and Agnes's. David's choices, far from being the most heroic or the most pragmatic, are in fact merely a few from the vast number of possible choices, all valuable in one way or another. We need to see why David chooses as he does and what those alter egos actually represent, aside from David's necessary distortion of them.

It is difficult to look beyond David's viewpoint because there is no artistic impulse drawing attention outward. Dickens' signposts are all we have, and Dickens' surface intent was the recreation and exorcism of childhood bogeys. He would not take us below, even if he could. Yet 'David's life is not presented to us in a way that can reasonably be called significant,'[9] nor is that life in any way significant itself. Even the apparent structure of autobiography holds the reader within David's vision. What is needed is an outside vantage point from which to view the novel. Such a vantage point would permit us to ask interesting questions: how does Dora feel? who is Steerforth? whence arise Heep's infamy, Wickfield's weakness? Of course, as Dostoevsky says about Raskolnikov's regeneration in Siberia, 'that is another story.' But that other story—those other stories—provide the omniscient viewpoint necessary to the sort of understanding we seek of *David Copperfield* or of any work. As Mark Spilka has said in his story of mutual interpretation of Dickens and Kafka,

One great advantage of influence study is that it cuts both

ways; it tells as much about old as new creations. From the familiar ground of the source, we can better survey the new terrain; and from that outlook, we can often perceive new aspects of the source.[10]

Before turning to Dostoevsky's re-vision of *David Copperfield*, I want to look at another re-creation of Dickens' novel by a noted writer. Robert Graves, in *The Real David Copperfield* (1933), purports to improve the novel through elimination of Dickens' 'continual readiness to sacrifice straightforwardness in writing to a tradesmanlike exploitation of the now extinct Dear Reader' and his 'temptation to economise in inventive effort by diluting.'[11] Apparently Graves saw in *David Copperfield* an organic whole whose meaning was somehow obscured by Dickens' style. He attempted 'the restoration of the novel written by Dickens for publication in 1850 to what appears to be its natural length and plot,'[12] which for Graves turned out to be half its length and strictly autobiographical. Graves appears to offer the reader just such a critical re-vision as Dostoevsky offered for Little Nell, and it is worth looking into in some detail for the portrait of David it paints, for Graves' David is as inherent as Dostoevsky's Steerforth in *David Copperfield*, and Graves' failure to create a living David is a useful caveat to the critic who attempts a reverse influence study.

Of course, cutting out half of Dickens' words has its losses, and these losses often fall most heavily upon characterization. Graves chooses to omit many Dickensian touches that have proven memorable to readers: David's doubt that Miss Murdstone sleeps with one eye open, for he himself was never able to manage the trick; David looking at himself in the mirror to be sure his grief at his mother's death is visible in his reddened eyes; Mr Micawber's delightful elocutions, his extensive letters (which Graves summarizes drily), and even his expressive explosion of the infamy of Heep, which is reduced to a clear, concise and disappointing statement of the intent to unmask; David fainting in a dishevelled heap before astonished Aunt Betsey. These omissions sadly truncate both David's characterization (upon which Graves will later rely so heavily for substantive changes in the novel) and the independent life of the book.

The latter is further diminished in other ways. The Orfling and Red Whisker are never named by Graves. The goroo man loses most of his speeches and for no reason is beset by schoolboys taunting him to give David his eighteenpence; but his locutions inexplicably reappear in David's mouth after his drunken dinner party: 'My mouth, my throat, my head, my stomach! Goroo, goroo, oh!' We also miss Julia Mills' diary and Martha's shadow at the door of the inn where David talks with the newly returned Peggotty. Besides the loss of delightful detail, we lose in Graves' version the plenitude of reporting that makes David a sympathetic narrator. The knowledge of David's soul that we get from his choice of detail is lost in a pragmatic, almost Benthamite emphasis upon the most plot for one's money.

Even in his concentration on David, Steerforth, and Emily, Graves has wrought substantial changes in characterization. Steerforth is at Mr Creakle's school 'a sort of magistrate for the boys,' an official rather than a casual authority. Nor is Steerforth made to be the haughty revealer of David's falseness to Mr Mell, for it is the bodyguard Tungay who says, 'Yesterday I overheard two of the other boys talking about Mr Mell's mother. They said she was an inmate of an almshouse.'[13] Steerforth gains no pleasure from the incident: 'There was no triumph in Steerforth's face either, only a cold look which may either have been contempt for Mr Creakle or the remains of his anger with Mr Mell.'[14] The childhood potential for disregard of others' feelings disappears in Graves' Steerforth.

Steerforth's relations with the Peggotty group are also subtly altered. While with them he sings songs presaging Emily's elopement and his own death and tells a mock shipwreck story obviously intended to prefigure the storm in which he dies. All his self-questionings are faithfully reproduced, while his formerly peaceful sleep is disturbed, when David enters, by a violent dream of unrest. Steerforth becomes, in Graves' hands, an ill-disciplined youth with leadership abilities and a firm sense of honour.

David's character undergoes more serious changes. Graves

omits almost entirely the sense of childhood Dickens is so careful
to include. To replace David's childish—and therefore immensely
revealing—thoughts, Graves allows him to reminisce about the
Murdstones' unpopularity at his mother's funeral, although
Dickens rightly understood that this was too astute an observation
for the young David to make. Graves' David is never truly a
child, nor does he undergo the adolescent trial of the warehouse
experience. David's wineshop days, on which Dickens spent so
many words of anguish, are dismissed in a few lines, serving
merely as the source of a future revelation of snobbery.

In keeping with his criticism of Dickens' unconscious class
snobbery, Graves gives David a true love of Emily in spite of her
lower class and then makes him reject it: 'I was trying to forget
about her by telling myself that, however anxious she was to
become a lady, she came of the common people and belonged
with them.'[15] Likewise he scorns Ham, calling him a 'booby' and
saying that he 'could not help but despising [Ham]
somewhat.' He is explicit in his knowledge of his own and
Steerforth's elevation above the Peggotty group. Graves even
attributes to David some of Steerforth's feelings about the
Peggotty group. When Barkis is dying, David misinterprets
Emily's emotion as only grief and, finding it excessive, thinks

> about 'that sort of people' and their capacities for feeling and
> suffering. I decided that they were capable of much stronger
> emotions than ourselves. Broad humour, family affection,
> dread of death, delight over trifles and religious enthusiasm
> stirred them often to an absurd degree. What they lacked was
> emotional fineness: that was the difference.[16]

David's class consciousness is reinforced when Graves
reintroduces Mick Waller from the wine warehouse. David gives
Mick, now a van-driver, his gold watch and chain and reflects
with evident satisfaction that it doubtless took some time 'before it
occurred to him to open the back of the watch to see if my name
was engraved inside—as it was.'[17] David's undisguised and
almost disgusting sense of superiority is nowhere better presented

than in this scene; yet a reader might well wonder why Graves omitted the early scene in which David checks his mirror to make sure his tear-stained eyes express evidence of suitable grief over the death of his mother, for this scene surely prepares us, as Dickens well knew, for David's later public posturings.

Also omitted is much of David's love affair with Dora. When David first meets Dora, Graves allows him to reflect sagely that 'I fell in love with her the moment I saw her, simply because I was looking for someone like that to fall in love with, and here she was.'[18] The mystery of love, the agonies, the ecstasies, the doting affections and remembrances, are there no longer. Graves' view of their marriage is close to that of many modern critics (see, for example, Q. D. Leavis in *Dickens the Novelist*), for his David explicitly recognizes Dora's resemblance to his mother and knows that he loves her for this reason. Wise beyond his years (and, we are tempted to say, beyond human believability), David is always sure of the springs of his behaviour. Presumably Graves thinks Dickens always was as well, for *The Real David Copperfield* is made specifically autobiographical by Graves' depiction of David as a hack writer, writing in 'the incompatible styles of the natural and the burlesque [with] an uncomfortable strain of melodrama', who 'was paid by the page, and had no interest in the stories as contributions to English literature.'[19] The autobiographical elements are taken seriously rather than as artistic devices for the exploration of character.

But it is Little Emily's character that undergoes the most serious alteration. From the beginning Graves has denied Emily her contracted nickname, probably as evidence of David's consciousness of speaking more correctly than the Peggotty group. Upon Emily's return to London, Graves grants David an interview with her, on the very day of Dora's death. In this interview Emily confesses that she was never Steerforth's mistress and ran away with him only because she saw that David considered himself so far above her that he would never marry her. Once her purity and gentility are established, Graves can allow David to admit his love for her. This ending, writes Graves, 'gives the three principal characters of the first part of the book—

David, Emily, and Steerforth—the fate that was foredoomed to them there.'[20] Such an ending is emotionally suitable for a number of reasons. Dickens' failure to resolve the Steerforth-Emily-David triangle creates part of the tension out of which Graves' virtual polemic against Dickens grows. By rewriting the book, Graves can realign each story's strings and knot them neatly up.

Graves' ending also creates a new Steerforth, one who acted out of love and honour rather than desire. Of course, Emily's purity is dependent upon a loving Steerforth. And Steerforth's inability to marry Emily because of an earlier vow to his mother merely shows how honourable he is. David's questioning of Emily about her relationship with Steerforth reflects his concern that Steerforth maintain his image. When he learns that Emily has not been ravished, his immediate response is not relief at her salvation but delight at Steerforth's behaviour: 'Thank God that Steerforth is what I always thought he was!' This one happiness seems to be not only sufficient but the one thing necessary—his continued belief in Steerforth.

> Steerforth had come alive for me again. He was not a villain any longer. Rather, he was a victim. … My friends all believed the story of his villainy. How could I untell it, as I was bound in honour to do, without betraying my secret of secrets?[21]

By insisting on secrecy and refusing Emily's tacit offers, David retains the real Steerforth for himself alone. Graves' story meets Dickens' again momentarily when Steerforth lies face down on the sands at Yarmouth, and David is, in a much more logical but far less compelling way, able to love Steerforth at the last. But this love, born out of a feeling of superiority resulting from Emily's preference of David, is as cheap as David's earlier 'knowledge' of how and why he loved Dora, uncomplicated by real emotion and rising only from the self-satisfaction David feels in being able to love one who will ever be thought a villain (although close-lipped David knows better). But there, unable to expose David, lies a body on the storm-washed sands.

I went. And it was Steerforth. He was lying with his head on his arm, as when I had seen him last.[22]

Thus ends Graves' version. The four-page Epilogue places all the characters on the road to victory or defeat, as they deserved and without so much as a bow toward the vagaries of life.

The change in David's characterization serves to give him a constancy of heart which the original has often been said to lack. In Graves' version it becomes possible for David to marry Agnes without Dickens' necessarily maudlin love scenes between two obviously non-sexual beings. David's position on class differences is clarified, at once bringing out the harmful nature of such snobbery and accentuating its needlessness: Emily was always lady enough for David, and both their lives were blighted by David's failure to recognize it. However unrealistic it may be to suppose that Emily would resist Steerforth's genuine love for more than two years, her resistance gives credence to her love for David.

At the same time, however, Graves' version makes David the creator of his own character. Steerforth sets an example of honour, love, and forbearance, but David seems to learn none of these traits. In contrast to Steerforth, David is unable to alleviate anyone's suffering but rather has to be relieved himself; although he is well liked, he is never able to get far enough out of himself to be completely at ease with those not on his level; he sacrifices love first to a childhood memory of his mother and later to convenience—and does so consciously; and he lives secondhand, through his novels, rather than directly. There is no indication how he learns these behaviour patterns. Graves' book is so close to David the Snob that the reader can get no other perspective and so must finally either lose interest in him or participate in his self-congratulatory class superiority.

Graves' second major revision of Dickens is the character of Steerforth. He is not Emily's seducer but instead her true lover, an honest charmer. David says at the end: 'Thank God that Steerforth is what I always thought he was!' Well, not quite, however, for Steerforth appears to be responsible for Rosa's 'ruin'; but David makes it clear 'that this must have happened when Steerforth was not of an age to have been the aggressor'—in other words, Rosa had seduced him. As for Steerforth's feeling for Emily, 'It was true love on his side,' she tells us. So Steerforth's main fault seems, in Graves' mind, to lie in the secrecy with which he pressed his proposal upon Emily. In actuality Steerforth becomes the book's touchstone, showing us what David could have done. Steerforth is David's good half; he reorganizes the school, he charms people, he is able to allow love to overcome class feeling, and he dares to confront life directly rather than retire into the safety of non-action, although even he is never fully active or assertive. David's love for Emily is shown to be passive and recallable, while Steerforth's requires action and defiance of tradition, particularly class tradition. Graves has Steerforth do what David would not do: try to marry Emily in spite of her apparent low-class background. And Steerforth's class standing is even higher than David's!

Thus, although David is the central character of *The Real David Copperfield*, Graves' structure and characterization have inadvertently raised Steerforth to the position of hero. David recognizes this by hiding Steerforth's secret, and Graves acknowledges it by ending the book with Steerforth's calm corpse, unchanged both in fact and in David's imagination now and forever. It is significant that Graves has omitted Dickens' opening statement about David's potential heroism, for Graves' pages show David as the central story-teller and Steerforth the source of all positive action and therefore as the hero of David Copperfield's life. Even David recognizes this.

In attempting to emphasize one aspect of David—his snobbery—Graves is forced to distort Dickens' plot and characterization. His sense that David needs explanation results in a reworking of the novel which produces that explanation at the cost of the balance of the novel. The story becomes a rapid character revelation rather than a character building, and when that character turns out to be disgusting, the reader is forced to take a holier-than-David attitude out of simple self-defence. There's no reason to read *The Real David Copperfield* more than once: in fact, you might find yourself wondering why you bothered to read it at all. Certainly none of Dickens' sense of the likeness between David and the reader (not to mention that between David and the author) remains. Steerforth becomes a sort of honour-hero who has no effect on David, a throw-away character serving the mere plot function of showing how David might have behaved toward Emily, who herself becomes another plot function. In the end there is no one left but David, and we don't like him well enough to remember him, as we remember Dickens' David. Graves is so intent upon exposing David as a snob that he is unable to show how he got that way.

The Real David Copperfield offers an excellent example of the usefulness of a less than fully conscious artistic absorption by one author of another. Perhaps one reason people today continue to read both Dostoevsky's and Dickens' novels but not Graves' is exemplified by the failure of insight that inadvertently 'discovers' Steerforth while destroying David. We don't want to read about a destroyed David; yet the vision of Steerforth Graves presents is closer to the compelling creature David saw and mythified than Dickens could allow us to get. We must, like Graves, find some way of casting off the veil the *Bildungsroman* form wraps around Steerforth while yet retaining, as Graves cannot, a vital David whose life is worthy of whatever heroism he is able to bring to it.

In recreating *David Copperfield*, Graves purposely limits Dickens, circumscribes him. His is not a revision but a parody; not a transmutation but a caricature. At the risk of invoking the intentional fallacy, I must argue that the intent of parody is disagreement, while the intent of re-vision is illumination. And so, while Graves' recreation of *David Copperfield* makes useful points about David's shortcomings and gives an insightful interpretation of the kind of influence that Steerforth might have had over David, it falls short of artistic re-vision because Graves quite frankly doesn't like Dickens and wants to do him one better. *Caveat emptor*: re-vision requires community of spirit. Graves lacked it. Dostoevsky did not.

But David is not the focus of Dostoevsky's re-vision. Instead, as George Katkov convincingly argues,[23] Steerforth is the model for

Stavrogin in *The Possessed*. Apparently Dostoevsky was not much interested in David himself; although he did read *David Copperfield* several times, he later mentions the book as a negative model for *A Raw Youth*, and the only character he ever refers to is Micawber, who is certainly anti-heroic. It appears that Dostoevsky did not consider David as a hero in the sense that David meant the word in the opening line of his autobiography. Instead he takes Steerforth's heroic characteristics—the same ones Graves unwittingly emphasized and clarified—as the basis for his compellingly ambiguous hero-villain, Stavrogin. The result is a Steerforth who throws new light on the growth of David's character.

Stavrogin with Steerforth in a pioneer article in comparative literature.[2] Like the early recognition of Dostoevsky's reworking of Little Nell, however, Katkov's work has never been followed up. Any discussion of Steerforth as a model for Stavrogin must rely heavily on Katkov's careful analysis. Although Katkov himself drew no conclusions, his comparison of the two men gives us a way of looking at Steerforth and his relationship to the galaxy of potential David-doubles which expands *David Copperfield* in ways Dickens could not.

Of course, I do not wish to suggest either that Steerforth was the only pattern for Stavrogin or that *The Possessed* as a novel relies in any way on *David Copperfield* for its genesis. The political ancestry and intent of *The Possessed* is too well known to require review here. The Nechaev incident of 1869 is at least the inspiration for the murder of Shatov; and there is extensive evidence that both Bakunin and Speshnev, the latter a member of the Petrashevsky circle whose activities resulted in Dostoevsky's Siberian imprisonment and exile, were in Dostoevsky's thoughts when he created Stavrogin.[3] Indeed, at the beginning he probably even had Tolstoy's *War and Peace* in mind, for Stavrogin was initially named 'Prince A.N.', probably after Andrei Bolkonsky.[4] There are also similarities to Herman in Pushkin's *The Queen of Spades* and to Faust.[5] Nonetheless, the similarity between Steerforth and Stavrogin is too strong to be mere coincidence.

We know that Dostoevsky read and admired *David Copperfield*. It was one of the two books he specifically asked for during his ten-year imprisonment and exile. By 1867 he had read *David Copperfield* for a second time, as his wife notes in her Dresden diary on 27 May of that year. Two years later he began *The Possessed*. During the Dresden period Dostoevsky refers to himself as Mr Micawber because of his poverty, a reference he repeats later in a letter to A. N. Maikov: 'I am positively in a terrible situation now (Mr Micawber). Not a kopek of money' (*Pis'ma*, II 262). In his notebooks for *A Raw Youth* (1875) he has his protagonist, Dolgoruky, the epitome of the callow, insensitive youth, state that in telling of his life he doesn't 'want<to make any "David>Copperfield" <out of this>' for he 'hate[s] the biography of Copperfield'* (*N*: *R*, 307, 309). This novel, which immediately followed *The Possessed*, seems to be based on *Copperfield* in a negative way, as if Dostoevsky were asking himself how one could depict youth and adolescence in another way than Dickens had done. It is well known that in *The Idiot* (1868–69) Dostoevsky tried to depict a Pickwick, a 'perfectly good man', and ended up studying instead the nature of evil and its inextricable relationship with good. Between his anti-Pickwick and his anti-David came *The Possessed*.

Katkov outlines the basic similarities between the two men:

They are both handsome, powerfully built, and of great physical prowess. The dominating feature of their character is pride and lust for domination, together with a sombre determination to use ruthlessly the privileged position in which they are placed.... They are both born leaders of men who attract weaker characters. ... Insults, betrayal, perfidy, and the injuries inflicted by them on those who look up to them for inspiration, are forgiven them by their followers and 'friends'. Under the mask of magnanimity they conceal total egotism, under that of charm, an emotional and moral coldness.... The final victory of the destructive forces in their soul is treated not as the exposure of the villain, but as the tragic issue of a struggle between equally real parts of their split personality.[6]

In a number of more specific respects, they are alike. Both have mysterious, undominated childhoods in which they in effect form themselves; there is a strange identity in their relationships with their mothers; they are often shown to the reader in similar poses; and they tend to treat women the same way. But most important is their effect upon the men whose lives shape the events of their respective novel-worlds.

Stavrogin is raised by his tutor, Stepan Trofimovich Verkhovensky. His mother loved him, but she had little to do with his upbringing, merely providing him with an example of

---

*Dostoevsky was notoriously inconsistent in the notebooks and used all sorts of strange shorthand. This is the form in which the editor transcribed them.

aristocratic behaviour. Although he appears never to have exerted himself, he received a military award and became an officer in the Russian army following a brilliant but debauched social career in Petersburg. He was always elegant, 'accustomed to culture and refinement.' Intellectually he seems to be superior, travelling to Europe and the Middle East and 'attending lectures in a German university' following 'some scientific expedition to Iceland.' Similarly, Steerforth appears to have been brought up 'at school'. He distinguishes himself at Oxford but doesn't much care to buckle down for a degree. When David meets him again he sees Steerforth as 'a handsome well-formed young man, dressed with a tasteful easy negligence.'

Both boys are loved by their mothers and seem to maintain a similar sort of distant respect for them from the first. Stavrogin 'knew that his mother loved him very much.' The monk Tihon, the most reliable observer in *The Possessed*, tells Stavrogin that 'although there is no external likeness, there is much internal, spiritual resemblance' (*P*, 646) between him and his mother. Even at the first moment of their meeting following his return from abroad, she feels 'his invariable and irresistible ascendency over his mother.' He is unfailingly courteous and respectful in her presence, although out of her household he is always self-willed; when asked how his mother will respond to the news of his marriage to lame and insane Marya Timofeevna Lebyadkina, he answers, 'Well, she must do as she likes,' dismissing her as a significant influence on his actions. After he leaves on his final journey toward death, his mother disowns him, saying, 'I have no son'. She feels betrayed by her ignorance of his actions, her sense of being outside the current of his life. To avoid her curse, Stavrogin leaves without seeing her. Yet even her curse becomes insignificant in the end, when she responds to his need and insists, unasked, upon accompanying him to Switzerland.

Steerforth's mother is equally entranced with her son. The first thing David notices about Mrs Steerforth is her devotion: 'It was no matter of wonder to me to find Mrs Steerforth devoted to her son. She seemed to be able to speak or think about nothing else.' Yet she sent him away to school and exacted of him the most respectful manner, creating a formality in their interchanges which is typical of Stavrogin's intercourse with his mother as well. Her air is 'always lofty' when she speaks of Steerforth, and she likes David precisely because he is 'quite devoted' to Steerforth, an emotion of which she approves. Steerforth uses extreme courtesy and attentiveness when he wishes to reinforce her delight in him, yet he shuts her out from all knowledge of his real activities. After his elopement with Emily she would refuse him her love if she could, as would David; yet both choose to recall him in the ideal. It is in keeping with Steerforth's sense of personal honour that he refuses to marry Emily because of his childhood vow to obtain his mother's consent to his marriage; likewise, Stavrogin agrees to his mother's request that he betroth himself to Lizaveta Nikolaevna, even though he knows the hollowness of such an agreement. Both men try to act in ways that will satisfy their mothers. And it is worth noting that as Mrs Steerforth denies the existence of her son, he is sailing toward his death, yet when he dies she moves into his bedroom, as if seeking the same sort of reunion Mrs Stavrogin seeks when she decides to fly to Switzerland to care for her son.

In spite of the fact that Mrs Stavrogin plays a larger role in *The Possessed* than merely 'mother of Stavrogin' and Mrs Steerforth does not occupy a similarly important place in *David Copperfield*, Katkov concludes that 'as far as her position as the mother of Stavrogin is concerned [Mme Stavrogin] does not display any features other than those to be found in the mother of Steerforth.'[7]

The character likeness between Steerforth and Stavrogin is supported by similarities of scene and plot. Both characters' bedrooms are described, and both men are shown asleep or in trance-like states as a means of character revelation. David describes Steerforth's bedroom thus:

It was a picture of comfort, full of easy-chairs, cushions and footstools, worked by his mother's hand, and with no sort of thing omitted that could help to render it complete. Finally, her handsome features looked down on her darling from a portrait on the wall, as if it were even something to her that her likeness should watch him while he slept. (*DC* 297)

Dostoevsky animates this scene and moves it into primary forms by having Stavrogin's mother watch as he sleeps:

> Seeing that Nikolay Vsyevolodovitch was sitting strangely motionless, she cautiously advanced to the sofa with a throbbing heart. She seemed struck by the fact that he could fall asleep so quickly and that he could sleep sitting like that, so erect and motionless, so that his breathing even was scarcely perceptible. His face was pale and forbidding, but it looked, as it were, numb and rigid. His brows were somewhat contracted and frowning. He positively had the look of a lifeless wax figure. ... He slept a long while, more than an hour, and still in the same rigid pose: not a muscle of his face twitched, there was not the faintest movement in his whole body, and his brows were still contracted in the same forbidding frown. ... But he suddenly opened his eyes, and sat for ten minutes as immovable as before, staring persistently and curiously, as though at some object in the corner which had struck him, although there was nothing new or striking in the room. (*P* 212–13)

Katkov points out the similarity in these apparently opposing pictures of repose: we see Steerforth three times in a sleep-like state:

> The three scenes, the serenity of innocent sleep, rigidity of the corpse, and the mother looking at her sleeping son, led Dostoevsky to a psychological discovery which could be roughly expressed in the following words: she, the mother, when looking at the features of her darling, would have recognized that the serenity of his sleep was nothing but the rigidity of death, which had already frozen his heart and paralysed him as a moral being. This discovery led to the construction of the scene in Stavrogin's study.[8]

Steerforth's divided motives are made evident when David introduces him to the Peggotty group and later finds him sitting before the fire:

> He was so intent upon his own reflections that he was quite unconscious of my approach.... Even my entrance failed to rouse him. I was standing close to him, looking at him; and still, with a heavy brow he was lost in his meditations. (*DC* 321)

The apparent tranquillity with which Steerforth sleeps (and dies) shows not only David's desire to believe his friend untroubled but also a concentration, a removal into himself, that Dostoevsky later attributes to Stavrogin.

Both men are shown to be capable of the ultimate insult to those beneath them. In an early draft of *The Possessed*, the 1869–70 'Jealousy', the Stavrogin-prototype Prince insults a teacher who was intended as the positive hero of the piece; the teacher's mother is involved in the insult. We are reminded of Steerforth's attack on Mr Mell through his mother's poverty. The Prince of 'Jealousy' lent almost all his features to the later Stavrogin.

As Katkov points out, biting is predominant in both books. David bites Murdstone in rebellion. Three times in *The Possessed*, rebellion against a superior is expressed through biting: an officer bites his general; Kirillov bites Petr Verkhovensky in fury over the latter's attempt to control his supreme act of identity, suicide; and Stavrogin himself bites the governor's ear in a public display of wordless scorn of what the man represents socially and politically. As in his repetition in *Crime and Punishment* of the incident of spontaneous combustion from *Bleak House*, Dostoevsky appears to select unusual physical acts as evidence of psychic misalignment with the external world.

There are other small similarities, such as between Betsey Trotwood and Varvara Petrovna, and between Miss Betsey's relationship with Mr Dick and Varvara Petrovna's with Stepan Trofimovich, the latter of whom was forever writing his own version of Mr Dick's Memorial. Stavrogin's estate, Skvoreshniki, from 'skvorets', meaning starling, may be reminiscent of David's first home, 'The Rookery'. Both Steerforth and Stavrogin have autoscopic-double hallucinations of devils.

The major plot similarity, however, is between the scene in Varvara Petrovna's drawing room when Stavrogin denies his marriage to Marya Timofeevna and the one in Mrs Steerforth's when Peggotty confronts her. Katkov shows both mothers facing what they view as the source of their sons' degradation. Both are in their drawing rooms accompanied by the wards whom their sons have ruined. Both women stiffly resist hearing the unpalatable truths about their sons, and both petitioners fail to press their moral rights 'out of real or faked magnanimity.'[9] Nothing is accomplished by either visit, and both petitioners are humiliated. This is a superb instance of Dickens' direct scenic influence on Dostoevsky.

Dostoevskian scene construction has often been likened to Dickens'. For instance, Futrell notes the similarity between the scene in *The Old Curiosity Shop* in which Brass plants a five-pound note on Kit Nubbles and then arranges an elaborate search which discovers the 'theft', and a similar scene in *Crime and Punishment* where Svidrigailov plants a ten-rouble note on Sonia and goes through the same elaborate search in front of her family and friends. Lary comments on the similarity between Jonas Chuzzlewit's suicide, in which Chevy Slyme eats nuts while waiting outside Jonas's door then enters to find him standing in a corner, and Kirillov's in which Petr Verkhovensky eats chicken, waits, and then finds Kirillov standing in an angle of the wall. There is also the climactic scene in *The Idiot* in which Myshkin breaks the Chinese vase; his disgrace and the stir it causes are strongly reminiscent of Mr Dorrit's reversion to his 'Father of the Marshalsea' role at Merdle's banquet and the commotion this causes.

Minor scenic similarities such as those between Zina's conversations with her mother about that woman's attempts to marry her off to the Prince (*Friend of the Family*) and Edith Dombey's nearly identical conversation with Mrs Skewton, or

Little Nell's and Nellie's deathbed scenes, further support the idea of a shared similarity of scenic concept. Thus Katkov's schematization of the scenes in Varvara Petrovna's and Mrs Steerforth's drawing rooms is plausible. His drawing of a likeness between Lebyadkin and Peggotty is less plausible. However, Peggotty's failure to assert Emily's just claim to reparation of the moral injury Steerforth has done her does weaken his argument; were he to argue for this basic human right, he might, as Katkov suggests, have become a tragic figure. As it is, he remains merely an ineffectual apologist for ineradicable class differences. Katkov's main inconsistency on this point comes about as a result of the fact that no one knows that Lebyadkin has a claim upon Varvara Petrovna similar to Peggotty's.

Both Steerforth and Stavrogin seem to gain a sense of identity through their relationships to women. Their peculiar sort of attractiveness to women is compounded of extreme courtesy and unquenchable sexual attraction. One could say of Stavrogin as David says of Steerforth:

> There was an ease in his manner—a gay and light manner it was, but not swaggering—which I still believe to have borne a kind of enchantment with it. I still believe him, in virtue of this carriage, his animal spirits, his delightful voice, his handsome face and figure, and, for aught I know, of some inborn power of attraction besides (which I think a few people possess), to have carried a spell with him to which it was a natural weakness to yield, and which not many persons could withstand. (*DC* 104)

This charm is exercised without apparent effort on Steerforth's part whenever he encounters someone who might be worth charming, such as Emily. His charm seems to work upon almost any woman. Even Peggotty cannot resist 'his easy, spirited, good humour; his genial manner, his handsome looks, his natural gift of adapting himself to whomsoever he pleased, and making direct, when he cared to do it, to the main point of interest in anybody's heart' (*DC* 310). Only Agnes, touchstone of good, can resist him—but then Agnes never meets him.

Stavrogin acts out what Dickens implies about Steerforth's attractiveness to women. The fawning Liputin warns Stepan Trofimovich even before Stavrogin's return that he'd better 'bolt your door against our prince. ... Every berry is worth picking if only he's in the mood for it' (*P* 128). Also before Stavrogin's return, a rumour circulates 'that Shatov's wife had at one time had a liaison with Nikolay Stavrogin' (*P* 128), and later it turns out that he has fathered her child. It was also 'whispered that he had ruined Lizaveta Nikolaevna's reputation, and that there had been an intrigue between them in Switzerland' (*P* 194). Marya Timofeevna Lebyadkina calls him her 'prince' and continues, in her madness, to believe he will rescue her.

Both Steerforth and Stavrogin share their households with young women whom they have ruined, dependents enchanted by the carelessly charming behaviour of their seducers. Although Stavrogin's Darya Pavlovna is but a shadowy representation of Rosa Dartle, the two girls' lives are parallel. Rosa Dartle is intractable to everyone except Steerforth, to whose charms she succumbs:

> Steerforth exerted himself with his utmost skill, and that was with his utmost ease, to charm this singular creature into a pleasant and pleased companion. That he should succeed, was no matter of surprise to me.... I saw her features and her manner slowly change; I saw her look at him with growing admiration; I saw her try, more and more faintly, but always angrily, as if she condemned a weakness in herself, to resist the captivating power that he possessed; and finally, I saw her sharp glance soften, and her smile become quite gentle. (*DC* 434–35)

She is even charmed into playing her harp for him. Knowing, however, that he will merely play with her but never love her, she soon retreats into her ascerbic, self-protective mannerisms, to emerge only once, when she learns of his death and is finally able to admit, bitterly, that she loved him and would have been his slave for life for a single loving word from him each year. Rosa's hardness is the result of her unsuccessful effort to resist Steerforth's power to charm and then depart.

Stavrogin's relationship with Darya Pavlovna Shatova is similar to Steerforth's with Rosa, although there are significant differences. As Katkov carefully details, both Rosa and Darya have been marked by aggressive acts by Steerforth and Stavrogin respectively. Rosa's 'scar can safely be regarded as a conventional symbol for some kind of sexual aggression committed by Steerforth in the past,'[10] which causes Rosa's intense fixation on him both physically and morally. (Graves made explicit this very connection.) There is little doubt that sexual contact took place between Stavrogin and Darya Pavlovna in Switzerland. Both events occur in times prior to the novels themselves and are pre-existing conditions rather than continuing actions. Like Rosa, Darya Pavlovna grew up in the family of her aggressor. Her initial nature was 'quiet and gentle, and capable of great self-sacrifice,' as Rosa's must have been, to hear Mrs Steerforth speak of it. She is well-educated, talented, and pretty; Rosa, even with her scar, is deemed handsome by David, and her harp-playing attests to her talent. Darya has loved Stavrogin since childhood and has sacrificed her life for him. She waits for his eventual return to her, counting on the fact that at the end everyone else will forsake him. Although Rosa never says so, one suspects that she too is waiting for Steerforth's eventual return.

Stavrogin has his Emily, too. However, here Dostoevsky has split Dickens' character into two people, for Emily is represented in Stavrogin's life by both Lizaveta Nikolaevna and Marya Timofeevna. Over the latter, his insane wife, Stavrogin exercises the same sort of charm as Steerforth exercises over Emily. And over Liza he has the same influence for action as Steerforth has over Emily.

It comes as little surprise to the reader that Steerforth charms Emily; Emily is so much more pliable than Rosa that we cannot be surprised at her helpless capitulation. When Steerforth first comes to Yarmouth, she is shy of the beautiful stranger, 'but she soon became more assured when she found how gently and respectfully Steerforth spoke to her; how skilfully he avoided anything that would embarrass her; ... how lightly and easily he carried on, until he brought us, by degrees, into a charmed circle, and we were all talking away without any reserve (*DC* 316). She is still wary of such charm, however, and tries to keep as far away from him as possible, both physically and emotionally. That she cannot merely attests to the power of his attractiveness. Each time David returns she has become more restive, more obsessed with a sense of worthlessness and ingratitude, and more repulsing of her betrothed Ham, who must have been a sorry figure in comparison to the dashing and handsome Steerforth whose manner is at once so dangerous and so alluring.

Even after she has eloped with Steerforth and knows the wrong she has done, Emily continues to be torn between her knowledge of right and her unquenchable desire for Steerforth. As she says in her letter, 'if you knew how my heart is torn.' Only when Steerforth tries to 'give' her to Littimer can she extricate herself from his charm, but she never ceases to recognize its existence, telling Rosa that 'if you live in his home and know him, you know, perhaps, what his power with a weak, vain girl might be. I don't defend myself, but I know well, and he knows well, or he will know when he comes to die, and his mind is troubled with it, that he used all his power to deceive me, and that I believed him, trusted him, and loved him!' (*DC* 720)

Display of the charming part of Stavrogin's nature is reserved for Marya Timofeevna. Every time he sees her he tries to be as pleasant to her as possible, although the impatience of his nature makes him a much poorer hand at it than Steerforth. When they first meet at Varvara Petrovna's house he speaks to her 'in a caressing and melodious voice' and has 'the light of an extraordinary tenderness in his eyes.' His attitude is respectful and his speech coaxing, in order to induce her to do what he wishes. We will not see him more charming than when he escorts that unfortunate woman from his mother's drawing room.

Stavrogin's second meeting with Marya Timofeevna occurs at her flat. He has come to tell her he is going to announce their marriage and is willing to take her away with him if she wishes to come. Again his manner is tender and his speech conciliating. He wears 'a still more friendly and cordial smile,' a 'cordial and amiable smile.' When he asks her to go away with him to Switzerland, he uses the same enticements of quiet, peace, comfort, and attentiveness that Steerforth doubtless used to convince Emily to run away with him.

With Lizaveta Nikolaevna, Stavrogin becomes a catalyst for action. Liza is pulled, like Emily, toward her own destruction (in nineteenth-century terms) by Stavrogin's irresistible charm. At their first meeting he is 'courteous', but 'apart from his courtesy his expression was utterly indifferent, even listless.' Such is to be his manner with Liza throughout. Their second meeting is antagonistic, and Liza almost strikes him; yet soon afterward her fiancé tells Stavrogin that she loves him, noting that 'you are trying to get her, you are pursuing her.' He senses the attraction Stavrogin's charm has for Liza and senses too thât Stavrogin purposely acts to attract, even though in Liza's case his behaviour toward her does not seem to be the same sort of charming friendliness he shows Marya Timofeevna. But Liza is a different sort of woman; she acts by contraries and would refuse to be charmed by outwardly charming behaviour. Therefore, although it seems that Stavrogin is trying to repel Liza, he is in fact doing just the opposite, consciously, by acting in a way he knows will attract her. Likewise Steerforth acts respectful rather than romantic toward Emily in order to draw her to him of her own apparent free will.

In the remainder of their meetings, Liza and Stavrogin speak little to each other. Although their elopement is ostensibly set up by Petr Verkhovensky, actually both Liza and Stavrogin plan it subconsciously. Stavrogin seeks to love and lose himself in love, and Liza seeks to act in a way which will define her. Given the world in which these two characters live, the only action which can accomplish both aims is a wilful flaunting of community morals in an act which has as its sole sanction the personal expression of love. With such motivation on both sides, the extraordinary morning-after scene between Liza and Stavrogin becomes explicable. Liza refuses to consider continuing the relationship because she embarked upon it not for future gain but for an instant of full self-realization; that instant gone, she is ready to stand before the world possessed of something it could never have given her and likewise can never take away. Stavrogin, on the other hand, desires to pursue the ideal of love which he has fastened onto his relationship with Liza. By making him acknowledge that what he seeks is an illusion, she forces on him the reality that nothing can exalt him above the status of simple human being. He cannot lose himself in love, or in anything else; like her, he will have to live for those few moments in which love preponderates.

The sexual statement Stavrogin enables Liza to make is in many ways similar to Emily's statement. By running off with Steerforth, with no real hope of marriage, Emily acknowledges her sexual nature and her need to stand apart from her family, to be herself, no matter what. As Peggotty's niece, Ham's future wife, but never Emily, she seeks her hour of selfhood as does Liza. Herein lies the basic charm, regardless of exterior behaviour, which these two free male souls, uncommitted to any value in life save existence, offer two tradition-bound women for whom they form the only avenue of escape. In this sense both Steerforth and Stavrogin charm in the same way, a way Dostoevsky doubtless saw when he read of Dickens' hero-villain.

Liza elopes with Stavrogin through the agency of Petr Verkhovensky, who both worships Stavrogin and hopes to gain from acquaintance with him; in this respect he is like Littimer. Emily elopes in a real boat; Liza elopes in a metaphorical boat of Verkhovensky's creation: 'a boat and ... maple-wood oars out of some Russian song.' The romantic idea of escape by water is a sort of baptism and rebirth into a new existence for both women.

Nor does Stavrogin care any more for Liza than Steerforth for Emily. He ruins her as it were incidentally, in the search for new excitements, and by the next morning he is already weary of her in spite of his desire that she stay. According to Littimer, Steerforth's devotion lasts a bit longer, indeed 'for a longer time than anybody could have expected.' Steerforth remains with

Emily because of his sense of honour. Stavrogin would do likewise, but Liza sends him away, seeks for—perhaps as Emily unconsciously did—the means of making a statement, realizing a dream, living fully for an hour; the future is of no concern to her.

The full effect of both Steerforth's and Stavrogin's charm, however, is reserved for the men whose lives they will invade and change. Kirillov speaks to Stavrogin of what he has meant in his life and says he considers him a god. Shatov looks upon him 'as a sort of sun,' exclaims that he can't tear Stavrogin out of his heart, and asks 'Why am I condemned to believe in you through all eternity?' Petr Verkhovensky feels that the idea of Stavrogin will never let him free, calling him 'my better half.' In an explicit outburst Petr Verkhovensky says to Stavrogin: 'Stavrogin, you are beautiful ... You are my idol! ... I know no one but you. You are the leader, you are the sun and I am your worm. ... You are beautiful and proud as a God' (*P* 392, 393, 396). It is obvious that Stavrogin exercises a mysterious spell over these three men, who are so bound to him emotionally and morally that they almost worship him. Even minor characters feel the attraction: Lebyadkin calls himself Stavrogin's Falstaff and says that 'you meant so much in my life!'; Tihon, to whom Stavrogin confesses his rape of the young girl, admits an irresistible love for the man; the convict Fedya feels that Stavrogin has the power to compel his obeisance. Even the shadowy narrator finds him 'uncontestably beautiful'.

Steerforth's attractiveness begins with Mr Creakle, whose respect for the youth combines greed, fear, and attraction, and extends through David to Traddles, to Mr Peggotty: to everyone but Agnes, who is less a woman than a figure in a morality play, or the chorus in a Greek drama, speaking the eternal verities as a sexless oracle. David is helpless, must love Steerforth even after he has caused Emily's downfall and Ham's death, because he cannot help being drawn under by the charm of this man, 'ni bon, ni méchant, ennuyé, sympathique et dangereux, amoral.'[11]

Steerforth's main influence, however, is over the women in his life and not over men, because he does nothing in the world of men. His Oxford sojourn is a minor episode in which he becomes attached to no one. Stavrogin is different; his major influence is over the revolutionaries, men whose lives he has shaped one way or another and who form his various doubles. The difference in novelistic conception and in social background accounts for much of this difference in the objects of these two men's charm. Steerforth lives in a world in which standard masculine accomplishments are accorded standard acclaim but in which no revolutionary activities, political or otherwise, are possible. In his world Steerforth could never he a hero. In him Dickens creates 'a portrait of the utterly English concept of the "gentleman and amateur." '[12] He is stringently confined as to what he can do. He can be an indolent moneyed gentleman; but this would not suit his restive nature. He can become a minister, a soldier, an attorney, but those are unsatisfactory for two reasons: Steerforth does not wish to apply himself to prepare for such occupations, and once in them he would be stultified by their repetitiveness. He needs the sort of profession which would allow for variety and activity and would generate a sense of meaning and individuality.

Had England bred revolutionaries, Steerforth would have been one of their leaders. But the world to which David can accommodate himself so easily is merely boring to Steerforth. In his search for active involvement, the sexual realm offers the only possibility for outrageous behaviour which could perhaps lead to, or proclaim, freedom. Steerforth, fettered with no social conscience yet endowed with a very Dostoevskian drive for meaningful behaviour beyond the confines of society, has only women to turn to. Therefore he exercises his power most upon women (or upon sensitive men, like David, whose minds, containing some of the saving 'feminine' graces, can be violated by his outrages).

It is surely Dickens' intent to show the pathos—for he does not seem to think it tragic, nor is it—of such a life. Indeed, he tacitly condemns a society which offers no place for the energies and wits of a Steerforth. Dickens' fascination with his type leads to Eugene Wrayburn of *Our Mutual Friend*, a reincarnation of Steerforth.[13] Wrayburn, the indolent lawyer with no proclivity for his profession and a driving need for forbidden stimuli (like Lizzie Hexam), finds almost as little enticement to life as does Steerforth and learns to live only by nearly dying. Steerforth is the type of a problem figure whom Dickens never loses sight of; in *David Copperfield* he is too peripheral to offer the means of a major statement, but he and his predicament recur. Even in *David Copperfield*, however, Dickens recognizes his social strictures.

Stavrogin, on the other hand, lives in a world in which revolutionary behaviour is possible and masculine moral standards fluctuate. The nature of the Russian soul (if indeed one can speak of the Russian soul since Bloomsbury popularized it to the point of disrespectability) permits such wildness in its men, and therefore Stavrogin has an outlet, namely nihilism, for his unwillingness to accept any single value of society. This makes it unnecessary that he violate women except for his pleasure, for he can violate men's minds with greater effect, thus earning the ultimate self-inflicted moral punishment. This is why the men in *The Possessed* are so attracted to Stavrogin: they need a leader, and he needs to have followers to violate. Dostoevsky's radicalism causes him to see energies such as Stavrogin's as an essential part of the polity and a natural reaction to it. This is not necessarily 'the Russian character', for Goncharov saw Oblomov's sloth as an equally valid depiction of a portion of the Russian character. It is, however, the Dostoevskian character par excellence.

Thus, Stavrogin's political actions are in no way a denial of his kinship to Steerforth. Although the effect of these two men's charm is different because of the nature of the world in which they live, its springs are the same and its desired ends similar, if not identical. The difference in expression is one imposed in part by the view of society each author wished to present and by social and political constraints each felt operative within the world of the novel. While not underestimating the difference between Steerforth and Stavrogin, I do want to emphasize that the gap is more social than artistic and need be no major barrier to an understanding of the restless charm of these two.

The difference between Stavrogin's power over men and

Steerforth's relative lack of such power is also due in part, of course, to the difference between the two novels. Steerforth can be seen only through David's eyes; we are limited to what David needs to see or can allow himself to see. Stavrogin we get nearly whole. This difference in point of view is extremely important, for through it Dostoevsky gains a vantage point that Dickens' novel's structure denied him.

There are enough similarities between Steerforth and Stavrogin, both in characterization and in structural function, to warrant the sort of close comparison between the two that Nellie Valkovsky's partial identity with Little Nell elicited. Although the political sources for Stavrogin cannot be ignored and indeed dictate many of his actions, the politics of the novel occurs only within an already-developed characterization of Stavrogin. And 'Stavrogin is the source of the chaos that streams through the characters,' says Irving Howe.

> All but one of the major characters are his doubles. Pyotr is his social double, Liza the Byroness his emotional double, and Marya, the cripple he has married, his double in derangement. Fedka the peasant murderer is a double through the link of the intellectual Kirillov, while Lebyadkin and Liputin are doubles in the dress of burlesque. The most important doubles are Kirillov and Shatov, who act out the two sides of Stavrogin's metaphysical problem.[14]

In fact, in *The Possessed* Dostoevsky seems to be working out the idea, broached long ago in *The Double*, of human interresponsibility as a determinant of individual personality. Viewed in this light, Stavrogin is an extraordinarily copious source of human multiplicity. Through him, Steerforth can be examined in the light of a similar multiplicity.

CHAPTER VII

Stavrogin and the Idea of the Double

> ... *the peculiar mark of Dostoevsky's psychology—opposite emotions simultaneously manifesting themselves.*
>
> DOROTHY BREWSTER, *East–West Passage.*

Dostoevsky carefully developed and expanded the idea of the double in the course of his career. Although most readers believe his short novel, *The Double*, to be his ultimate statement, in fact Golyadkin and his double are an elementary form of doubling, as Dostoevsky realized later when he admitted that the story should have been written entirely differently. The rewriting of *The Double* takes place again and again in his novels.

Nor was the experience of duality foreign to Dostoevsky. The Soviet critic Vyacheslav Polonsky says: 'The author of *The Double* was himself a double—not without reason did he love duality in people, and he studies the double in his pages from the first works to the last.'[1] To see the struggle between one's good and evil tendencies as the root of human suffering is to find duality in each soul; to cure that suffering by reconciling the good and the evil is to acknowledge and learn to control one's duality. Thus the idea of the double is at the heart of all Dostoevsky's writings.

Robert Rogers, working with Otto Rank's studies of the double, differentiates four basic types of double.[2] Dostoevsky's doubles fall into all four groups, beginning with Golyadkin in the first group and ending with Karamazovshchina[3] in the fourth.

The first group is the mirror-image or autoscopic double which Lawrence Kohlberg also calls the 'hallucinatory double',[4] a terminology I will not use because of its potential confusion with actual hallucinations, which can be symptomatic of other types of doubling as well. Many of the traditional doubles in literature are autoscopic: Catherine and Heathcliff are mirror images of each other, differing only in sex; William Wilson has a double who is like him physically but his exact opposite in behaviour; Spencer Brydon finds a mirror-image double. Golyadkin in Dostoevsky's *The Double* is perhaps the clearest literary example of this classification. He creates an autoscopic double who is at once just like him and exactly his opposite, as Dr Jekyll creates in Mr Hyde a release for his unrealizable despicabilities. In all these cases the doubles cannot long coexist because their mutual exclusivity makes coexistence impossible; thus one of the pair must die, leaving the other free either to reject forever the knowledge of his duality or to incorporate and internalize the fullness of his character. Some sort of resolution of autoscopic doubling is mandatory. Such doubles are manifest; the author and the reader are explicitly aware of the fact of doubling. But because they are manifest, they often lack complexity, for the entirety of physical and psychic identity must be laid open. *Dr Jekyll and Mr Hyde* is interesting not because it explores the nature of the duality inherent in human beings, for it does not, but because we do not know until the end which half is going to survive. Since resolution of the duality is impossible and destruction of one of the halves inevitable, curiosity may be satisfied but little knowledge can be gained from the study of such doubles. This is why Dostoevsky later rejected Golyadkin as any sort of 'solution' to the problem of the double.

A second kind of double is the dissociative, opposing-self double, the psychological half-brother. Two separate characters serve as doubles of each other, for instance Leggatt and the Captain in *The Secret Sharer*. Destruction of one character, although it may occur, is not necessary for resolution of the story.

Such a double is frequently latent; the story can be read on a superficial level without a realization of the duality, thus allowing readers a larger range of interpretation and an increase in complexity and ambiguity (and therefore interest). Lydgate and Dorothea, Elizabeth and d'Arcy, Lily Briscoe and Mrs Ramsay, are all dissociative doubles who concurrently oppose and complement one another. Raskolnikov and Svidrigailov are in part dissociative doubles, for Svidrigailov represents the ultimate application, and folly, of Raskolnikov's megalomania. In Dickens we find Ralph and Nicholas Nickleby as dissociative doubles, as well as Sir Leicester Dedlock and Mr Rouncewell.

A third type of double is the set of characters (it can be more than two) who represent complementary traits, all of which are possessed by a focal character who represents either the genesis or the reconciliation of the various complementary doublings illustrated by the other characters. This is the double of decomposition—one full personality decomposed into its constituent parts.[5] *Pierre* presents Isabel and Lucy as the warring factions of passion and intellect which Pierre unsuccessfully attempts to reconcile. In *Wuthering Heights* both Catherine and Edgar merge in young Cathy, whose elemental force is tempered by Edgar's softness. The double of decomposition is perhaps most evident in *The Possessed*; the revolutionary youths are fractions of Stavrogin. In *David Copperfield*, as we shall see, David, Traddles and Uriah Heep are all decompositions of Steerforth.

The fourth type of double, most evident in *The Brothers Karamazov*, is the composite or multifaceted double, in which a single human whole is represented by a number of characters, none of whom separately is able to achieve the full spectrum of humanity. Obviously this sort of double deals more with differences than with likenesses; it is the unlikeness of Ivan, Dmitri, Alyosha, and Smerdyakov that makes up the full human soul which is the essence of Karamazovshchina. This type of double is almost mandatorily latent, for there is no individual who represents the composite of traits, values, or responses which the author implies as ideal or complete.

It can be seen by the way Dostoevsky uses doubles that he is moving towards an integration of human emotions and traits. And with each successive type of double he gets closer to a resolution of duality that will allow both freedom and survival. In this, of course, the 'great psychologist' follows the path of many who have written before him, just as Freud did not invent psychology but merely made it manifest.

> Because Dostoevsky's protagonists are usually split personalities, the psychological and philosophical drama in a Dostoevsky novel is expressed in terms of a conflict between opposite poles of sensibility and intelligence, self-sacrifice and self-assertion, God-Man and Man-God, or sometimes 'good' and 'bad'. To dramatize this conflict, Dostoevsky often gives his characters several alter egos or doubles, each projecting one of the extremes of the split personality. Even when the hero is not present in the scene, he may represent the centre of interest because the characters present, represent different facets of his personality.[6]

Although J. M. Beebe said this of *Crime and Punishment*, it is equally true of *The Possessed*. Stavrogin represents all extremes, is explicitly the source of all action and belief, exhibits all character traits. 'Each of a number of characters "represents" an aspect of Stavrogin or a force in his life, and Stavrogin is in all of them.'[7] Petr Verkhovensky says he is 'beautiful and proud as a god,' and Liputin attributes to him 'the most subtle and refined intelligence'. He is fearless and has 'complete self-control' yet is capable of being sensible and modest and even of appearing to Marya Timofeevna Lebyadkina as 'a diamond set in the dirty background of her life.' Because Stavrogin is taciturn, the reader can only learn of him through his doubles. The usual characterization devices of authorial narrative comment (here largely lacking because of the narrator's feebleness) and personal action (Stavrogin 'does' nothing but sleep with Liza and then commit suicide) are largely replaced by the actions of doubles who represent Stavrogin's conflicting ideals.

This idea is not new. In 1914, Nicholas Berdaiev had noted:

In this symbolic tragedy there is only one person—Nikolai Stavrogin and his emanations. From Stavrogin's soul come both Shatov and P. Verkhovensky, both Kirillov and all the characters of *The Possessed*. In Stavrogin's soul were begot and from him emanated not only the bearers of ideas but also all these Lebyadkins, Lutugins [sic], all the lower hierachy of *The Possessed*, the elementary souls. From the eroticism of a Stavroginesque soul were born also all the women in *The Possessed*. All lines come from him.[8]

Five years later an anonymous Soviet critic wrote in the short-lived *Meteor*:

Made up of popular contrasts, Stavrogin is for everyone a riddle and a mystery, for everyone an 'idol'. All the dramatis personae of the tragedy live on crumbs from Stavrogin's table, endlessly obliged to him, 'condemned to believe in him forever' ... They deify him as an idol and hate and insult him at the same time. Everything revolves around him as around the sun. Thus he must stand in the centre of the tragedy.[9]

The same ideas are repeated today: Irving Howe, studying the political bases of the novel, finds that 'all but one of the major characters is a double of Stavrogin.'[10] Mikhail Bakhtin, in a study of Stavrogin's inner dialogue, decides that 'in *The Devils* [sic] there is not a single idea which does not find a dialogical response in Stavrogin's consciousness.'[11]

Yet in spite of the almost universal consensus that many of the characters in *The Possessed* are decomposite doubles of Stavrogin, only one critic, Irving Howe, has specified just how facets of Stavrogin as multifarious as assuming Godhead through suicide, cementing political affiliations through murder, and affirming identity through ruin and death are natural outgrowths of Stavrogin's life. And not even Howe suggests what such doubling shows.

Shatov is in a certain sense one of the real reflections of

Stavrogin, one of his vampireish doubles which he has gathered around himself, and they adhere by suction to his heart and drink the blood of their prisoner—Shatov as well as Kirillov.[12]

We first meet Shatov, as we do Kirillov and Petr Verkhovensky, through the story's narrator, who gives us our most objective picture of Shatov, completely apart from whatever changes or inspirations Stavrogin's presence might cause. The two had been friends in Geneva; following the breakup of their friendship, Shatov went to America with another of Stavrogin's doubles, Kirillov. He never forgot Stavrogin's great influence, however, and continued to love him, believing that Stravrogin's teaching had raised him from the dead intellectually. Shatov's public attack on Stavrogin in his mother's drawing room is the focal point of their relationship, a relationship based largely on the duality revealed in their confrontations with one another.

'I [struck you] because you meant so much to me in my life,' Shatov confessed. Stavrogin's representation of God as 'the synthetic personality of the whole people' has become the basis of Shatov's faith, so much so that he is able to repeat nearly verbatim Stavrogin's 'weighty words' and to consider Stavrogin his 'teacher'. To Stavrogin Shatov is a philosophical embodiment of his former self: 'In your words I recognize my own mood two years ago.' However, Shatov persists in seeing Stavrogin as the root of his beliefs, beliefs which have brought him to the verge of resigning from the secret society and seeking somehow to gain the faith in God that he believes is necessary for a life of dedication to the Russian people. Ironically, Shatov does not believe in God, although he assures Stavrogin that: 'I ... I will believe in God.' Stavrogin merely claims atheism, but his acknowledgement that Shatov has accurately reproduced his ideas and fervour indicates that he too must have at least tried to believe when he held those ideas, else there would have been little reason for passing them on.

In lieu of belief in God, however, Shatov exhibits an unquenchable belief in Stavrogin: 'Why am I condemned to believe in you through all eternity?' he cries out in anguish. 'Such dialogues,' writes Albert Guérard, 'are confrontations as of beings "come together in infinity," inward debates in a sense, or debates with the suppressed thoughts of one's spiritual brother.'[13] As the source of Shatov's beliefs, Stavrogin indeed becomes a kind of God—surely a position he seeks as well as evades. This God-man, or father-son, relationship is the first full-blown doubling of Stavrogin. Indeed, Polonsky has said that the two represent 'UNBELIEVING AND BELIEVING SIMULTANEOUSLY' [capitals in the original].[14]

There is also a symbiotic doubling of these two characters. Both Shatov and Stavrogin are married to women named Marya. Dostoevsky usually avoids repeating names within a novel, so this obvious duplication must point to an identity between Shatov and Stavrogin in their choice of wives. Stavrogin seduced Shatov's wife in Switzerland, impregnated her, then left her. When her baby is born, Shatov accepts it as his own, thus *becoming* Stavrogin through the convenient fiction of paternity. The two join in being respectively the symbolic and the literal father of the boy, who is the symbol of the renaissance of Stavrogin's ideas and Shatov's faith in them.

As Stavrogin's double, Shatov obliquely 'delivers' Stavrogin's child to him when he announces that Marya Timofeevna claims to have had a child. Stavrogin, in stating that Marya Timofeevna is still a virgin, denies himself the possibility of regeneration.

The two men stand in peculiar relationship to Marya Timofeevna. Stavrogin marries her out of a desire for personal degradation and a seemingly genuine wish to protect her. Yet because of her simple-mindedness and because Stavrogin is physically repelled by her, he turns to the wife of one of his doubles. Upon Shatov's wife he can wreak his lust and can satisfy his desire for the child Marya Timofeevna will never bear him. Still, he continues to send Marya Timofeevna money and is invariably polite and respectful to her, duplicating Shatov's behaviour toward her. Shatov too saves her from insult; when Lebyadkin is beating her, Shatov 'dragged him off by the hair. He tried to beat me, but I frightened him, and so it ended.' The two men share a protective feeling toward the deranged woman which is accentuated by Shatov's residence in the house in which Marya Timofeevna lives, paralleling Stavrogin's residence with Shatov's wife in Geneva. Stavrogin consciously desires to extend this identity by asking Shatov to take care of Marya Timofeevna but, diverted by his obvious unease at the possibility of responsibility for Shatov's 'idea', he forgets.

It is this 'idea' that ties the two men most closely, however. Both are idealists, although Stavrogin embraces a number of ideas which Shatov chooses to reject but which are picked up by Stavrogin's other doubles. Shatov has adopted Stavrogin's Slavophilism based on belief in Russia's mission as the true embodiment of nationalism. But such a doctrine requires faith, which Shatov does not yet have and which Stavrogin denies ever having had. Because of his belief in Stavrogin, Shatov is able to acknowledge his dissatisfaction with the policies of the group and seek straightforwardly to begin a new life. Stavrogin recognizes this impulse—no doubt feels it himself—yet also recognizes its impossibility. He knows of the plot to murder Shatov and thus knows that Shatov's plans can never be realized. At the same time he suspects the same death for himself ('I believe I'm sentenced to death too') whether or not he seeks a new life. Thus Stavrogin sees the futility of Shatov's 'idea'. At the same time, however, Shatov's commitment to Stavrogin's 'idea' ennobles him above his teacher. Shatov fully believes in the possibility of change and improvement. Commitment need not be eternal, and a change of commitment need not be immoral.

The return of Shatov's wife parallels his decision to resign from the secret society. Stavrogin's child becomes the objective correlative of his new sense of purpose. Honour can now reside in a social artifact, namely the family, which will provide him with a structure for belief in his 'idea'—a new commitment. Shatov exemplifies both the possibility of orderly change and the assurance that even though a new social structure is not immediately visible, it can be found.

Stavrogin, on the other hand, recognizes that Shatov's striving toward belief is one of his own needs, yet because he feels he cannot will himself to have faith he must deny the desire to do so, thus repelling Shatov and all he stands for. Shatov's position as Stavrogin's believing half is set forth as explicitly as Dostoevsky ever set such a correspondence forth; it is used to tell us what Stavrogin himself cannot, that he is at war internally in ways he is not willing to admit. The fact that we like Shatov helps us like Stavrogin. Even though the reader may be largely unaware of this aspect of the doubling of the two men, the other proofs of doubling create a sufficient identity between them that Stavrogin's weakness (his desire to believe) becomes less despicable in his own mind because he sees Shatov wrestling with it.

The most intimate contact between the two comes at Varvara Petrovna's when Shatov strikes Stavrogin. Dostoevsky often uses such sudden violent acts to show what cannot be told. We learn later that Shatov struck him because of Stavrogin's lie regarding his marriage, but even without knowing the reason the reader is arrested by the significance of the act to the two participants. Shatov strikes once and then remains standing in front of Stavrogin. Stavrogin, who is capable of killing a man out of sheer anger, reacts uncharacteristically to the blow by merely standing facing the waiting Shatov for a second, then grasping him by the shoulders; 'but at once, almost at the same instant, pulled both hands away and clasped them behind his back. He did not speak, but looked at Shatov' (*P* 191).

When the two men are considered as doubles, this scene becomes clear. Shatov, as a representative of Stavrogin's sense of truthfulness, confronts him with his lie. It is enough that the confrontation occurs; Shatov need not continue the attack, nor need he flee. Stavrogin, chastised by the meaning of the blow, wishes to retaliate, to insist that it is not so, and thus he grasps Shatov to shake him or throw him to the ground. His sense of the truth of Shatov's reprimand, however, keeps him from acting further, and so he drops his hands in a silent acknowledgement of Shatov's right (as his double) to challenge him thus. Shatov presents Stavrogin with his falseness, and Stavrogin acknowledges it as a part of himself he wishes to fight against but, in the end, cannot. The narrator describes Stavrogin's anger at the blow as '*reasonable* anger' (emphasis Dostoevsky's), i.e. anger which flows not from the emotions but from the reason. Only because he is determined to commit himself to nothing does Stavrogin fail to respond violently to Shatov's challenge to him to rectify all lies. Because Stavrogin encompasses so much of the variety and contradiction of human nature, however, he is later able to admit the rightness of Shatov's action by announcing the fact of his marriage. Shatov, his conscience, works slowly, but in the end Stavrogin is unable to disavow this shared conscience because to do so would be to take a position—that he wishes to hide the marriage and will work toward that end—and he refuses to take a position. This, and not Stavrogin's role in making Shatov a Slavophile and a revolutionary, is the significance of their doubling.

As with Shatov, the narrator first introduces Kirillov and presents his 'idea' from what is supposed to appear an objective perspective. Like Stavrogin, he is aloof, taciturn, intellectual. Like Stavrogin, he tries to help Marya Timofeevna, saving her from a whipping. He bites Petr Verkhovensky's finger in an act of fury at the latter's failure to understand him, as Stavrogin bit the governor's ear in a similar protest against unreasoned acquiescence to authority.

Kirillov too sees himself as a protégé of Stavrogin's. 'Remember what you have meant in my life.' Shatov confirms that Kirillov's 'idea' comes from Stavrogin: 'He is your creation'. Because Shatov desires to live, he sees Kirillov's 'idea' as 'poison'; Kirillov, however, is an enthusiast for one of the sorts of meaning which all the characters in *The Possessed* seem to think Stavrogin is capable of defining. Basically, Kirillov is convinced that if God does not exist, then man has the capacity to become a God himself. Only fear prevents a man from taking upon himself the ultimate act(s) of will. By killing himself for no reason, thus ridding himself of the fear of death, Kirillov believes he will become free of this final fear and therefore will prove that God does not exist and all mankind is free.

Both Kirillov and Shatov attribute to Stavrogin the source of belief in the possibility of a truly significant cause or act. Kirillov's 'idea', like Shatov's, is merely an attempt to find something to believe in. As Stavrogin articulates: 'If you were to find out that you believe in God, then you'd believe in Him; but since you don't know that you believe in Him, then you don't believe in Him' (*P* 221). Kirillov's willed lack of belief is as necessary to his 'idea' as is willed belief to Shatov's.

Both fearlessness and independence are part of Kirillov's 'idea'. If he kills the ultimate human fear (of death), he can prove himself—and, by extension, all people—fearless. We have learned that Stavrogin would not hesitate to kill an opponent and that his 'was one of those natures that know nothing of fear.' To attain a Stavroginesque fearlessness, Kirillov must maintain his independence to act, which he does quite consistently by refusing to accept or acknowledge Petr Verkhovensky's obvious desire to influence the cause of his suicide. Even the murder of Shatov does not sway Kirillov for long. Such tenacity would normally be culturally approved (Shatov's imperturbable dignity is heightened by its intensity). Kirillov is willing to sacrifice himself for a principle he believes in. However, willingness to act for all keeps him from acting to save Shatov. The adoption of Stavrogin's teaching of the possibility of significant action on behalf of humanity limits Kirillov, as it does Shatov, to action within a tiny range which precludes other courses of action. It is Kirillov's adoption of Stavrogin's independence and fearlessness which prevents him from doing the only positive action the novel presents: saving Shatov.

Just as Shatov represents the possibility of belief in life which Stavrogin cannot surrender himself to, so Kirillov represents the possibility of significant action. Both show the impossibility of living without direction. Shatov defines himself by what he is; the significance of Kirillov's doubling of Stavrogin is that he is able to define himself by what he does. The definition may be wrong, as is Raskolnikov's; but then one has to find a better one. Those who fail suffer, as do Golyadkin and Ivan Karamazov. Those who succeed are at last able to begin to live: Raskolnikov in Siberia with Sonia; Dmitri Karamazov in his search for forgiveness from all; Aloysha Karamazov as he moves toward the fulfilment of his full Stavroginesque potential in the projected 'Life of a Great Sinner'. Both the potential to be and the potential to act lie within Stavrogin. But as he himself refuses to settle upon a single potential, it remains for his doubles to show the character he cannot show. Like Shatov, Kirillov adopts one of Stavrogin's beliefs and turns it to what he conceives as a benefit for mankind. To rid the world from fear would be to release the human energy channelled into a futile struggle against, or a forced capitulation to, emotional bondage. For such an aim Kirillov gains our respect; and again, the fact that we respect Kirillov helps us respect Stavrogin.

There is an obvious correspondence between Kirillov and Shatov. Although they illumine different portions of Stavrogin's soul, as polar opposites of him they also become doubles (autoscopic) of one another. Irving Howe summarizes:

> Though at opposite poles ideologically, Shatov and Kirillov are in close emotional dependence, functioning as the split halves of a hypothetical self.... They represent in extreme form the issues thrown up by Stavrogin and debased by Verkhovensky. ... Shatov believes in a God who is a man, Kirillov in a man who will be God.... Shatov hungrily pursues God, Kirillov admits that 'God has pursued me all my life.' A man of pride, Shatov worships humility; a man of humility, Kirillov develops an ethic of pride.... To Shatov is assigned Dostoevsky's most cherished idea, to Kirillov his most intimate sickness. Shatov suffers from an excess of self, Kirillov from ideas that can only destroy the self. The two are bound together by a thousand dialectical ties, neither has meaning without the other; Dostoevsky's image of the ideal man implies a unity of Shatov and Kirillov.[15]

Shatov represents much of Stavrogin's yearning toward life. But while Stavrogin is unable to accept Lizaveta Nikolaevna's love or Darya Pavlovna's sympathy because he is tormented by the human flaws visible in any relationship, Shatov accepts Marie, with her illegitimate child and her querulous inability to confess her need for him, for he sees in her the possibility of human contact and warmth. Kirillov, on the other hand, refuses this possibility in favour of another: the possibility of an ultimately significant action. Stavrogin too seeks such action; Kirillov tells Verkhovensky that 'Stavrogin, too, is consumed by an idea.' That idea, Kirillov says, is faith. But whereas Shatov wills himself to have faith and Kirillov wills himself not to have faith, Stavrogin is unable to will himself into any belief. All possibilities lie open before him, and each action merely confirms that no single possibility is adequate. And so Shatov and Kirillov, as doubles of one another, serve as the two positive forces flowing through Stavrogin.

Mikhail Bakhtin said of Prince Myshkin in *The Idiot* that as a double of other characters he is 'the carrier of the penetrant word (proniknovennoe slovo), i.e. of a word which is capable of actively and confidently intervening in the interior dialogue of another person, helping that person to recognize his own voice.'[16] Stavrogin can inspire both the irrational will to live and the rational will to die, yet he himself can choose to do neither. Both Kirillov and Shatov are outgrowths of his fantasies of the possibility of good and the feasibility of living as if values existed. Yet these very values doom them. Kirillov would prefer that Shatov not be killed, but to prevent the murder would require that he found his actions on a belief in the possibility of significance within fear. Shatov, on the other hand, is crippled by his belief in life; he becomes unable to see the reality of death and so is an easy prey to the revolutionaries. So in a way Stavrogin is right: commitment is doom.

Kirillov and Shatov, as builders of meaningful lives out of the chaos of human existence, are inherent in Stavrogin himself, who has before him all their choices, and more, but who is unable to take advantage of them because of an excess of ratiocination which dooms him to see the fatal flaw in any positive action, even his own. The use of such doubles as Shatov and Kirillov makes it possible for Dostoevsky to create Stavrogin. Those avenues Stavrogin cannot explore can be explored by others, and their

relative success or unsuccess can be shown without having
Stavrogin himself pursue all paths, which is an obvious
impossibility. Thus, in no other way could the complexity of
Stavrogin be shown so fully and yet so economically.

The third major double of Stavrogin is Petr Verkhovensky. This
young man is the most fully developed of the revolutionaries.
Bulgakov has said that 'Stavrogin "means" for Verkhovensky no
less, if no more, than for Shatov and Kirillov, he is his unmasked
"I", his outward projection, a living "impostor" ... for him
Stavrogin is also only a mirror, a double. That pretender, whom
Verkhovensky wants to find in Stavrogin, is, of course, he
himself';[17] Rex Warner finds that 'Verkhovensky, in spite of his
efficiency and his genius for organization, is simply "Stavrogin's
ape".'[18] Stavrogin's connections with both Shatov and Kirillov are
developed early in the book and then dropped, but his
relationship with Petr Verkhovensky begins more slowly and
becomes a more integral part of his character revelation.

The two men are alike in the rapidity of their social success in
the town; the multitude of rumours intended to offset each man's
basic secrecy about himself; the town's conviction that both have
significant connections with the revolutionary movement. More,
Verkhovensky sees himself as different from Stavrogin and yet
the same. Stavrogin is his 'chief' and he the chief of the
revolutionaries. The similarity is a derivative one. 'You are my
idol! ... You are the leader ... Without you I am a fly, a bottled
idea: Columbus without America ... My better half' (P 393, 499).
He suggests himself as a rival for Lizaveta Nikolaevna and even
draws his own clothes from Stavrogin's trunk. The metaphors of
love and clothing indicate a sexual and social identity as well as a
philosophic one.

Unlike Shatov and Kirillov, who assume a physical duality
with one another rather than with Stavrogin, Verkhovensky
becomes Stavrogin's physical double. When Verkhovensky takes
Stavrogin to a meeting of the revolutionaries, Stavrogin walks in
the middle of the sidewalk, forcing Verkhovensky to dodge
'round him with obsequious alacrity, at one moment trying to

walk beside his companion on the narrow brick pavement and at the next running right into the mud of the road' (*P* 359). The inferior/superior relationship is unmistakable. Later, Verkhovensky asserts his superiority in exactly the same manner: 'Pyotr Stepanovich walked in the middle of the pavement, taking up the whole of it, utterly regardless of Liputin, who had no room to walk beside him and so had to hurry a step behind or run in the muddy road if he wanted to speak to him' (*P* 517–18).

Verkhovensky also becomes Stavrogin's agent. Stavrogin, like Ivan Karamazov after him, considers himself the moral murderer of the Lebyadkins even though he neither committed the murder nor knew specifically that it was to take place. The actual murderer, Fedya the convict, tells Verkhovensky that *he* is 'the chief murderer'. As in *The Brothers Karamazov*, moral, instrumental, and physical guilt are shared; and Verkhovensky assumes Stavrogin's identity by fulfilling one of his wishes. As with Shatov and Kirillov, Verkhovensky's responsibility in the Lebyadkins' murder makes him a double of only one part of Stavrogin. In acting out that part he destroys the other part of Stavrogin that, like Shatov, wishes to care for Marya Lebyadkina and to nurture what is holy in her rather than destroy what is mad.

Like his assumption of identity with Stavrogin through the murder of the Lebyadkins, Verkhovensky also assumes partial identity through his 'idea' of revolutionary activity. He shocks Stavrogin by attributing his ideas, beliefs, even actual words to Stavrogin, speaking of 'our fellows' and 'our cause'. He speaks as if he *were* Stavrogin, were the executor of Stavrogin's 'idea'. The fact that he does in fact arrange the tryst between Stavrogin and Lizaveta Nikolaevna shows him the doer to Stavrogin's thinker. In this way, as in the murder of the Lebyadkins and the literal assumption of middle-of-the-sidewalk ascendancy, Verkhovensky acts out another side of Stavrogin's character—the side that seeks influence over others. His 'idea' is power, through the formation of revolutionary groups whose sole allegiance will be to him.

Yet like Shatov and Kirillov, Verkhovensky fails to encompass Stavrogin. Because of his commitment to gaining power, he becomes an enthusiast, visibly surrendering himself to his idea. As a double of Stavrogin he shows the innate superiority of Stavrogin's lack of commitment to his own commitment, to whatever cause. When the fire is started by the labourers, Petr Verkhovensky's main weapon of terror is taken out of his hands; his idea, in effect, is stolen by others. Any idea lends itself to such theft by one who can execute it soonest. If one of the other revolutionaries had become enamoured of Kirillov's theory he could have shot himself first, thus removing all reason for Kirillov to commit suicide himself thereafter. If Stavrogin were to have to represent all the facets of his idea himself, he would have to commit himself to one (or some) of them and therefore would be susceptible, as Petr Verkhovensky is, to having the idea(s) stolen. If Shatov and Kirillov represent the possibilities of success through commitment, Verkhovensky represents the possibility of failure. He in effect justifies Stavrogin's choice. At the same time, Verkhovensky emerges as ultimately powerful precisely because he takes risks. Power requires risk; Dmitri Karamazov risks being denied the forgiveness of the peasant and thereby doomed to unexpiated guilt. In *The Possessed* Dostoevsky is unable to reconcile risk and power, however, and so Petr Verkhovensky serves as a double of accusation, highlighting as much the way Stavrogin could fail as the ways he could succeed.

It can be seen, then, that Petr Verkhovensky acts out an entirely different set of features for Stavrogin than do Shatov and Kirillov. They build on Stavrogin's ideas, whereas Verkhovensky destroys—and in so doing he destroys part of Stavrogin. With such warring impulses as Stavrogin exhibits through his doubles, it is little wonder that he assumes a lassitude that keeps him on the brink of action yet restrains him from the failure of potential that comes with action. Only after the deaths of Shatov and Kirillov and the doom of Verkhovensky's revolutionary plot can Stavrogin raise his hand decisively. But without his saving dualities, he can only raise his hand against himself.

Although in many ways the minor characters in *The Possessed* are also doubles of Stavrogin, it is enough to show his three major doubles and the ways in which they duplicate portions of Stavrogin's character which he is unable to express. His power in the novel comes from his inaccessibility; he is 'an enigmatic and romantic figure ... an extremely advantageous position' for influencing others but unfortunately not for delineation of character. For that, and for assessment of influence, Dostoevsky is forced to create doubles to show what Stavrogin cannot act out. He cannot seek life itself, as does Shatov, because that path requires a belief he cannot express (although, ironically, one he may well possess). He cannot believe in the importance of a single act and therefore is prevented from seeking Kirillov's solution. Nor can he, because of his reverence for life and love, adopt Verkhovensky's factitious leadership. He is at once a source of love and a source of destruction. Kirillov and Shatov, who seek to ease the pain of humanity, die; Verkhovensky and Fedya, the murderers, live. It is as if those who would have others live must themselves die. Stavrogin, encompassing all beliefs, can do neither.

Such a Stavrogin is in the direct line of development of Dostoevsky's sufferers. Dostoevsky's early flirtation with the idea of the double as an alleviation of suffering was a failure, as he almost immediately recognized. Golyadkin could not throw off his inadequacies onto a double without also losing his humanity. Stavrogin's doubling, while an interesting exercise on Dostoevsky's part, is similarly a failure, but for different reasons. Whereas the dissociative double allows one to develop a self in opposition to selected models, the double of decomposition is death to the decomposite character. All his choices are co-opted by his doubles; each choice representing a denial of dissociative double traits and an assumption of a particular life-fiction which shapes values and gives self-chosen meaning to existence. The strength of the decomposite double is that he can conjoin all life-fictions; in Stavrogin Dostoevsky is able to examine moral vacuum, a radiative source of power shown full spectrum. But the weakness of the decomposite double, e.g. Stavrogin's, is that he relinquishes humanity (here probably synonymous for Dostoevsky with limitation) in order to retain plenitude. As

Pereverzev has noted, 'Dostoevsky was unable to find any conclusive solution for the doubled heroes of his novels.'[19]

Dostoevsky approaches this problem again in *The Brothers Karamazov*, and here, as with the problem of evil and suffering, he has much greater success—ironically, because he risks greater failure. Dmitri Karamazov offers his life in recompense for the guilt of humanity. Through this offering he learns the value of suffering and gains what Dostoevsky intended to be conclusive salvation, unlike Raskolnikov's continued search for self through suffering. To find his salvation, Dmitri must commit himself as Stavrogin is unable to do. He must recognize his fraternity with the rest of humanity (as shown in the novel through his brother-doubles) and share the distorted ugliness of Karamazovshchina. The composite double allows this as the decomposite does not; the latter requires a characteral encompassment of humanity that prevents the creation of a life-fiction, while the former offers choices that allow participation in humanity. One need not be everything. It is enough to understand and accept differences, and above all to love them.

Doubles of separation—autoscopic or dissociative—do not allow for this acceptance and thus may be no more than convenient ways of defining self. Through decomposite doubling Dostoevsky shows the possibility of choices, although the decomposite figure himself cannot make them. It is only through the composite double that Dostoevsky finds adequate means of accepting and expiating suffering and thus truly rising above innate human evil. With Stavrogin, Dostoevsky concludes that only a chosen life-fiction, a commitment to belief or action, can provide a coherent identity. It is this that Stavrogin offers but cannot realize for himself. And it is this which Dostoevsky saw Steerforth offering in *David Copperfield*.

CHAPTER VIII

The Ascent of Steerforth

*Dostoevsky was, compared with Dickens or almost
anyone else, exceptionally unrepressed, and did
not block understanding that most writers would
find intolerable.*

ALBERT GUÉRARD

Of course *David Copperfield* cannot be viewed in the same way as
The Possessed. The latter's political content and third-person
narrative allow for an objective presentation of a man in a social
milieu. Indeed, it is only through such an objective structure that
Dostoevsky can adequately develop a double of decomposition.
Stavrogin's perceptions alone, dimmed by what he does not know
and warped by what he cannot afford to believe, would curtain
the reader from the doubling which explains (better than
Stavrogin himself could) Stavrogin.

The form of *David Copperfield* prevents such revelation.
Omniscient narration would destroy the tension between hero
and environment necessary for David's development of conscious
selfhood. But without omniscient narration, a figure like
Stavrogin is prevented from revealing himself. Insofar as
Steerforth is like Stavrogin, insofar as he influences the actions of
others in the novel, it is vital for a more complete understanding
of David that we know Steerforth better in ways that the
autobiography of David cannot provide. It is here that

Dostoevsky's choice of Steerforth as a model for Stavrogin's psyche (as opposed to his politics, for which Dostoevsky properly chose other models) provides the illumination of reverse influence. Dostoevsky must have seen decomposite doubling possibilities in Steerforth, especially as Steerforth's behaviour is tacitly a model for David's major character development. Even the rather shallow happiness David attains can be re-evaluated in the light of the possibilities Steerforth offers as a double of David.

To say that there are doubles in *David Copperfield* is not a startling critical novelty. 'Dickens is full of [the] concept of the double,' writes Angus Wilson.[1] The closest critical approach to the idea of the double of decomposition in *David Copperfield* is Leonard Manheim's; he sees that the Dickens hero may be 'a whole panoply of figures in the same novel embodying aspects of the hero from black to white, with shades between like the following pattern: Ham Peggotty→ Tommy Traddles→ David→ Steerforth→ Uriah Heep.'[2] But it is not enough to merely see the fact of doubling. Although A. E. Dyson feels that David is 'sure that Steerforth is his twin soul in all spiritual matters,'[3] even Dickens' own recognition of the existence of such doubling is questioned by Richard Dunn, who says that 'instead of definitely suggesting the tantalizing idea that Steerforth represents a psychic double who vicariously gratifies David's repressed desires, Dickens neglects even a convincing presentation of David's gradual recognition of Steerforth's character.'[4] Their sexual opposition as lovers of Emily in exclusively filial versus exclusively sexual ways is often mentioned, yet there is no identity suggested between David's coy sexual love of Dora and Steerforth's sexual pursuit of Emily. David's struggle to rise to Steerforth's social class makes them doubles; but no one has suggested that Uriah Heep's similar struggle makes him even momentarily admirable, as it does David. If Steerforth and Heep are at the same end of the duality spectrum, why is David unable to hate Steerforth while conceiving the utmost feeling of repulsion toward Heep? And why doesn't he love Ham, if Ham is Heep's opposite? Even Manheim, in 'The Personal History of David Copperfield,' in which he specifically designates those parts of

David to be found in Steerforth, Uriah, Traddles, and Ham,[5] sees them merely as dissociative doubles of David: they show ways he might have gone, choices he might have made. And the dissociative double, focused upon David and seen through David's eyes, is the strongest doubling pattern Dickens presents, but surely not the only one. Nor is it most useful to linger over the dissociative double.

I want instead to move beyond the dissociative double, to the double of decomposition and the composite double, by means of the Steerforth-Stavrogin comparison. The Steerforth Dostoevsky saw allows us to examine Dickens in a wider light and to place *David Copperfield* within the realm of his continuing artistic concerns elucidated in Part I of this study.

One glance at *David Copperfield* will convince most readers that David himself could never be a double of decomposition. Although Manheim sets up dissociative-double situations between David and Steerforth, David and Uriah and to a lesser degree David and Ham and David and Traddles, he does not attempt to link them all as David manqués. It would be impossible to do it. David's is not a strong character, and the very nature of his learning processes, in which he takes on various value systems in order to find the ones he can live within, prevents him from having a significant impact on the world around him within the time span of the novel itself. (After David has married Agnes and become a successful novelist, he might be able to impart to others some of what he has internalized; but that would be another story and not the one Dickens wrote.)

David's development is a result of the forces impinging upon him, and he is not a significant force in the lives of others. Because he is undeveloped morally, he cannot act as anchor for others similarly drifting with the moving tides which sweep through his and others' lives. This is illustrated by his helplessness as Rosa accosts Emily while he looks on in the hall, rationalizing why he dare not save Emily the humiliation he so eagerly watches, and again by his agonized helplessness in the face of Uriah's machinations over the Wickfields. He is unsure enough of his position and his motives that he is unable to step forward and act definitively. In addition he is 'sexually inadequate'.[6]

His attachment to Steerforth shows an awareness of passion and an ability to value it in others, but in all his relationships with women he is romantic rather than passionate. Dora's death as the result of a miscarriage is a thinly disguised statement about the undesirability of passion and the harm it can bring. By the time he comes to love Agnes, David is totally devoid of any passionate feelings for her; their relationship is a return to the comfortable friendliness of childhood and, in spite of the children they produce, is totally unsexual.

Third, David's upward mobility takes him out of the class of the Peggotty group and into Steerforth's class. As Graves' *The Real David Copperfield* shows so painfully, David must use others as models to achieve behaviour appropriate to the class he wishes to join. He is thus prevented from being himself a model or from providing assistance to others. As with his moral underdevelopment and asexuality, so David's classlessness unfits him for a position of influence. And once again the *Bildungsroman* form requires that this be so. The pupil cannot be the teacher. Thus David cannot be a double of decomposition, for such a double must be a whole character before he can become fragmented. David is not a whole character; one could argue that he becomes one, or close to it, by the end of the novel, but that does not qualify him as a decomposite double figure during the course of the novel.

Now, of course, it is not necessary for David to be the cause of the action. It is enough that he be its focus. The novel is, after all, his. Yet it interests us to know not only what David becomes but why. The more we can understand of the sources of his choices and of the world that shapes him, the better we will be able to understand the novel.

It is clear that only Steerforth is a significant model for David. Micawber has been suggested as a father figure: 'he represents neither half of Copperfield senior but both halves together,' says Christopher Mulvey, and 'is the most representative of the father figures.'[7] But however fully formed, however whole, Micawber is hardly influential upon David and in fact owes his ability to influence anyone in the novel to a startlingly unrepresentative diligence in the dull menial job Uriah Heep offers him. Murdstone is both formed and influential, but his influence is harmful and therefore almost universally resisted. Mr Peggotty and Ham are too idealized to serve as realistic models, especially for urbane, class-conscious David. Traddles turns out to be a man of some strength and ability, but we see too little of him and the early actions he performs are too insignificant for him to influence David. Agnes, being a woman, can only influence indirectly, however beneficially. Wickfield is hopeless; Dr Strong is peripheral. Uriah Heep is perhaps the closest we come to a formed and influential centre, and he certainly tries to take over the world the novel creates. But he lacks something which could make others wish to follow and emulate him.

Only Steerforth has the presence to be 'the Stavrogin angel-devil whose charm so dominates the novel.'[8] Like Stavrogin, Steerforth remains outside the novel's moral framework. In fact, George Katkov has noted that 'as a reader of Dickens, Dostoevsky reconstituted the elements of Steerforth's character and saw that the evil actions he committed were not the result of yielding to the temptations of the flesh, or of social ambition, but sprang from an autonomous daemonic desire for evil as such.'[9] To this concept readers have intuitively assented, feeling Steerforth indeed to be a daemonic force of irrational evil, as if representing absolute evil in the world. The existence of such a force is fully consonant with Dickens' expanding investigation of the nature of good and evil and human responsibility for the evil within. I wish to consider the effect of viewing Steerforth (as Dostoevsky did) as a double of decomposition.

David is Steerforth's most obvious double and the one who best reflects his influence. David is a social, intellectual, professional, and sexual double of Steerforth; and in some cases he is conscious of the doubling and in fact strives to bring Steerforth's beliefs and behaviour into line with his own values so that he can continue to believe Steerforth a 'good Angel'.

Socially David emulates Steerforth. The world he aspires to in childhood is Steerforth's world. Its manners and values are inherent in Steerforth. In it one does not keep secrets from one's best friend; one does not hesitate to introduce one's friend to the family and friends of home and childhood, although one may feel compelled to apologize for unpolished manners. In it David feels it would be 'unfriendly' for him to show sympathy for Mr Mell. In it Traddles is a dullard, Mr Mell an inferior; Steerforth's is the only approval to be desired.

From their first meeting at Mr Creakle's school, Steerforth influences David's intellectual development and eventually his career. David is the new boy; Steerforth, the most powerful in the school, appears to know everything. The two become one in the expenditure of David's small store of funds, David supplying the money and Steerforth doing the buying. Whenever Steerforth acts, David is still; it is as if there is only one person who resides alternately in Steerforth's and in David's body, moving from one to the other with ease but allowing only the ascendant one to act or think. And because of David's low status, it is Steerforth who does most of the acting and thinking. The exception is David's knowledge of stories, in which he becomes the actor (the teller) and Steerforth plays the inactive role of listener. In exchange Steerforth helps David with the rest of his studies. This is a dissociative-double exchange, where one person makes up what the other lacks. Steerforth is intelligent enough to learn the stories David tells him; he has time enough to do so, for he has time enough to listen to David tell them, a much longer affair than reading them himself.

The stories, however, represent a side of Steerforth, which he is reluctant to develop, namely imagination. Imagination is dangerous to him because it threatens to carry him willy-nilly out of the realm of reality in which he has full control of himself and his surroundings, and into a realm where he must be the follower. Imagination is a hard taskmaster and demands subservience from those who wish to know it; it must lead, for in following it extinguishes itself. Therefore Steerforth cannot allow it any play in his mind. For its expression he turns to David and

David's stories of Peregrine Pickle or the Arabian Nights. Early in *David Copperfield* David becomes an expression of Steerforth's inexpressible desire to live in imagination without submitting to it. David's mature professional life is an incarnation of one of Steerforth's hidden faces.

In his school career David strives to become a second Steerforth. At Mr Creakle's, what takes David long hours of study seems to come naturally to Steerforth, and it is obvious that with suitable direction he would be able to master any profession. David, on the other hand, is long in developing this trait, although it lies in him; his eventual success as an author bespeaks a natural aptitude, albeit one that must be carefully cultivated before it bears fruit. Steerforth's apparently unreachable superiority in school, however, proves to be illusory, for David himself achieves the same status in Dr Strong's school and probably appears to the younger boys much as Steerforth appeared to him and Traddles. Yet David never makes friends with any of the younger boys at Dr Strong's. If he is indeed like Steerforth, we can assume that he made such friendships but that they were of little account to him in the wider scope of his life, just as Steerforth appears never to have cared a great deal for David. David has left enough of a gap in his account of his school days that we suspect he too formed friendships which did not mean enough to him to warrant commitment to them in any significant way. In this lack of commitment he is a double of Steerforth.

Even David's professional activities are a reflection of his belief in Steerforth. He drifts into the profession of proctor, but Spenlow's death conveniently releases him from a bondage which he has come to feel oppressive. Writing is a respectable profession, but it is a restless one, leading in various directions and depending for inspiration upon a muse which, as Dickens well knew, was not always timely. David ends by making a living from the creation of fictions, the shaping of worlds, and the ordering of lives. We hear the echo of Steerforth's words: '*I* take a degree! ... Not I! ... I have never learned the art of binding myself to any of the wheels on which the Ixions of these days are turning round and round' (*DC* 327, 294). David gives as little indication of a commitment to hard work. He flees the wine warehouse labour and would prefer to live without labouring at all, if he could. He certainly didn't learn much as an apprentice proctor. And his three years abroad, during which he establishes his reputation as a novelist, are skimmed over in a pair of pages devoted mostly to the Swiss climate, his Swiss friends, and memories of Agnes. The autobiographical nature of the novel accounts for much of David's apparent industry versus Steerforth's self-proclaimed (but never proven) indolence (sheer brilliance alone would not have created for him such a reputation at Oxford). David definitely inclines toward work which does not tie him down to specific times and places or to physical labour.

David's tendency toward restlessness is obviously a double of Steerforth's inability to be bound on any wheel. The reader is told, of course, that David leaves the wine warehouse because he seeks a better life and that he transfers his affections from Emily to Dora to Agnes because he is learning the nature of love, whereas Steerforth seems merely to delight 'to find a vent in rough toil and hard weather, as in any other means of excitement that presented itself freshly to him.' But David's departure from the wine warehouse is an impetuous flight from his natural heritage of steady, grinding labour, for there is little reason to suppose that David (or Oliver Twist or Pip, for that matter) is entitled to a natural and easy rise into the gentle classes. So too, although he does not literally set forth in a ship upon stormy seas, he figuratively embarks in a frail craft in rough weather when he persists in marrying Dora despite her obvious unfitness for adulthood. Because of the *Bildungsroman* form the objective insubstantiality of David's character is lost in the mass of detail about his *feelings* toward his labours and choices, feelings which are denied us in Steerforth's case. Yet the doubling is there.

David is also a sexual double of Steerforth in several ways. Most obvious is Steerforth's fulfilment of David's desire for Emily: he acts out what David is unable to acknowledge. David's unflagging pursuit of Dora reflects the energy and attention Steerforth devotes to seducing Emily. Even Steerforth's relationship with Rosa Dartle is a pattern for David: the girl, loved in childhood and then deserted, whose subsequent behaviour reflects an attempt to justify and at the same time disprove her earlier devotion, could be David's Emily. One is reminded most strongly here of Stavrogin's seduction of Shatov's wife and the identity created between the two men through their love for the same woman. The sexual identity between David and Steerforth is heightened by Steerforth's appropriation of David as his 'property' and the many suggestions of latent homosexuality. David's nickname of Daisy is at once feminine and compliant. He becomes an object of Steerforth's self-love—both self and beloved.

In his relation to the Peggottys, David assumes the role he sees Steerforth play with his mother. As Steerforth reigns over Mrs Steerforth and enchants (but refuses) Rosa, so David is with the Peggottys. They are surrogate mother and father to him and show the same uncritical approval of all his actions that Mrs Steerforth shows toward her son. Steerforth's opinions about social class are literally echoed by David, who says, 'they *are* that sort of people that you mentioned.' David's subsequent desire to believe that Steerforth's ease with Mr Peggotty and Ham indicates a real liking for and sympathy with them is wish-fulfilment, an attempt to deny Steerforth's (and by extension, his own) sense of superiority. Steerforth chides David for seeing what he wishes to exist rather than what really exists—a class gulf that neither young man would eliminate *even if he could*. (If Steerforth could raise Emily to the status of lady by marrying her, David could have done the same. Yet this possibility *never occurs* to him.) Such willed belief in his own and Steerforth's egalitarianism in the face of the physical and emotional evidence to the contrary is strikingly similar to Shatov's conviction that he 'will believe' in God and that Stavrogin too 'must' believe because such belief seems necessary to the completion of Stavrogin's Slavophile ideals.

David falls victim to Steerforth's version of social and sexual reality. In so doing, he lives out one of the possibilities Steerforth is unable to choose. Like Shatov, David is naïve and thus falls prey—not to revolutionaries, for in Dickens' world, remember,

there can be no revolutionaries—but to snobbery, on whose brink
Steerforth teeters. Both sin. Steerforth's are sins of commission:
he deflowers Rosa, abducts Emily. David, striving for what
Steerforth naturally has and is, cannot afford to soil himself
similarly, but his sins lead to equal personal defilement. His are
sins of omission. He stands listening to Rosa's attack on Emily,
well knowing the pain it is causing Emily, yet he chooses not to
intervene on the weak excuse that he felt it better to wait for Mr
Peggotty to rescue her. (Yet he was not even sure Mr Peggotty
would arrive at all!) Even George Gissing cannot allow himself to
believe that his beloved David is capable of listening without
intervention.[10] Likewise, David permits Uriah Heep to continue
persecuting Agnes and Mr Wickfield without once trying to
ascertain whether there were anything he could do about it,
although Micawber's uncharacteristic actions make it clear that
much could be done, and in a short time, by anyone interested
enough to investigate the situation minimally. David obviously
seeks uninvolvement, a disengagement from the workings of the
world. His final profession, which allows him to create worlds
according to his own desires, and his marriage, which is too
obviously made in heaven to allow it many of the normal human
joys and pains, are both withdrawals from experience. Although
Steerforth is the one who effects Mr Mell's dismissal and seduces
Emily, the impetus for both those acts originates with David. He
shares with Steerforth the innate evil of which even a Little Nell is
capable.

Steerforth's superiority over David comes from his recognition
of the evil within. He stares into the fire and says he is a 'torment'
to himself as well as others. He acknowledges his lack of
direction: 'I wish to God I had had a judicious father these last
twenty years!... I wish with all my soul I could guide myself
better!' (*DC* 322) He sees something within which frightens him:
'I have been afraid of myself ... and may have something to be
afraid of too.' Building the self unaided is a frightening and
haphazard task. Steerforth can barely allow himself to view the
finished product; except for the scene in his Highgate bedroom,
when he as much as confesses to David that he will not sleep

easily, this is the only time he indicates dissatisfaction with himself. In both instances the dissatisfaction haunts him and poisons his repose. As both source and sharer of all the action in *The Possessed*, Stavrogin suffered and expressed his suffering through restlessness and sleeplessness just as Steerforth does. Like Stavrogin, Steerforth will not refrain from evil and thereby lessen his sufferings. It is almost as if he is driven to act on the evil in his soul in order to keep it alive so he will remain whole. He cannot choose to restrain himself; he will not renounce any action or satisfaction that demonstrates continued freedom.

Sylvère Monod, in a brief article, analyses Steerforth as the source of all evil in the novel. In fact, he sees two Steerforths: the charming one David presents and loves, and the destroyer of all happiness. Steerforth is 'une incarnation du Mal' and, unfortunately for David, 'le Mal est séduisant.'[11] Monod believes that Steerforth's evil seduces David into introducing him into the Peggotty group; David, by participating in Steerforth's evil, becomes responsible for the unhappiness of those worthy people. Yet David's action is necessary, according to Monod, because without it David would never have been able to comprehend the fullness of life.

> Jamais il n'aurait pu nous raconter sa vie comme il le fait, et nous révéler les aspects authentiques et objectifs du personnage de Steerforth si Steerforth ne lui avait fait découvrir la différence entre le Bien et le Mal.... C'est Steerforth qui a révélé à David sa faiblesse et sa vulnérabilité.[12]

Monod sees in *David Copperfield* a Blakean progression toward maturity. Innocence must recognize and incorporate experience before that higher innocence based on knowledge can lead to an acceptance of life as it is coupled with the amelioration that Dickens firmly believed good people to be capable of. Mr Dombey has already been 'saved' by the time *David Copperfield* is written; the sterility of the Garlands' goodness has led Dickens to drop such characters, substituting instead Captain Cuttles, who can give only temporary aid to individuals, or Betsey Trotwoods, whose goodness flows from self-deception succeeded by bitter knowledge. Innocent goodness must learn the ways of the world. And so, as Monod views him, Steerforth represents the world which threatens to pollute David even as it entices him, and which he must resist even as he loves it. Evil is indeed seductive, but, as Monod points out, it is only through a knowledge of evil that David can learn to be truly good. The child must grow up.

But David does not grow up; he never acknowledges his part in the seduction of Emily and consequently is unable to confront the evil which he shares with Steerforth. As Ivan Karamazov's hallucinatory devil-double revealed parts of Ivan's character that his self-image prevented him from acknowledging, so Steerforth could reveal to David the deep split which keeps him from recognizing why he has chosen as he has. But David's final inability to admit his own participation in the evil of the human soul cuts him off from the deepest sources of human understanding. The resolution he will not attain for himself he gives instead to Steerforth when he chooses to see him lying in death as he had lain at school of old, his head upon his arm, in a peaceful posture at variance with both the violence of his life and the violence of his death. David's transformation of the living Steerforth, whose reality threatened the rather precarious life David had built of selected shreds of the whole cloth, tames those things David needs to leave unacknowledged. David must keep his image of Steerforth whole and untarnished; therefore, he recreates it into a peacefully sleeping figure for whom he has 'romantic feelings' of friendship and whom he can now believe loved him better and treated him more kindly than any other. Steerforth becomes what David wants him to be: a silent pattern, an image. David is able at last to *become* his image of Steerforth— not through his own actions but through a revision (in all senses) of Steerforth.

Through David's latent doubling with Steerforth, Dickens can both show the sources for David's behaviour and retain the reader's sympathy for him. Like Shatov, David tries to assume and transform vital aspects of Steerforth. He succeeds insofar as he continues to live and becomes a responsible member of society—a high priority for Dickens at this point in his career. He fails by choosing not to see the repression and conflict that society requires of human wholeness. This failure causes a blandness that elicits the sorts of critical comments I included at the beginning of Chapter Five. David must choose to be colourless in order to succeed. Nor should we fault Dickens for this: just as the child must retain the safety of home to test out new skills, so the development of full humanity is at first fragile and must be shielded. Dickens could not have brought Steerforth to flower in 1850. Only David, as colourless and self-protecting as we may decide he is, can emerge victorious within social strictures Dickens is unready to attack. At the same time, however, a knowledge of the extent of David's doubling with Steerforth helps us see the depth of his weakness just as the *Bildungsroman* form emphasizes the relative success of his choices.

But of course no doubling between Steerforth and David, however profound and central, makes of Steerforth a double of decomposition. Other aspects of Steerforth, unrealized by David, must appear in other characters who form the novel's phalanx of values. And indeed Traddles and Heep are as much decomposite doubles of Steerforth as David is, or as they are of David.

On the surface, Traddles would appear to be as different from Steerforth as David is from Uriah Heep. He is cheerful, hard-working, constant, practical, and good. Even at school he is merry and good-natured; throughout life he is honourable and often seems a patsy because of his unswerving devotion to right behaviour. His bravest act is to stand up to Steerforth when the latter has effected Mr Mell's dismissal. In this confrontation of Traddles' goodwill with Steerforth's evil, Traddles, unlike David, will not capitulate and forsake his values. Once embarked upon a law career, he impresses everyone with his ability. Only his reluctance to put himself forward makes it seem as if he is never going to amount to much.

These good qualities are counterbalanced by his failings. David several times describes him as 'unfortunate', and his actions support that description. He breaks windows by accident,

habitually occupies corners rather than the centre of the room, is
so incautious as to lend Micawber his name on a bill, and seems
unable to claim his beloved from the demands of her family.
Indeed, in all his dealings with Sophy's family Traddles is at a
disadvantage because he puts the most generous construction on
all they do. Therefore he quite naturally ends up married to the
whole lot of Creweler girls, having to fetch and carry for The
Beauty and sympathize with Sarah's complaints about her spine.
He must live amidst ribbons and giggles because he hasn't the
heart to say no. His whole courtship and marriage are examples
of extreme sexual, social and emotional naïveté.

Practical, however, he always is. We have an early hint of
Traddles' practical nature when, instead of railing against
injustices he can do nothing about, he draws skeletons until his
humour returns. Later he seconds David's idea of taking up
shorthand in order to become a court reporter. He also suggests,
practically, that Mr Dick become a copyist to help support
himself, and attempts to dissuade Micawber from hoping to
become a judge. When shorthand becomes difficult for David,
Traddles suggests that he dictate so David can practice. He does
David a further service by convincing Dora's aunts that David is
worthy to court their niece, 'confirming me in good round terms,
and in a plain, sensible, practical manner, that evidently made a
favourable impression' (*DC* 598). But his most stunning practical
accomplishment is to aid Micawber in unearthing and unmasking
Heep's schemes. David is conscious, during the unmasking, that
'this was the first occasion on which I really did justice to the
clear head and the plain, patient, practical good sense of my old
schoolfellow' (*DC* 758).

There seems to be remarkably little of Steerforth in Traddles.
Certainly the older boy did not influence Traddles' choice of
lifestyle or values. Yet there are a number of ways in which
Traddles appears to be a double of Steerforth, and these doublings
point to a decomposite relationship between the two.

Traddles' practicality on behalf of others is no greater than
Steerforth's practicality on his own behalf. In a matter of weeks
Steerforth learns enough from the Yarmouth fishermen to handle

a seagoing boat by himself. His brilliance at Oxford could not, as has been mentioned, have been achieved without effort. We see Traddles' efforts merely because David's are dependent upon them rather than upon Steerforth's. Nor is Traddles' apparent quietude a bar to likeness with Steerforth; he draws skeletons—images of death and decay—while Steerforth actually wreaks destruction, but the impulse is present in Traddles as it is in Steerforth. Third, Traddles' misfortunes are remarkably similar in kind to Steerforth's: he fails to marry because of parental interference; it appears to outsiders he will never get ahead because of his incapacity for singleminded devotion in the face of personal desires (for Traddles, others' desires; for Steerforth, his own).

The effect of Traddles' actions is like the effect of Steerforth's. Traddles and Sophy in their rather juvenile married bliss may well be a double of Steerforth and Emily in Europe, when, as Littimer recounts, Steerforth 'was more settled, for a length of time, than I have known him to be since I have been in his service.' Similarly, Steerforth's ability to charm and fool the Peggotty group while secretly plotting their disruption is paralleled by Traddles' insinuation into the affairs of Heep (via Micawber). Both extreme good and extreme evil are vulnerable to invasion. To be effective, Traddles must be like Steerforth. Thus, much more than a double of David or a representative of the ineffectuality of goodness, Traddles stands as a decomposite double, like David a limitation of Steerforth to a single line of development.

Although his goodness seems to parallel Shatov's, in fact Traddles is more like Petr Verkhovensky in the singleness of his purpose and the distance which the reader feels between him and Steerforth. And in Dickens there actually is such a distance, for Traddles is not shaped and influenced by Steerforth as David is. The shaping is more negative: Steerforth's behaviour gives Traddles a chance to refine and express his own feelings. His silent approbation of Mr Mell could have effect only after Steerforth had denounced him; his sense of honour over not tattling can be expressed only because Steerforth allows him to take the blame. And while he shares some traits with David—which we see very clearly because we are looking through David's eyes—he actually realizes Steerforth's potential for thought and action. He takes opportunities, as David does not, for positive action. He strives to eliminate suffering in the world; David concentrates on alleviating his own suffering.

Many readers find Traddles the most likeable fellow in *David Copperfield*; he seems to represent the sort of unequivocal social force Dickens had sought in earlier novels. The energies that David himself could not realize are balanced in practical, self-sacrificing Traddles. His eye is upon the goal of honest behaviour, not upon the main chance. David may laugh at his home life, with Beauty and the other sisters bringing him his pipe and ruffling his hair, but Traddles represents something Dostoevsky sensed in Steerforth. In part he redeems Steerforth, for he puts Steerforth's virtues into action. Dostoevsky sought illumination of Steerforth, Dickens transformation. Transformation has its drawbacks: Traddles' marriage is a 'Creweler' one even than David's fiasco with Dora. Dickens' goal of melioration is reflected in the novel's structure, social background, and characterization. But this does not lessen the validity of Dostoevsky's vision that Steerforth's positive qualities are the ones that move the world.

As Stavrogin's negative qualities set in motion forces opposing the realization of good, so too Steerforth's negative qualities are reflected in Uriah Heep (and to a much lesser extent in David, as I have already noted), who puts them into effect. Heep seems to be a dissociative double of just about everyone. Traddles is unlike him, Steerforth strangely like, and David fights recognition of likeness.

Leonard Manheim's spectrum places Traddles as far from Uriah as it is reasonably possible to be:

Ham→ Traddles→ David→ Steerforth→ Uriah Heep.[13] Of the four characters able to function in the novel's world, Traddles and Uriah are direct opposites. Traddles is devoted to a belief in honest work at the expense of success, while Uriah aims at success regardless of means. Traddles' patient love for Sophy incites Dickens to reward him with perhaps disproportionate happiness at the end, whereas Uriah's crawling pursuit of Agnes arouses in both author and reader the utmost disgust and desire to punish (few readers find Dickens' ultimate disposal of Heep harsh enough to be satisfactory). Traddles, without pride, is lovable; Uriah's pride alone would suffice to create a reader dislike ineradicable by good deeds. And yet, as Christopher Mulvey had noted, both Traddles and Uriah (as well as Steerforth and David) seek 'a position'; both have received a shaping inheritance from fathers (Traddles an indifference that spurs him on to honest efforts, Uriah the pride that mocks and manipulates honesty); and Uriah's downfall is a direct result of Traddles' investigative efforts. Therefore, although the doubling at first appears quite straightforward, it soon becomes clear that there are ties as well as disjunctions between the two, suggesting more than mere dissociative doubling.

The identity between David and Uriah is established early and strongly, despite David's thin attempt to disavow it. David consciously models himself on Steerforth, so it is quite easy to trace the ways in which his behaviour parallels Steerforth's, even in negative ways. Yet the same sort of doubling takes place between David and Uriah; we don't see it so clearly because, again, David's point of view shuts us off from a direct comprehension which David is at pains to disavow. Steerforth's attraction is obvious, Uriah's less obvious but no less attractive to David. When the two first meet, David is left in a room with a view of Uriah's writing desk. He sits on a chair which is 'opposite a narrow passage which ended in a little circular room' where Uriah writes. Now, it would seem an easy matter for David to shift his position so he would not have a view through this narrow passage into Uriah's small room, yet he stations himself so that Uriah can look at him the whole time he is there. Although he says he tries to get out of the way of Uriah's eyes, he fails to take the obvious expedient of moving his stool three feet to left or right. He clearly wants to be able to see Uriah. Later, he offers to shake Uriah's hand in order to have physical contact with him, although he is aware that such contact is bound to be repulsive to him. Eventually he seeks out Uriah and admits to 'feeling myself attracted towards Uriah Heep, who had a sort of fascination for me.'

This spiritual brotherhood is deepened when Uriah spends the night in David's room but will not usurp his bed; it is consummated when David returns to the Wickfields' and finds Uriah living in his old room and, at last, sleeping in his bed. In so doing Uriah has become David, occupying the place (with Agnes) that we know David is to occupy later in life. This identity between David and Uriah moves into the plane of David's consciousness when David admits a similarity between Uriah's pretensions and his own. David's schemes to join Spenlow and Jorkins and marry Spenlow's daughter are expressed in only slightly balder terms than those Uriah uses to describe his aspirations for Mr Wickfield's practice and daughter.

Uriah also serves as a receptacle for feelings David cannot own about Steerforth. At one point Uriah's accusations of Annie Strong enrage David so much that he strikes Uriah, offering Dickens the strange possibility (which he even more strangely accepts) of showing Uriah the superior as he genuinely turns the other cheek.

Many critics have faulted the relationship between Annie and the good Doctor, pointing out that Dickens never did resolve the problem of Annie's behaviour toward her cousin (Graves goes so far as to have Annie run off with Jack Maldon as soon as the doctor dies). It is Uriah who first sees the possibility of falseness in the triangle, a falseness which David himself comes to believe until Dickens quite factitiously relieves him of his suspicions by unconvincingly negating them. But in order to deny both his suspicions and any thought of a parallel between the Annie–Doctor–Jack confluence and his own uneasy complicity in Steerforth's abduction of Emily, David strikes out physically, giving body to his denial and seeking vent for his need to punish someone for that sense of complicity—and who better to punish than Steerforth, the villain of the piece? And so when he strikes Uriah he is able to punish Steerforth for hurting Emily and Mr Peggotty, for whom he is in a moral way responsible. Against Uriah he can vent feelings he could not vent against his friend and against himself. And indeed, Mark Spilka has noted that 'David's inconsistent slap seems aimed ... at a subdued aspect of himself.'[14] In this scene, Dickens gives David the chance to learn what Uriah's unadulterated evil can tell him about himself, but David is afraid to delve for fear of what he might find. Instead, he simply chooses to view Uriah as the source of undisguised evil. Uriah is attractive to David because he is a secret sharer and yet repulsive because David does not want to acknowledge his confraternity with him. Traddles is exactly the opposite; David likes Traddles' honesty but does not find it attractive, in the same way evil attracts him, because it strikes no hidden but responsive chord in his secret soul.

Uriah's peculiar attractiveness to David is a major factor in drawing David off his scent, for Agnes early warns David not to 'resent ... what may be uncongenial to you in him.' This is in direct opposition to her warning about Steerforth. David is to suspect what he admires of Steerforth and to like what repulses him in Uriah Heep. He must create a dichotomy between the two in order to remain clear about himself. This clarity, as we have seen, is the major thrust of the book and the one which has made it, as autobiography, so attractive for a century and a quarter. David's dissociative doubling with Uriah Heep is quite real and illuminates a discovery that David proves finally unable to make—that there is a conspiracy of evil existent in the human soul. Although David would deny it, the novel shows that David shares evil with Uriah. And Uriah quite as clearly shares it with Steerforth, becoming Steerforth's surrogate when David strikes him for the expression of David's own evil thoughts.

The genesis of Steerforth and Uriah Heep is strikingly similar and leads to similar ends. Both are, as boys, left with widowed mothers who rest all their pride and hope upon their sons. Uriah's mother is as 'humble' as Steerforth's is proud, and these controlling characteristics shape their behaviour toward David. Both mothers work for and are interested in nothing else than the social welfare and progress of their sons, unlike David's mother who cared for his soul and spirit, and Traddles' mother who seems to have had time to care for very little. Both Steerforth and

Uriah attend bad schools where they learn to survive through cunning, charm, and a high degree of development of their respective character foci, pride and humility. Both have a generalized desire to do what they wish with the other people in their worlds; this desire is not veiled either by Steerforth's charm or by Uriah's seeming devotion to selfless labours. Steerforth apparently lusts for Emily with as little genuine emotion as Uriah for Agnes, and surely the result of Steerforth's lust is no more degrading to Emily socially than Uriah's lust is to Agnes emotionally. Mr Peggotty as the bearer of the reader's reactive hatred toward Steerforth parallels Mr Wickfield as the agonized and helpless viewer of Uriah's machinations.

David himself makes the strongest connection between Steerforth and Uriah when he dreams of Uriah 'that he had launched Mr Peggotty's house on a piratical expedition, with a black flag at the masthead, bearing the inscription "Tidd's Practice", under which diabolical ensign he was carrying me and little Emily to the Spanish Main to be drowned.' Aside from the obvious link between Steerforth's future villainy and David's subconscious desires, this dream is an exact description of Steerforth's abduction of Emily. The ship he 'gives' Mr Peggotty goes on a piratical expedition to bear away its trophy, the black flag symbolizing the death of Emily's virtue and the inscription, 'Tidd's Practice', standing for the same thing in Uriah's life (Mr Wickfield's practice and Agnes's body) as the 'Little Em'ly' stood for in Steerforth's. Steerforth does carry Emily to Europe, where she 'drowns' to respectable society forever. David's dream thus connects Uriah to Steerforth, giving them a common motive in life and showing that Uriah's actions flow from the same self-centred springs as Steerforth's. In his unmitigated evil, Uriah Heep is the overdevelopment of one of Steerforth's qualities. That it is a quality we dislike makes him no less a double; that it is a quality under-developed in David and Traddles makes Uriah the final decomposition of Steerforth.

Well, yes, one says. Steerforth and Uriah are indeed 'alike' in that 'they take ways David might have taken,' representing 'two shameful directions, ... the antitypes of the crime-free David.'[15]

And of course it is clear why David chose to pattern himself after Steerforth rather than Uriah. Uriah is ugly, Steerforth handsome; Uriah awkward, Steerforth graceful; Uriah demeaning, Steerforth uplifting. It is not pleasant to look at or speak to Uriah. His affected humility is a thousand times worse than Steerforth's easy and natural pride. Uriah seeks out and forces himself physically upon others when they would prefer to have no contact, while Steerforth never seeks to attract but apparently cannot avoid doing so. It is preferable for David, and therefore for the reader, to disavow a connection between the two. Yet Uriah's successes, when placed beside Steerforth's utter failure, must cause us to question whether they are merely two of the awful ends David might reach or whether there is a deeper connection between the two.

David's one act of physical violence is to strike Uriah. It is a repudiation of all that is evil within him, an attempt to distance himself from what Uriah seems to represent. However, his simultaneous attempt to absorb Steerforth's nature—a nature so similar to Uriah's as to make them clearly dissociative doubles of evil—thus creates a large part of the tension inherent in David's struggle to grow up. Steerforth and Uriah Heep never meet, and there is no suggestion that Uriah 'learned' from Steerforth as Shatov, Kirillov and Verkhovensky learned from Stavrogin. Yet the evil inherent in Steerforth is the *same* evil inherent in Uriah. Indeed, both represent ways David might have turned out. That he doesn't turn out at all 'like' Uriah is misleading; for indeed he does marry Agnes, does take pride in his own 'humility' in dealing with characters from low life that he creates in his novels. The reader doesn't notice these absorptions at first glance, only because David himself doesn't notice them.

All four major male characters in *David Copperfield* are doubles. But rather than being doubles of David, they are more accurately doubles of Steerforth. All around him as he grows up David sees patterns of what a person can choose to be like. If he chooses prudence and diligence he will perhaps become a Traddles. If he chooses deceit—the supremacy of evil over good—he may be a Uriah Heep. If he chooses them all he will be a Steerforth, tossed among choices and values without ability to crystallize around any one of them. Only Steerforth possesses the wholeness of character to stand, as did Stavrogin in a much more frank way, as a double of decomposition. David, Traddles, and Uriah together show all that Steerforth could be. He is the pattern of which they are variations, and they, drawing on the universality he represents, illustrate directions in which the human being can choose to move during the process of growth which shapes the personality. Like Stavrogin, Steerforth contains all possibilities and cannot give up any of them; therefore, he is unable to act in any meaningful way. David, Traddles, and Uriah are all possible ways in which Steerforth could have chosen to limit himself. But such wholeness as Steerforth represents is paralyzed, prevented from acting and thus dead to all human purpose. Stavrogin, in order to retain wholeness, had to eschew the assumption of values; Steerforth does the same, and his actions throughout *David Copperfield* indicate that he consciously chooses to do so. His elopement with Emily, so intricately planned over such a long period of time, shows us the depth of his commitment to actions based only upon personal desire and devoid of principle. Had he adhered to any principle, he would have become a David or a Traddles, or even a Uriah; that he did not shows his Stavroginesque refusal to limit himself.

And yet this is not wholly negative. David and Traddles choose well (from a social viewpoint) and are able to make positive contributions to the welfare of human society. Uriah chooses poorly and is cut off from that society. However, Steerforth, in his freedom from commitment, stands in the novel as the unreachable goal, the unrealizable dream, the unquenchable quest for the core of existence. This existence contains the Manichaean as well as the progressive, the Byronic as well as the Benthamite. And while Dickens thoroughly approved individual effort and responsibility, he was able to see that Benthamism did not always correspond to this ideal, as we see in *Hard Times*. So too he can allow David to honour and adore Steerforth without celebrating Steerforth's Byronic nature.

I do not think we need posit for Dickens a belief in the

purposelessness of endeavour to suggest that he recognized the existence of such a belief in others. It is not true to say, as Edgar Johnson does, that 'the cynicism and disillusion of a Byron was not inwardly conceivable.'[16] Indeed Dickens was capable of conceiving it. The progression of his recognition of evil in the world throughout the novels shows not only that he could recognize evil but that he came to see that it pervaded the very idea of goodness. Dickens doesn't much like Steerforth himself (in fact, in the early years of his career he probably would have liked to have eradicated him), but the idea of Steerforth turns out to be inescapable. It undergoes transformations: Esther Summerson comes to recognize her unintentional participation in the spiral of evil that threatens to bring the whole world, like Tom-All-Alone's, tumbling down around her; Amy Dorrit and Arthur Clennam despair of overcoming the multifaceted evil of *Little Dorrit* that moves from the motiveless rancour of Blandois/ Rigaud through Casby to Flintwinch to Mrs Clennam's fully purposeful destruction of good.

Probably the best example of the way Steerforth as a double of decomposition fits with Dickens' purposes comes in *Great Expectations*, which is in many ways an advanced parallel to *David Copperfield*. Pip himself becomes the decomposite double in *Great Expectations*. Orlick is his evil self, the self responsible for willed destruction and smug assumption of superiority, while Joe is the 'good Angel' of faith, love, and forbearance. Through Magwitch, himself a dual personality representing both contamination and expectations, Pip brings to focus all his opposing tendencies and makes the same sort of decision David made about how to live. But unlike David, Pip learns to accept himself fully. He does not need to abate Magwitch's ugliness and Orlick's malevolence in order to recognize them in himself, nor does he need to minimize Joe's goodness to recognize that he does not fully share it. Critics and readers prefer Pip to David precisely because of this recognition. With Pip as the source rather than the recipient of action and values, *Great Expectations* becomes what *David Copperfield* is not: a story of maturity.

Pip becomes one of the 'redemption[s] of Steerforth' of whom

Angus Wilson has spoken. The line of redemption leads through Pip to Eugene Wrayburn, but 'before that redemption came about, the figure of Steerforth had suffered under many guises and, in the course of his translation to hero, had borne witness to many changes in Dickens's social and moral outlook.'[17] These changes place the hero within social bounds and force the sorts of choices that Steerforth is unwilling to make. Eugene, while clearly a descendent of Steerforth's, admits his faults and eventually learns to rise above them. The society Dickens places him in forces him to confront himself in ways David's society did not. There is evidence of an advance in Dickens' conception of the complexity of society which is paralleled by increasing complexity of characterization and subtler and (paradoxically) more forceful presentation of the human bases for social responsibility. *David Copperfield* is, like *The Old Curiosity Shop*, an early shadow of the framework of Dickens' mature artistic consciousness and opens avenues of investigation that Dickens was not to explore fully for more than a decade.

I need not emphasize again the differences between Dickens and Dostoevsky. Nor do I wish to discount Dickens' belief in the efficacy of personal and purposeful striving toward the sort of goodness exemplified in social responsibility. This is what *David Copperfield* presents—what Dickens wanted it to present and what his readers have accepted it as presenting. But it is equally false to discount Dickens' insight into human nature and his increasing artistry, both of which allowed for a growth in complexity and allusiveness which a study of Dickens' later novels suggests is quite pervasive and which helps delineate the extent of his social concerns and document the growth of what can only be called pessimism about human nature.

John Jones says that even 'when [Dickens] suggests, as he does repeatedly, that *Copperfield* is really about "the mistaken impulse of an undisciplined heart", we don't believe him; this is a clear case of "Never trust the artist, trust the tale"—the tale being not an affair of theme, of subjects, at all.'[18] If we trust instead the tale as Dostoevsky saw it, we will agree with Sylvère Monod that, c'est un des miracles de l'art dickensien dans ce roman de forme autobiographique qu'il soit constamment donné au lecteur d'entrevoir la réalité a travers les illusions de David.[19]

Dostoevsky offers a way of viewing Steerforth more roundly than Dickens can present him and thus gives the critic a further insight into the reality that lies behind David's illusions. The idea of the decomposite double, which Dickens uses as a major means of character revelation in *Great Expectations*, begins with Steerforth, the Steerforth Dostoevsky saw and re-created in Stavrogin. A complete understanding of Steerforth's power in no way damns David; his choices remain meaningful and poignant, and their poignancy in the face of the other choices he might have made adds to David's charm. It is only when we see the full extent of David's possibilities that we can assess his choices.

At the same time, such a clarification of Steerforth's potential suggests a further identity between the Russian and English authors. Stavrogin's inability to reach any sort of synthesis mirrors Dostoevsky's own inability to transcend Steerforth's incipience. There seems to be no way to get beyond full potential, and Dostoevsky quite clearly shows, through Stavrogin, that incipience itself may be a special norm which cannot be transcended. Life requires polarity, decisions. That decisions are limiting is a fact of the human condition. The attempt to overcome the bonds of humanity is so utterly doomed to failure, both for Dostoevsky and for Dickens, that it cannot even be celebrated. Myshkin could never become a 'perfectly good man'; in fact, the attempt led not to an acme but to a nadir, to identity with Rogozhin over the body of their mutually beloved Nastasya Filippovna.

The drab success of *Little Dorrit, Great Expectations*, and *Our Mutual Friend* suggests that Dickens felt much the same way. But such a sombre conclusion can be reached only through experiment with other possibilities. It is a great and glorious thing to celebrate the fullness of the human soul. Both Dickens and Dostoevsky so celebrated, albeit in different worlds, peopled by different types heading down different roads. The success of

Eugene Wrayburn in marrying Lizzie Hexam, of Pip in forgiving
and befriending Magwitch, is paralleled by Dmitri Karamazov's
recognition of the need for perpetual, universal forgiveness for the
sins occasioned eternally by the mere act of living. Esther sees
that she is responsible for all, but she has no one she can save
through that knowledge; Pip moves a step further and sees that he
can be responsible for Magwitch and for himself. Dmitri takes
upon himself repentance and atonement for his sins both
personally and as they expand into the body social and politic. But
such acceptance of responsibility requires a self-knowledge that
both authors make possible for their characters through
presentation, in Dickens' case at first instinctive but later nearly
fully conscious, of the sorts of choices possible and the results of
application of those choices.

What I have had to say about Steerforth unbalances *David
Copperfield* in much the same sort of way a Freudian analysis of
Little Nell unbalances *The Old Curiosity Shop*. But once the
invesitgation is made and the balance restored, Dostoevsky's re-
visions of Dickens make it possible for us to imagine more nearly
the progression and totality of Dickens' ideas. And it is clear to
me that Dickens is primarily a novelist of ideas. Within the social
framework which he saw as the only locale for the working-out
of human concerns, he strove to tell the truth about human
beings. The closer we can get to those human beings, the more
distinctly we can see that truth.

CONCLUSION

Oui, vraiment ... Dostoevski nous ouvre les yeux
sur certains phénomènes, qui peut-être ne sont
même pas rare—mais que simplement nous
n'avions pas su remarquer.

ANDRÉ GIDE

I wish not so much to conclude as to open a door, to define a beginning. I have pulled *The Old Curiosity Shop* and *David Copperfield* rather out of shape in the preceding pages, then used the distortions to form a new shape and restore the novels to a measure of their former selves. But only a measure; the value of reverse influence lies in its power to broaden criticism and thus to change our overall conception of the works criticized.

> One great advantage of influence study is that it cuts both ways; it tells as much about old as new creations. From the familiar ground of the source, we can better survey the new terrain; and from that outlook, we can often perceive new aspects of the source.[1]

Thus does Mark Spilka commend the technique of reverse influence (which he calls mutual interpretation); but he is unable to define it because the technique *is* the definition: the material presented is its own conclusion. Nonetheless, I want to work toward such a definition, one that will discriminate among

creative influence, formative influence, and parody, the three
main forms that borrowing is likely to take.

Reverse influence is the illumination of artistry—including but
not confined to character, plot, technique, ideas, moral values—
through subsequent artistic re-rendering of that artistry. This
bare-bones definition requires some immediate addenda: there
must be a demonstrable bond between the two artists, such as in
influence, in similarity of thought and values; in shared belief in
the purpose of the artistic form(s) employed; the subsequent
rendering must be of sufficient artistic complexity to offer the
possibility of deeper understanding of the source, and it must
genuinely develop the original artistry; the artistry illuminated
must warrant interpretation in depth; and it must itself be
complex enough to bear the fruit of interpretation.

The first addendum is quite obvious. An interpretation of
Dickens through Dostoevsky can be valid only if Dostoevsky is
genuinely influenced by Dickens. It is the fact of his borrowing
that gives him the stature of one who has developed some sort of
understanding through knowledge. But often the evidences of
direct influence are lacking, although it is clear from a mutual
reading that ideas have been assimilated. In such a case influence,
although indirect, can be presumed to be present. Such may have
been the case with Kafka's developments of the ideas of *Bleak
House*, although he never formally acknowledges his debt to
Dickens.[2] It also seems possible that a re-use of form can provide
the basis for a reverse influence study. One need only think of
John Fowles' *The French Lieutenant's Woman* as a
redevelopment of the Victorian novel to see the usefulness of a
reverse study of the idea of the narrator and the sense of
historicity involved in the 'realism' sought by many mid-
nineteenth-century novelists. However, in the absence of a fairly
clearly definable model or precedent, the factual, influential base
for a reverse influence study cannot well exist.

Similarly, without sufficient depth and complexity, the re-
rendering can offer the critic little. The mere fact that the
spontaneous combustion of Krook in *Bleak House* is mirrored in
a similar conflagration in *Crime and Punishment* is nearly self-

consuming: aside from the weight it lends to an argument of the similarity of 'fantastic realism' in the two authors, the detail is a dead end. In contradistinction, Dostoevsky's growing concern with the meaning of relation, i.e. the nature of the family and its bonds, derives in part from, and is surely reflective upon Dickens' development of what Dostoevsky calls the 'casual family'— Esther Summerson's parents, the Dorrits, Pip and Magwitch. The latter is an idea Dostoevsky developed rather than repeated. Only such development can hope to show something about its source.

All the development in the world, of course, will be of no help in illuminating a work that has no depth. The surface interpretation of Charlotte Yonge's novels is sufficient, and the reader feels no need to probe much more deeply. But of course this caveat is unlikely to need stating, for no artist of the stature of Dostoevsky would bother searching for non-existent depths.

More important is the requirement that the artistic source be able to come to fruition under re-visionary scrutiny. Even a work worth re-rendering may prove no more comprehensible after we have seen it reviewed than before. It is possible that a study of Dostoevsky's criminals will illuminate Jonas Chuzzlewit and Dickens' conception of the criminal mind, leading to a better understanding of Rogue Riderhood and Bradley Headstone, of Honoria Dedlock, of Magwitch. Such understanding might even be brought to bear upon John Jasper in the eternal attempt to unravel the mystery that *Edwin Drood* leaves us with. Or perhaps not. We cannot tell until we have tried. Surely reverse influence's greatest successes will come with those works whose lowest depths it sounds.

This extended definition of reverse influence requires a distinction between formative influence and creative influence. In many cases formative influence, which helps shape an artist's ideas and techniques, may be merely what its name implies, a formal means of artistic development. In that case, of course, it will not meet the criteria of reverse influence: it may merely supersede the original artistry rather than attempt deeper understanding, or it may be assimilated from a work that cannot bear an advance in interpretation. Creative influence, on the other hand, leads to integration and development. When influence is assimilated creatively, which is by no means always the case even with great artists, it becomes part of the thought processes and creative processes, becomes entwined with the works and ideas of the borrower, and reappears in changed forms. The very changes, in fact, may make it difficult to pinpoint their sources. We need, as Carlyle suggested, to look beneath the clothing of a borrowed idea. Creative influence grows from and looks back to essences, lending itself beautifully to reverse influence studies.

There is also a great difference between creative influence and parody. Robert Graves' *The Real David Copperfield* is a parody; it seeks not development but definition. There is no bond, no sympathy between Graves and Dickens, nor is Graves' reworking of *David Copperfield* a development of Dickens' ideas. Rather, Graves tries to pin Dickens down, to force him to yield up an explanation. He seeks not expansion but stasis. There is no love in Graves, as there is in Dostoevsky. There is no seeking, only a sense of superior understanding (and a bit of smugness, I might add, at the idea of such superiority). Reverse influence is not inherent in all reworkings of an idea, any more than it inheres in all examples of influence.

Perhaps, then, it might seem that there is little scope for reverse influence. I think this is not so. In recent years our knowledge that Matthew Arnold was influenced directly by Goethe allows us to re-evaluate his works in light of the pervasiveness of the Goethean influence. Might not Arnold's uses of Goethe reflect upon that master? Faulkner and T. S. Eliot read Dickens; Dostoevsky read Balzac and Hoffman; Brontë read Thackeray. The possibilities are wide, and much remains to be said about even our greatest writers. My study by no means exhausts even the possibilities for a Dostoevskian re-vision of Dickens. There is the casual family; there is the criminal mind; there is the concept of 'goodness' Dostoevsky found in Pickwick and tried to transplant into Prince Myshkin; there are the larger ideas of the influence of the city upon human beings, the two authors' shared concept of man's social nature, the whole human/society interface.

I think it highly likely that some of these possibilities can be achieved in no other way than through reverse influence. Little Nell is a case in point. She has been largely impervious to standard critical methods of characterization analysis, yet Dostoevsky's re-vision of her allows a new perspective which goes a long way toward accounting for her force in the novel, both as Dickens saw it and as he could not see it. And while it might not matter much to our understanding of *David Copperfield* that Steerforth is the first in a series of flamboyant darers whom Dickens gradually shapes into a form that can utilize its potential for good, surely such an understanding adds to our appreciation of the extent of Dickens' artistry and gives weight to the seriousness of his concerns. New aspects of such works can sometimes be discovered only through reverse influence. The major value of the technique is that it permits us to re-see what we have come to view from a constant, perhaps even a static, angle. In some cases the re-vision may turn out not to be worth the candle; but that is a critical evaluation rather than a technical one. The method itself remains, a useful tool in itself and a handmaiden of criticism.

Even the limited study presented here is useful in developing the latent critical perspective of reverse influence on Dickens' behalf. Following the English discovery of Dostoevsky in the early decades of the twentieth century, Dickens fell in estimation before the apparent superiority of depth and vision of the Russian author. From Edmund Wilson to Steven Marcus it has been fashionable to say, as Marcus does, that

for the best of reasons—reasons which have everything to do with the unique regard in which modern culture holds Dostoevsky—most of us now expect that in literature the powers of mind, the powers of truth, appear exclusively in company with the powers of suffering, negation and outrage. In contrast, *Pickwick Papers* is an imagination of life in which the powers of affirmation co-operate with the powers of truth, in which the ideals of virtue and regeneration, and the idyllic representations of innocence, stability and reconciliation transcend our most confidently prepared denials. Dostoevsky could appreciate Dickens, but our own appreciation of Dostoevsky tends to cut us off from Dickens.[3]

But this is becoming increasingly untrue. For one thing, our view of Dickens today moves him closer to Dostoevsky's tragic view of the fallibility of human nature. We have begun to see those 'powers of suffering, negation and outrage' in Dickens as well as in Dostoevsky, and this naturally moves the two closer in our minds.

It is perhaps coincidence that Dostoevsky read both *The Old Curiosity Shop* and *David Copperfield* and made them part of the artistic background of Nellie and Stavrogin; but I think not. It appears that whatever Dostoevsky read of Dickens he internalized, making it available for weaving into the fabric of the lives he created in his own novels. The nature of the transformation of Dickens into Dostoevsky will probably never be fully understood just because of the elusive nature of the artistic psyche. We can approach an understanding, however, by first comparing the two authors and then trying, as I do here, to isolate the specific visions which appear to have been transmitted from the Englishman to his Russian disciple. Angus Wilson sees that both Dostoevsky and Dickens stayed afloat in the negating worlds of their imaginations

by their extraordinary mixture of black and comic vision which allowed them to see how profound absurdity can be and how utterly ridiculous most of the profound things often are, to see that profound things and absurd things are totally mixed together. It is this vision that Dostoevsky and Dickens had, that they offered as the solution. ... They saw very deeply into our age, more deeply than any other men of their century, and they propounded the same answer which is much more important than their direct answers, the simple Christian things they said. They painted the same vision of the world which is their answer to the troubles of our time. What is perhaps most remarkable of all is that Dickens could paint so complex and ambiguous a picture of life while remaining quite sincerely an 'earnest' man in the best meaning of that great Victorian virtue.[4]

This study of two major examples of Dostoevsky's use of Dickensian material represents but an introduction to a new sort of study of literary influence upon both the borrower and the source. The door is open.

NOTES

Introduction

1. Dmitri S. Merezhkovskii, *Dostoievsky*, p. 8.
2. N. M. Lary, *Dostoevsky and Dickens*; Michael Futrell, 'Dostoevsky and Dickens', *English Miscellany*, 7 (1956), 41–89; Angus Wilson, 'Dickens and Dostoevsky', *Dickens Memorial Lectures, 1970*, pp. 42–61; Igor M. Katarsky, *Dikkens v Rossii*; and two unpublished dissertations: Terry Wade Murphy, 'Dostoevsky and Tolstoy on Dickens' Christianity', and Kenneth Klotz, 'Comedy and the Grotesque in Dickens and Dostoevsky'.
3. Donald Fanger, *Dostoevsky and Romantic Realism*; Stefan Zweig, *Three Masters: Balzac, Dickens, Dostoevsky*.
4. Vissarion Belinsky, 'Russkaia literatura v 1844 godu', in *Sobranie sochinenii*, ed. F. M. Golovenchenko, II, 700–701.
5. Quotation from 'Dickens in Russia', unpublished contribution by Igor M. Katarsky to the forthcoming, *Charles Dickens: An International Guide to Study and Research*, ed. Ada Nisbet (trans. Rodney Patterson), p. 1.
6. *Ibid.*, p. 6.
7. Dickens' own knowledge of Russian literature was limited. *Household Words* printed four of Turgenev's *Sportsman's Sketches* in 1855, curiously attributing only the first three to their author. The catalogue of his library, published after his death, reveals that he owned seven volumes of Turgenev's works in English and French and a volume of Gogol in French. *Reprints of the catalogues of the Libraries of Charles Dickens and W. M. Thackeray, etc.*, ed. J. H. Stonehouse (London, 1935), lists:

   Gogol, N. *Nouvelles Russes*; Traduction par L. Viardot, 1845.
   Tourguenef, (Ivan) Dimitri Roudine [sic]; *suivi du Journal d'un*

Homme de trop, et de Trois Recontres, Paris, n.d.

—*Une Nichée des Gentilshommes, Moeurs de la Vie de Province en Russie*, traduits du Russe par Comte de Sollogoub et A. de Calonne, Paris 1861.

—*Récits d'un Chasseur*, traduits par H. Delaveau, with woodcuts by G. Durand, Paris 1858. Presentation copy; inscribed, 'To Charles Dickens, one of his greatest admirers the author. Paris 1862.'

—*Liza [or 'Nest of Nobles']*, a Novel, translated from the Russian by W. R. S. Ralston, 2 vols. 1869. Presentation copy from the translator.

—*Scènes de la Vie Russe: Nouvelles Ruses*, traduits par X. Marmier, 2 vols. Paris 1858.

In addition, *Household Words* printed many articles on Russia and the Russians, the most famous of which are George Augustus Sala's 'A Journey Due North', which appeared in twenty-two instalments running from 4 October, 1856, to 14 March, 1857. Nor could Dickens have read Dostoevsky, for the only translation of Dostoevsky before 1870 was a German one, and Dickens knew but a few words of German. He was fluent in French, but the French translations all came out after 1870, and translation into English began only in 1886.

8. See Leonid Grossman, *Biblioteka Dostoevskogo*, p. 139.

9. Referred to in P. K. Mart'ianov, 'Iz knigi "V perelome veka"', in *F. M. Dostoevsky v vospominaniakh sovremennikov*, ed. A. S. Dolinin, I, 240. It is interesting to note that Dostoevsky read at least some of the Vvedensky translations, for these are the looser, less literal, more spirited of the major early translations. Vvedensky had no English-Russian dictionary (it was not until much later in the century that Vasilii V. Butuzov, also a translator of Dickens, published his dictionary of English idiomatic terms). When Vvedensky came to a particularly difficult passage for which he could not find the exact corresponding terms, therefore, he created a scene or conversation based on his intuition of Dickens' meaning and tone. In a conversation with me in 1974, Mira Perper, a Soviet philologist and colleague of the late Igor Katarsky, praised Vvedensky's intuition in creating non-literal translations which nonetheless corresponded so closely, in her opinion, to the spirit of the original that they were unmatched for a century. Thus Dostoevsky received a less literal but perhaps more lively impression of Dickens.

10. In *The Eternal Husband*, Dostoevsky has Velchaninov, Trusotsky, and Natalia Vassilevna 'read Dickens' novels' in their *ménage à trois* (EH 30). In *The Possessed* Stepan Trofimovich Verkhovensky writes

for 'a progressive monthly review, which translated Dickens and advocated the views of George Sand' (*P* 3). But Dickens' major appearance in Dostoevsky's novels is a recollection in *A Raw Youth* of a scene from *The Old Curiosity Shop*. Trishatov and Dolgoruky reminisce over memorable scenes from their childhoods, and Trishatov recreates Nell's arrival at the village church which is to be her grave (*R Y* 434–35). Although his recollection of the scene is technically inaccurate, his feeling for Nell's relationship to the church and old Trent's eventual worship of her is as precise as if Dostoevsky had read *The Old Curiosity Shop* the day before. In the notebooks for *A Raw Youth* there is another reference to Pickwick: 'In our days, a new breed of people can be seen walking around, all bearded, and all with that same thought, so that one can judge from their physiognomies: Are they or aren't they readers of "The Pickwick Club"?' (*N:R*, 295). In these same notebooks Dostoevsky refers three times to *David Copperfield*. His narrator, Dolgoruky, says: 'I don't want <to make any "David> Copperfield<" out of this>' (*N:R*, 307); 'I hate the biography of <David> Copperfield' (*N:R*, 309); and finally, merely the single word 'Copperfield' (*N:R*, 312). It seems Dickens was on his mind as he wrote his own story of a boy's growth into manhood.

11. Interestingly enough, this assertion of Russian superiority in translating and understanding Dickens was reiterated in our century by Prince Petr Alekseevich Kropotkin in *Russian Literature* in 1905, when he said that 'the sarcasm of Voltaire, the rollicking humour of Dickens, the good-natured laughter of Cervantes are rendered with equal ease' in the Russian language (p. 4).

12. *The Works of John Ruskin*, ed. Alexander Wedderburn and E. T. Cook (London, 1903–1912), V, 114–15.

13. 'Zapisnaia tetrad' 1875–1876 gg.', *Literaturnoe Nasledstvo: Neizdannii Dostoevsky*, ed. V. G. Bazanov, 83 (*Moscow, 1971*), 420; 441; 448; 616.

14. Anna Suvorina, 'Dostoevsky v vospominaniakh A. I. Suvovinoi ', in *Dostoevsky i ego vremia*, ed. G. M. Fridlender, pp. 299–300.

15. Anna Dostoevsky, 'Iz"Vospominanii" ', in *F. M. Dostoevsky v vospominaniakh sovremennikov*, ed. A. S. Dolinin, II, 70–71.

16. Aimée Dostoevsky, *Fydor Dostoevsky: A Study*, p. 203.

17. For other frequently noted comparisons, see Michael Futrell and Angus Wilson, (note 2, above).

18. Leonid Grossman, 'Dostoevsky i chartistskii roman', *Voprosy literatury*, (April 1959), p. 155.

19. Mark Spilka, *Dickens and Kafka: A Mutual Interpretation*, pp. 21–2.

20. *Ibid.*, p. 93.

21. *Ibid.*, p. 23.

Chapter I

1. Cornelius C. Felton, 'Dickens', vol. 56 (January 1843), in *Dickens: The Critical Heritage*, ed. Philip Collins, p. 131.
2. This is the full quotation given by Hesketh Pearson in *Oscar Wilde* (New York, 1946), p. 208; Pearson gives no source for it.
3. Paul Elmer More, 'The Praise of Dickens', *Shelburne Essays*, p. 34.
4. Rex Warner, 'On Reading Dickens', *The Cult of Power*, p. 27.
5. George H. Ford, *Dickens and His Readers*, p. 69.
6. G. K. Chesterton, *Charles Dickens: The Last of the Great Men*, p. 17.
7. James Joyce, *Finnegans Wake*, (London 1939), p. 434.
8. Charles Dickens, *Bleak House*, Preface; *Household Words*, I (30 March, 1850), 'A Preliminary Word', in Monroe Engel, *The Maturity of Dickens*, p. 9; J. Forster, *The Life of Charles Dickens*, II, 279.
9. J. Forster, *Life*, II, 278.
10. Aldous Huxley, 'Vulgarity in Literature', *Music at Night and Other Essays*, pp. 270–336. This essay first appeared in 1930 in *Saturday Review*. A. O. J. Cockshut, 'Sentimentality in Fiction', *Twentieth Century*, (April 1957), pp. 354–64.
11. The first to develop psychobiographical criticism of Dickens was Jack Lindsay, *Charles Dickens: A Biographical and Critical Study*.
12. See Rachel Bennet, 'Punch Versus Christian in *The Old Curiosity Shop*', *Review of English Studies*, n.s. 22, No. 88 (November 1971), 423–31; John Gibson, '*The Old Curiosity Shop*: The Critical Allegory', *The Dickensian*, 60 (September 1964), 178–83; John Holloway, 'Dickens and Symbol', *Dickens 1970*, ed. Michael Slater (London, 1970), pp. 53–74; Michael Kotzin, *Dickens and the Fairy Tale*, pp. 52–81.
13. Charles Dickens, *The Letters of Charles Dickens*, ed. Madeline House and Graham Storey (Oxford, 1965–   ), II, 199 (31 January 1841); hereinafter referred to as *Letters*.
14. Charles Dickens, *The Speeches of Charles Dickens*, ed. K. J. Fielding, p. 10.
15. J. Forster, *Life*, I, 123.
16. *Letters*, II, 233.
17. H., 'The Province of Tragedy—Bulwer and Dickens', *Westminster Review*, 47 (April 1847), 6. 'H' is possibly William E. Hickson, editor of the *Westminster Review* from 1840 to 1852.
18. Fitzjames Stephen, 'The Relation of Novels to Life', *Cambridge Essays, 1855*, p. 175.
19. *Ibid.*, p. 175.

20. Kathleen Tillotson, *Novels of the 1840's*, p. 50.
21. George Gissing, *The Immortal Dickens*, pp. 196–97.
22. Mark Spilka, 'Little Nell—Revisited', *Papers of the Michigan Academy of Science, Arts and Letters*, 45 (1960) 429.
23. K. J. Fielding, *Charles Dickens: A Critical Introduction*, p. 51.
24. Huxley, p. 331.
25. *Ibid.*, pp. 334–35.
26. George Santayana, 'Dickens', *Soliloquies in England and Later Soliloquies*, pp. 67–8. This essay first appeared in *The Dial*, 71 (1921).
27. G. K. Chesterton, *Appreciations and Criticisms of the Works of Charles Dickens*, pp. 53–4.
28. Ford, 'Little Nell: The Limits of Explanatory Criticism', *Dickens and His Readers* pp. 55–71.
29. Gabriel Pearson, 'The Old Curiosity Shop', in *Dickens and the Twentieth Century*, ed. John Gross and Gabriel Pearson, develops this idea.
30. James R. Kincaid, *Dickens and the Rhetoric of Laughter*, pp. 91–2.
31. Donald Fanger, *Dostoevsky and Romantic Realism*, pp. 16, 66–100.
32. *Ibid.*, p. 71.
33. Mark Spilka, 'Erich Segal as Little Nell, or The Real Meaning of Love Story', *Journal of Popular Culture*, 5, No. 4 (Spring 1972), 782–83.
34. Georg Lukacs, *Studies in European Realism*, p. 11.
35. Extracts from Dostoevsky's notebooks, published by Strakhov and Miller in *Biografia. Pis'ma*, 1883, p. 373, as quoted in Sven Linner, *Dostoevskij on Realism*. Stockholm Slavic Studies, I (1976) 203.
36. Fanger discusses this at length and very well.
37. David Magarshack, ed., *Dostoevsky's Occasional Writings*, p. 134.
38. Lukacs, p. 6.
39. René Wellek, *Concepts on Criticism*, ed. Stephen G. Nichols, p. 242.
40. Victor Hugo, *William Shakespeare*, in *Oeuvres complètes de Victor Hugo* (Paris, 1885–89), Vol. 18, p. 238.
41. Linner, p. 56.
42. Fanger, p. 100.

Chapter II

1. V. I. Kirpotin, Introduction, *Unizhennye i oskorblonnye*, p. 19.
2. N. A. Dobroliubov, 'Zabitye liudi', in *F. M. Dostoevsky v Russkoi kritike*, ed. A. A. Belkin, p. 54.
3. Albert Guérard, *The Triumph of the Novel*, p. 107.
4. Dobroliubov, 'Zabitye liudi', pp. 58–9.

5. Petr Polzinsky, *Detskii mir v proizvedeniakh Dostoevskago*, p. 44.
6. Igor M. Katarsky, *Dikkens v Rossii*, pp. 391, 393.
7. *Ibid.*, p. 395.
8. Angus Wilson, 'Dickens and Dostoevsky', *Dickens Memorial Lectures, 1970*, p. 59.
9. N. M. Lary, *Dostoevsky and Dickens*, p. 9.

Chapter III

1. Mark Spilka, *Dickens and Kafka: A Mutual Interpretation*, pp. 264–65.
2. *Letters*, II, 233.
3. J. Hillis Miller, *Charles Dickens: The World of His Novels*, p. 96.
4. Leonard Manheim, 'Dickens HEROES, *heroes*, and heroids', *Dickens Studies Annual*, 5 (1976), 13.
5. It is tempting to see the twin club-footed Garlands in a diabolical light, but there is no evidence that a club foot is to be associated with the devil, although Mario Praz does suggest as much in *The Romantic Agony* when, speaking of Byron's cultivation of a satanic nature, he asks, 'Does the whole Byronic legend then stand on no firmer pedestal than a club foot? A club foot, hence the besoin de la fatalité' (Cleveland, 1933, p. 70). Cloven hooves are, unfortunately, quite a different matter than club feet. However, because a deformed foot is so generally associated with a satanical disposition, it is entirely possible that Dickens intended some such diffuse association when he bestowed upon both male Garlands a conspicuous and congenital club foot. At the very least, Dickens warns the reader that none is free from deformity; none is so good as he might be.
6. G. K. Chesterton, *Charles Dickens: A Critical Study*, p. 191. Ada Nisbet has suggested that Chesterton and Dickens both recognize that a very real pleasure for the genteel poor was the possibility of doing something they saw as forbidden to them, such as enjoying on occasion the privileges of their betters. Yet, as is clear from Dickens' overall handling of Kit, he saw such pleasure as demeaning—as a weakness in those who (unlike Dick Swiveller) felt it even though he understood very well why the social mores and the false values of the time made them feel so.
7. Edmund Wilson, 'Dickens: The Two Scrooges', *The Wound and The Bow*, p. 22.
8. See Gabriel Pearson, 'The Old Curiosity Shop', in *Dickens and the Twentieth Century*, ed. John Gross and Gabriel Pearson; and James R. Kincaid, *Dickens and the Rhetoric of Laughter*.
9. See, for example, David Hume's *Dialogues Concerning Natural Religion*, Part XI.

10. B. S. Rurikov, Introduction, *Idiot* (Moscow, 1960), p. 17.

11. Kincaid, *Dickens and the Rhetoric of Laughter*, p. 104.

12. Pearson, in Gross and Pearson, p. 84–5.

13. Patrick Braybrooke, 'Little Nell', *Great Children in Literature*, p. 210.

14. Steven Marcus, *Dickens: From Pickwick to Dombey*, p. 150.

15. Laurence Senelick, 'Little Nell and the Prurience of Sentimentality', *Dickens Studies*, 3, No. 2 (October 1967), 153.

16. Leonard Manheim, 'Thanatos: The Death Instinct in Dickens' Later Novels', *Psychoanalysis and the Psychoanalytic Review* 47 (Winter 1960–61), 19. Interestingly, Dickens broke down and wept when his daughter Kate married; his other daughter Mamie became 'an odd old spinster'.

17. Rex Warner, 'On Reading Dickens', *The Cult of Power*, p. 32.

18. Joseph Gold, *Charles Dickens: Radical Moralist*, p. 104.

19. Until his death John Dickens was to be a constant drain on his son's cash and patience, and the man's improvidence comes through clearly in Dickens' letters even though it was 'family policy' to suppress 'reference to John Dickens' money affairs' (*Letters* III, 344n). Says Forster, 'the earliest impressions received and retained by him in London were of his father's money involvements' (J. Forster, *Life*, I, 11–12). In February 1834 Dickens complained that he had 'mortgaged' his salary to redeem his father from the Marshalsea again (*Letters*, I, 48–9), and in 1839 he established his father at Alphington (see *Letters*, I, 518–21, 528). As late as 1842 John Dickens continued to seek funds from any possible source, as sadly evidenced in his Micawber-like letter to Dickens' publishers asking for train fare to London to the sum of ten guineas a year (*Letters*, III, 575n). Dickens considered him the 'Great Unpaid' (*Letters*, I, 38n), a 'blood-petitioner' (*Letters*, III, 601), and the 'prodigal father' (see Ada Nisbet, 'The Autobiographical Matrix of *Great Expectations*', *Victorian Newsletter*, No. 15 [Spring 1959], 10–13). It is difficult to imagine what John Dickens could have been spending his money on, unless he were one of the many who frequented the shops Dickens describes so well in 'The Betting-Shops' (*Miscellaneous Papers* [London, 1914], pp. 341–48).

   The extent of gambling in nineteenth-century England at all class levels is well chronicled in such studies as Andrew Steinmetz's *The Gaming Table: Its Votaries and Victims, in all times and countries, especially in England and in France* (London, 1870, 2 vols.) It is the slow drain of the penny-and-shilling gambler that would precisely account for John Dickens' constant and exasperating, while yet manageably small, debts. Then too there is a suggestion that these debts (or the means of incurring them) could be controlled by watchfulness; Dickens writes that he is sending his brother to school as a weekly boarder because 'I should wish the boy, for more reasons than one, to be at home from Saturday night to Monday morning' (*Letters*, II, 2–25)—perhaps to keep watch on his father. But even if John Dickens did not gamble, Dickens' feelings about his father are certainly expressed in Trent, the gambler, and Nell's attitude toward him.

20. Sigmund Freud, *The Interpretation of Dreams*, trans. Dr A. A. Brill, p. 32. Brill's translation first appeared in 1913, the book having been originally published in German in 1900.

21. *Ibid.*, p. 52.

22. M. Elizarova, 'Dikkens', *Bol'shaia Sovetskaia Entsiklopediia*, vol. 22, p. 318. The emphasis is mine.

23. Both Dickens and Dostoevsky write about gamblers, and both write from personal experience. The possibility for comparison is intriguing but unfortunately beyond the scope of this study.

24. Manheim, 'Thanatos', p. 18.

25. Angus Wilson, 'Dickens on Children and Childhood', in *Dickens 1970*, ed. Michael Slater, p. 223.

26. Georg Lukacs, *Studies in European Realism*, p. 12.

Chapter IV

1. Nikolai Mikhailovski 'Zhestokii talant', *Sochinenie*, V, 1–78. The entire article describes in detail Dostoevsky's 'philosophy of suffering'.

2. M. Babovich, 'Sud'ba dobra i krasoti v svete gumanizma Dostoevskogo', *Dostoevsky: Materiali i issledovaniia*, ed. G. M. Fridlender, Vol. I, pp. 100–107.

3. *Young India*, 16 June 1920, and 11 August 1920, in Romain Rolland, *Mahatma Gandhi*, trans. Catherine D. Groth (New York, 1924), p. 67.

4. Mikhailovski, 'O Pisemskom i Dostoevskom', *Sochinenie*, V, 419.

5. For a survey of the use of the double in literature, see Claire Rosenfield, 'The Shadow Within: The Conscious and Unconscious Use of the Double', *Daedalus*, 92 (Spring 1963), 326–44.

6. Otto Rank, *Beyond Psychology*, p. 96.

7. I take this term from Robert Rogers, *The Double in Literature*, which gives an excellent and comprehensive analysis of the subject.

8. See Chapters VI and VII for a discussion of Dostoevsky's other uses of the double.

9. Edward Wasiolek, *Dostoevsky: The Major Fiction*, p. 131.

10. *Ibid.*, p. 75. The emphasis is Wasiolek's.

11. Eliseo Vivas, 'The Two Dimensions of Reality in *The Brothers Karamazov*', in *Dostoevsky: A Collection of Critical Essays*, ed. René Wellek, p. 74.
12. Rosenfield, 'The Shadow Within', p. 333.
13. Vivas, 'The Two Dimensions of Reality', p. 86.
14. Edmund Wilson, 'Dickens: The Two Scrooges', *The Wound and the Bow*, p. 61.
15. Monroe Engel, *The Maturity of Dickens*, p. 81.
16. *Ibid.*, p. 83.
17. *Ibid.*, p. 188.
18. J. Hillis Miller, *Charles Dickens: The World of His Novels*, p. 140.
19. Robert Barnard, *Imagery and Theme in the Novels of Dickens*, p. 41.
20. K. J. Fielding, *Charles Dickens: A Critical Introduction*, p. 79. The emphasis is Fielding's.
21. Engel, p. 107.
22. Julian Moynahan, 'Dealings With the Firm of Dombey and Son: Firmness versus Wetness', in *Dickens and the Twentieth Century*, ed. John Gross and Gabriel Pearson, pp. 121–131, shows this disgust quite clearly.
23. Miller, *Charles Dickens*, p. 198.
24. W. J. Harvey, 'Chance and Design in *Bleak House*', in *Dickens and the Twentieth Century*, ed. John Gross and Gabriel Pearson, p. 157.
25. Judith Wilt, 'Confusion and Consciousness in Dickens's Esther', *Nineteenth Century Fiction*, 32, No. 3 (December 1977), 293.
26. Miller, *Charles Dickens*, p. 207.
27. Wilt, p. 308.
28. *Ibid.*
29. Miller, *Charles Dickens*, p. 233.
30. *Ibid.*, p. 235.
31. Barnard, pp. 94–5.
32. Miller, *Charles Dickens*, p. 242.
33. John Wain, 'Little Dorrit', in *Dickens and the Twentieth Century*, ed. John Gross and Gabriel Pearson, p. 178.
34. Miller, *Charles Dickens*, pp. 271–72.
35. Engel, p. 167.
36. Barnard, p. 106.
37. Fielding, *Charles Dickens: A Critical Introduction*, p. 175.
38. See Julian Moynahan, 'The Hero's Guilt: The Case of *Great Expectations*', *Essays in Criticism* (January 1960), p. 70, and Dorothy Van Ghent, *The English Novel: Form and Function*, p. 170.
39. Moynahan, 'The Hero's Guilt', p. 67.
40. Barnard, p. 119.
41. Barbara Hardy, *The Moral Art of Dickens*, p. 13.

42. George Gissing, *Charles Dickens: A Critical Introduction*, p. 213.
43. Angus Wilson, 'Dickens and Dostoevsky', *Dickens Memorial Lectures, 1970*, pp. 56, 60.
44. Edmund Wilson, 'Dickens: The Two Scrooges', p. 61, pp. 82–83.
45. All the critics I cite in this chapter agree on this 'moral progression', although each finds in it particular symbols—love, the city, morality—as adhesive to hold the progression together. My own particular interpretation is intended not to refute others but to enrich all views of Dickens.
46. Hardy, *The Moral Art of Dickens*, p. 55.
47. Engel, p. 189.
48. *Ibid.*, p. 96.

Chapter V
1. James R. Kincaid, 'The Structure of *David Copperfield*', *Dickens Studies*, II, No. 2 (May 1966), 76.
2. James R. Kincaid, *Dickens and the Rhetoric of Laughter*, p. 165.
3. Stephen Leacock, *Charles Dickens*, p. 144.
4. E. M. Forster, *Aspects of the Novel*, p. 108.
5. Percy Lubbock, *The Craft of Fiction*, p. 130.
6. Q. D. Leavis, 'Dickens and Tolstoy: The Case for a Serious View of *David Copperfield*', *Dickens the Novelist*, p. 44.
7. G. K. Chesterton, *Appreciations and Criticisms of the Works of Charles Dickens*, pp. 137–38.
8. Christopher Mulvey, '*David Copperfield*: The Folk-Story Structure', *Dickens Studies Annual*, 5 (1976), 77. The emphasis is mine.
9. Arnold Kettle, *An Introduction to the English Novel*, Vol. I, p. 14.
10. Mark Spilka, *Dickens and Kafka: A Mutual Interpretation*, p. 175.
11. Robert Graves, *The Real David Copperfield*, p. 5.
12. *Ibid.*, p. 6.
13. *Ibid.*, pp. 64–65.
14. *Ibid.*, p. 65.
15. *Ibid.*, p. 189.
16. *Ibid.*, pp. 242–43.
17. *Ibid.*, p. 380.
18. *Ibid.*, p. 216.
19. *Ibid.*, pp. 363, 329.
20. *Ibid.*, p. 9.
21. *Ibid.*, p. 405.
22. *Ibid.*, p. 414.
23. See George Katkov, 'Steerforth and Stavrogin', *Slavonic and East European Review*, 17 (1949), 469–88.

Chapter VI

1. William Marshall, 'The Image of Steerforth and the Structure of *David Copperfield*', *Tennessee Studies in Literature*, 5 (1960), 65.
2. George Katkov, 'Steerforth and Stavrogin', *Slavonic and East Europe Review* 17 (1949), 469–88.
3. See Leonid Grossman, *Poetika Dostoevskogo*, p. 56 ff. for a wealth of information on the sources for *The Possessed*.
4. Katkov, 'Steerforth and Stavrogin', pp. 474–75.
5. See A. L. Bem, 'Faust v Tvorchestve Dostoevskogo', *Zapiski Nauchno-Issledovatel'skago obedineniia*, 5, No. 29 (1937), 27; and Katkov, 'Steerforth and Stavrogin', p. 473.
6. Katkov, 'Steerforth and Stravrogin', p. 474.
7. *Ibid.*, p. 479.
8. *Ibid.*, p. 476.
9. *Ibid.*, p. 482.
10. *Ibid.*, p. 479.
11. Romain Rolland, *Notebooks of Romain Rolland* (Paris, 1952), p. 153.
12. A superb phrase for which I thank my colleague and critic Michael Hollington of Griffith University, Brisbane.
13. Angus Wilson, 'The Heroes and Heroines of Dickens', in *Dickens and the Twentieth Century*, ed. John Gross and Gabriel Pearson, p. 8.
14. Irving Howe, 'Dostoevsky: The Politics of Salvation', *Politics and the Novel*, p. 64.

Chapter VII

1. Leonid Grossman and Viacheslav Polonsky, *Spor o Bakunine i Dostoevskom*, p. 181.
2. See Rogers, *The Double in Literature*, for an excellent and deep study of doubles. My account here is much indebted to Rogers.
3. This word, describing the behaviour exhibited by the Karamazov family and also the peculiar sort of family feeling they display toward one another, was coined by Maxim Gorky in a series of articles about the Moscow stage production of *The Brothers Karamazov*. See *Stat'i 1906–1916* (St Petersburg, 1918).
4. Lawrence Kohlberg, 'Psychological Analysis and Literary Form: A Study of the Doubles in Dostoevsky', *Daedalus*, 92 (Spring 1963), 357. For a study of doubles, see also Clare Rosenfield, 'The Shadow Within: The Conscious and Unconscious Use of the Double', *Daedalus*, 92 (Spring 1963), 326–44.
5. See Rogers, Chapter V.
6. Maurice Beebe, 'The Three Motives of Raskolnikov', in *Crime and Punishment and the Critics*, ed. Edward Wasiolek, p. 99.

7. Albert Guérard, *The Triumph of the Novel*, p. 286.
8 Nicholas Berdaiev, 'Stavrogin', *Russkaia mysl'*, No. 5 (May 1914), p. 82.
9. B.M., 'Obraz Stavrogina i ideya romana-tragedii *Besi*', *Meteor* (Nizhni-Novgorod), 1 May 1919, No. 1, p. 8.
10. Irving Howe, 'Dostoevsky: The Politics of Salvation', *Politics and the Novel*, p. 64.
11. Mikhail Bakhtin, *Problems of Dostoevsky's Poetics*, p. 60.
12. Sergei Nikolaivich Bulgakov, *Tikhiye dumi*, p. 22.
13. Guérard, *The Triumph of the Novel*, p. 276.
14. Grossman and Polonsky, *Spor o Bakunine i Dostoevskom*, p. 181.
15. Howe, pp. 65–6.
16. Bakhtin, p. 204.
17. Bulgakov, pp. 26–27.
18. Rex Warner, 'Dostoevsky and the Collapse of Liberalism', *The Cult of Power*, p. 60.
19. Valerian Pereverzev, *Tvorchestvo Dostoevskogo*, p. 225.

Chapter VIII

1. Angus Wilson, 'Dickens and Dostoevsky', *Dickens Memorial Lectures, 1970*, p. 57.
2. Leonard Manheim, 'Dickens' HEROES, *heroes*, and heroids', 216; originally listed in 'The Dickens Hero as Child', *Studies in the Novel*, 1, No. 2 (1969), 189.
3. A. E. Dyson, *The Inimitable Dickens*, p. 125.
4. Richard Dunn, '*David Copperfield*: All Dickens is There', *English Journal*, 54, No. 9 (December 1965), 793.
5. See *American Imago*, 9, No. 1 (April 1952), 32–4.
6. See Mark Spilka, '*David Copperfield* as Psychological Fiction', *Critical Quarterly* 1, No. 4 (Winter 1959), p. 300–301.
7. Christopher Mulvey, '*David Copperfield*: The Folk-Story Structure', *Dickens Studies Annual*, 5 (1976), 82.
8. Angus Wilson, 'Charles Dickens: A Haunting', in A. E. Dyson, *Dickens: Modern Judgements* (Nashville, 1969), p. 37.
9. George Katkov, 'Steerforth and Stavrogin', *Slavonic and East European Review* 17 (1949), 485.
10. George Gissing, *Charles Dickens: A Critical Study*, p. 97.
11. Sylvère Monod, 'James Steerforth ou le problème du mal dans *David Copperfield*', *Annales de l'Université de Paris*, 37, No. 2 (April–June 1967), 173.
12. *Ibid.*, p. 175.
13. Leonard Manheim 'Dickens' HEROES, *heroes* and heroids', p. 16.
14. Mark Spilka, *Dickens and Kafka: A Mutual Interpretation*, p. 193.

15. Mulvey, p. 77.
16. Edgar Johnson, *Charles Dickens: His Tragedy and Triumph*, II, 697.
17. Angus Wilson, 'The Heroes and Heroines of Dickens', in *Dickens and the Twentieth Century*, ed. John Gross and Gabriel Pearson, p. 8.
18. John Jones, 'David Copperfield', in *Dickens and the Twentieth Century*, ed. John Gross and Gabriel Pearson, p. 142.
19. Monod, p. 170.

Conclusion

1. Mark Spilka, *Dickens and Kafka: A Mutual Interpretation*, p. 175.
2. Spilka, *Dickens and Kafka*, pp. 199–266, gives details; see also his explanation of the lack of direct evidence for influence, p. 292n.
3. Steven Marcus, *Dickens: From Pickwick to Dombey*, p. 13–14.
4. Angus Wilson, 'Dickens and Dostoevsky', *Dickens Memorial Lectures, 1970*, p. 61.

SELECT BIBLIOGRAPHY

I. Works dealing with both Dickens and Dostoevsky

Fanger, Donald. *Dostoevsky and Romantic Realism*. Cambridge, 1965.

Fièbre, M. le M. 'Dostoevsky, Dickens and Others'. *The Dickensian*, 43 (March 1947), 102–103.

Futrell, Michael. 'Dostoevsky and Dickens'. *English Miscellany*, 7 (1956), 41–89.

Katarsky, Igor M. *Dikkens v Rossii*. Moscow, 1966.

Katkov, George. 'Steerforth and Stavrogin'. *Slavonic and East European Review*, 17 (1949), 469–88.

Klotz, Kenneth. 'Commedy and the Grotesque in Dickens and Dostoevsky.' Dissertation, Yale University, 1973.

Lary, N. M. *Dostoevsky and Dickens*. London, 1973.

Mason, Leo. 'Dickens and Dostoevsky.' *The Dickensian*, 13 (May 1957), 114–16.

Murphy, Terry Wade. 'Dostoevsky and Tolstoy on Dickens' Christianity.' Dissertation, Kent State University, 1973.

Nazirov, R. G. 'Dikkens, Bodler, Dostoevsky: K istorii odnogo literaturnogo motiva'. *Uchenye zapiski Baskhirskogo gosudarstvennogo universiteta, kafedra Russkoi literatury*, 17 (1964), 168–82.

Reizov, B. G. 'K voprosu o vliianii Dikkensa na Dostoevskogo'. *Iazik i literatura*, 5 (1930), 253–70.

Warner, Rex. 'On Reading Dickens' and 'Dostoievsky and the Collapse of Liberalism'. *The Cult of Power*. London, 1946.

Wexler, Alexandra. 'Dickens und Dostojewski'. *Deutsche Rundschau*, 88 (1962), 732–40.

Wilson, Angus. 'Dickens and Dostoevsky'. *Dickens Memorial Lectures, 1970*. Supplement to *The Dickensian* (September 1970), pp. 41–61.

Zweig, Stefan. *Three Masters: Balzac, Dickens, Dostoevsky*. Trans. Eden and Cedar Paul. New York, 1930.

II. Works dealing with Dickens

Anikst, Alexander. 'Dickens in Russia'. *Times Literary Supplement*, 4 June 1970, p. 617.

Bagehot, Walter. 'Charles Dickens'. *Literary Studies*, II, 127–67. Ed. Richard Holt Hutton. London, 1902.

Barnard, Robert. *Imagery and Theme in the Novels of Dickens*. Bergen, 1974.

Belinsky, Vissarion. 'Russkaia literatura v 1844 godu'. *Sobranie Sochinenii*, II, 647–704. Ed. V. I. Kuleshov. Moscow, 1948.

Bennet, Rachel. 'Punch Versus Christian in *The Old Curiosity Shop*'. *Review of English Studies*, n.s. 22, No. 88 (November 1971), 423–34.

Blount, Trevor. *Charles Dickens: The Early Novels*. London, 1968.

Braybrooke, Patrick. 'Little Nell'. *Great Children in Literature*. London, 1929.

Carlton, William J. 'The Death of Mary Hogarth – Before and After'. *The Dickensian*, 63 (May 1967), 68–80.

Chesterton, G. K. *Appreciations and Criticisms of the Works of Charles Dickens*. London, 1911.

—*Charles Dickens: The Last of the Great Men*. New York, 1942.

—*Charles Dickens: A Critical Study*. 1906 reprint. London, 1960.

Cockshut, A. O. J. *The Imagination of Charles Dickens*. New York, 1962.

—'Sentimentality in Fiction'. *Twentieth Century* (April 1957), pp. 354–64.

Collins, Philip, ed. *Dickens: The Critical Heritage*. Nlew York, 1971.

Coveney, Peter. 'The Child in Dickens'. *Poor Monkey: The Child in Literature*. London, 1957.

Daleski, Herman M. *Dickens and the Art of Analogy*. New York, 1970.

Dickens, Charles. *The Letters of Charles Dickens*. 4 vols. Ed. Madeline House, Graham Storey, and Kathleen Tillotson. Oxford, 1965– .

—*The Speeches of Charles Dickens*. Ed. K. J. Fielding. Oxford, 1960.

Dunn, Richard. '*David Copperfield*: All Dickens is There'. *English Journal*, 54, No. 9 (December 1965).

Dyson, A. E. '*The Old Curiosity Shop*: Innocence and the Grotesque'. *Dickens*. Nashville, 1966.

—*The Inimitable Dickens*. London, 1970.

Elizarova, M. 'Dikkens'. *Bol'shaia Sovetskaia Entsiklopediia*. Moscow, 1935.

Engel, Monroe. *The Maturity of Dickens*. Cambridge, 1959.

Fielder, Leslie. 'Good Good Girl and Good Bad Boy'. *No! in Thunder*. Boston, 1960.

Fielding, K. J. *Charles Dickens: A Critical Introduction*. New York, 1958.

Ford, George H. *Dickens and His Readers: Aspects of Novel-Criticism Since 1836*. Princeton, 1956.

Forster, John. *The Life of Charles Dickens*. 2 vols. London, 1966.

Gibson, John. '*The Old Curiosity Shop*: The Critical Allegory'. *Dickensian*, 60 (September 1964), 178–83.

Gifford, Henry. 'Dickens in Russia: The Initial Phase'. *Forum for Modern Language Studies*, 4, No. 1 (January 1968), 45–52.

Gissing, George. *Charles Dickens: A Critical Study*. 1898 reprint. Port Washington, 1966.

—*The Immortal Dickens*. London, 1925.

Gold, Joseph. *Charles Dickens: Radical Moralist*. Minneapolis, 1962.

Graves, Robert. *The Real David Copperfield*. London, 1933.

Gross, John and Pearson, Gabriel, eds. *Dickens and the Twentieth Century*. Toronto, 1962.

Hardy, Barbara. *The Moral Art of Dickens*. New York, 1970.

—'The Complexity of Dickens'. *Dickens 1970*. Ed. Michael Slater. London, 1970.

Holloway, John. 'Dickens and Symbol'. *Dickens 1970*. Ed. Michael Slater. London, 1970.

Huxley, Aldous. 'Vulgarity in Literature'. *Music at Night and Other Essays*. London, 1960.

Johnson, Edgar. *Charles Dickens: His Tragedy and Triumph*. 2 vols. New York, 1952.

Katarsky, Igor M. *Dikkens*. Moscow, 1960.

Kincaid, James R. *Dickens and the Rhetoric of Laughter*. Oxford, 1971.

—'The Structure of *David Copperfield*'. *Dickens Studies*, II, No. 2 (May 1966).

Kotzin, Michael. *Dickens and the Fairy Tale*. Bowling Green, 1972.

Lane, Lauriat Jr. 'Dickens and the Double'. *The Dickensian*, 55 (1959), 47–55.

Leacock, Stephen. *Charles Dickens*. Garden City, 1936.

Leavis, F. R. and Q. D. *Dickens the Novelist*. London, 1970.

Lindsay, Jack. *Charles Dickens: A Biographical and Critical Study*. London, 1950.

Lucas, John. *The Melancholy Man: A Study of Dickens' Novels*. London, 1970.

Manheim, Leonard. 'Thanatos: The Death Instinct in Dickens' Later Novels'. *Psychoanalysis and the Psychoanalytic Review*, 47 (Winter 1960–61), 17–31.

—'Floras and Doras: The Women in Dickens' Novels'. *Texas Studies in Language and Literature*, 7, (Summer 1965), 181–200.

—'Dickens' HEROES, *heroes*, and heroids'. *Dickens Studies Annual*, 5 (1976), 1–22.

Marcus, Steven. *Dickens: From Pickwick to Dombey*. New York, 1965.

Marshall, William. 'The Image of Steerforth and the Structure of *David Copperfield*. *Tennessee Studies in Literature*, 5 (1960), 57–65.

Miller, J. Hillis. *Charles Dickens: The World of His Novels*. Cambridge, 1959.

Monod, Sylvère. *Dickens the Novelist*. Norman, 1967.

—'James Steerforth ou le problème du mal dans *David Copperfield*'. *Annales de l'Université de Paris*, 37, No. 2 (April–June 1967), 166–76.

More, Paul Elmer. 'The Praise of Dickens'. *Shelburne Essays*. 5th series. New York, 1905.

Mulvey, Christopher. '*David Copperfield*: The Folk-Story Structure'. *Dickens Studies Annual*, 5 (1976), 74–94.

Orwell, George. 'Charles Dickens'. *A Collection of Essays*. New York, 1954.

Petersburg Literary Gazette, 20 July 1844, p. 472.

Russkaia Mysl', 5 (1891), p. 213.

Santayana, George. 'Dickens'. *Soliloquies in England and Later Soliloquies*. New York, 1922.

Senelick, Laurence. 'Little Nell and the Purience of Sentimentality'. *Dickens Studies*, 2, No. 3 (October 1967), 146–59.

Sil'man, Tamara. *Tvorchestvo Dikkensa*. Moscow-Leningrad, 1948.

Spilka, Mark. *Dickens and Kafka: A Mutual Interpretation*. Bloomington, 1963.

—'*David Copperfield* as Psychological Fiction'. *Critical Quarterly*, 1, No. 4 (Winter 1959), 300 ff.

—'Little Nell—Revisited'. *Papers of the Michigan Academy of Science, Arts and Letters*, 45 (1960), 427–37.

—'Erich Segal as Little Nell, or the Real Meaning of *Love Story*'. *Journal of Popular Culture*, 5, No. 4 (Spring 1972), 782–98.

Steig, Michael. 'The Central Action of *The Old Curiosity Shop*, or Little Nell Revisited Again'. *Literature and Psychology*, 15, No. 3 (Summer 1965), 163–70.

Stephen, Fitzjames. 'The Relation of Novels to Life'. *Cambridge Essays, 1855*. London, 1855.

Symons, Julian. *Charles Dickens*. London, 1951.

Times Literary Supplement, The. '*The Old Curiosity Shop*—Dickens and Disney', 6 April 1940, p. 167.

Wilson, Angus. 'Dickens and the Divided Conscience'. *The Month*. Series 2, 1 (May 1950), 349–60.

—'Evil in the English Novel'. *Kenyon Review*, 29 (1967), 167–94.
Wilson, Edmund. 'Dickens: The Two Scrooges'. *The Wound and the Bow*. New York, 1970.
Wilt, Judith. 'Confusion and Consciousness in Dickens's Esther'. *Nineteenth Century Fiction*, 32, No. 3 (December 1977) 293.
Winters, Warrington. '*The Old Curiosity Shop*: A Consummation Devoutly to be Wished'. *The Dickensian*, 63 (September 1967). 176–80.
Woolf, Virginia. 'David Copperfield'. *The Moment and Other Essays*. London, 1952.

III. Works dealing with Dostoevsky

Alekseev, Mikhail Pavlovich. 'Russkii Dikkens'. *Charl'z Dikkens*. Ed. Iu. V. Fridlender. Leningrad, 1946.
Amenitski, D. A. 'Psikhiatricheskii analiz Nikolaia Stavrogina'. *Sovremennaia psikhiatriia*, No. 1 (January 1915), pp. 28–41.
Anikin, G. V. 'Idei i formy Dostoevskogo v proizvedeniiakh Angliiskikh pisatelei'. *Russkaia literatura 1870–1890 godov*, Sbornik 3 (Sverdlovsk, 1970), pp. 19–36.
Askol'dov, S. 'Psikhologiia kharakterov u Dostoevskogo'. *F. M. Dostoevsky: Stat'i i maierialy*. Ed. A. S. Dolinin. Leningrad and Moscow, 1925.
Babovich, M. 'Sud'ba dobra i krasoti v svete gumanizma Dostoevskogo'. *F. M. Dostoevsky: Materiali i issledovaniia*. Ed. G. M. Fridlender. Leningrad, 1974.
Bakhtin, Mikhail M. *Problems of Dostoevsky's Poetics*. Trans. R. W. Rostel. London, 1973.
Beebe, Maurice. 'The Three Motives of Raskolnikov'. *Crime and Punishment and the Critics*. Ed. Edward Wasiolek. San Fransisco, 1961.
Belinsky, Vissarion. 'Vzglad na Russkuiu literaturu 1846 goda'. *Sobranie sochinenii*, III, 641–83. Ed. F. M. Golovenchenko. Moscow, 1948.
Bem, A. L. 'Faust v Tvorchestve Dostoevskogo'. *Zapiski Nauchno-Issledovatel'skago obedineniia*, 5, No. 29 (1937), 1–27.
Berdaiev, Nicholas. 'Stavrogin'. *Russkaia mysl'*, No. 5 (May 1914), pp. 82–89.
—*Dostoievsky*. Trans. Donald Attwater. London, 1937.
Bulgakov, Sergei Nikolaievich, *Tikhiye dumi*. Moscow, 1918.
Carr, Edward Hallet. *Dostoevsky: 1821–1881*. London, 1949.
Chizhevsky, Dmitri. 'The Theme of the Double in Dostoevsky'.

Dostoevsky: A Collection of Critical Essays. Ed. René Wellek. Englewood Cliffs, 1962.

Dobroliubov, N. A. 'Zabitye liudi'. *F. M. Dostoevsky v Russkoi kritike*. Ed. A. A. Belkin. Moscow, 1956.

Dolinin, A. S., ed. *Dostoevsky: stat'i i materiali*. 2 vols. Petersburg, 1922–25.

—ed. *F. M. Dostoevsky: Materiali i issledovaniia*. Leningrad, 1935.

—ed. *F. M. Dostoevsky v vospominaniakh sovremennikov*. 2 vols. Moscow, 1964.

—ed. *Dostoevsky: Materiali i issledovaniia*. Leningrad, 1974.

Dostoevsky, Aimée. *Fydor Dostoevsky: A Study*. Trans. Anon. New Haven, 1922.

Dostoevsky, Anna Grigor'evna. *The Diary of Dostoevsky's Wife*. Ed. René Fülop-Miller. London, 1928.

Freud, Sigmund. 'Dostoevsky and Parricide'. Trans. D. F. Tait. *Yearbook of Psychoanalysis*, 2 (1946), 231–49.

Fridlender, G. M. *Tvorchestvo Dostoevskogo*. Moscow, 1959.

—*Realizm Dostoevkogo*. Moscow-Leningrad, 1964.

Fridlender, G. M., ed. *Dostoevsky i ego vremia*. Leningrad, 1971.

Fülop-Miller, René. *Fyodor Dostoevsky*. Trans. Richard and Clara Winston. New York, 1950.

Gide, André, *Dostoievski: Articles et Causeries*. Paris, 1923.

—*Dostoevsky*. London, 1925.

Grossman, Leonid Petrovich. *Biblioteka Dostoevskogo*. Odessa, 1919.

—*Tvorchestvo Dostoevskogo: 1821–1881–1921*. Odessa, 1921.

—*Poetika Dostoevskogo*. Moscow, 1925.

—'Dostoevsky i chartistskii roman'. *Voprosy literatury*, (April 1959), pp. 147–58.

Grossman, Leonid Petrovich and Polonsky, Viacheslav. *Spor o Bakunine i Dostoevskim*. Leningrad, 1926.

Guérard, Albert. *The Triumph of the Novel*. New York, 1976.

Hingley, Ronald. *The Undiscovered Dostoevsky*. London, 1962.

Holquist, Michael. *Dostoevsky and the Novel*. Princeton, 1977.

Howe, Irving. *Politics and the Novel*. New York, 1957.

Ivanov, Vyacheslav. *Freedom and the Tragic Life: A Study in Dostoevsky*. New York, 1952.

Kabat, Geoffrey. *Ideology and Imagination*. New York, 1978.

Khrapchenko, M. 'Dostoevsky i ego literaturnoe nasledie'. *Kommunist*, 16 (1971), 108–24.

Kirpotin, Valerii Iakovlevich. *F. M. Dostoevsky: Tvorcheskii put'*. Moscow, 1960.

—*Unizhennye i oskorblennye*. Introduction. Moscow, 1964.

Kohlberg, Lawrence. 'Psychological Analysis and Literary Form: A

Study of the Doubles in Dostoevsky'. *Daedalus*, 92 (Spring 1963), 345–62.

Lavrin, Janko. *Dostoevsky and His Creation: A Psychocritical Study.* London, 1920.

Lesser, Simon. 'The Role of Unconscious Understanding in Flaubert and Dostoevsky'. *Daedalus*, 92 (Spring 1963), 363–82.

Linner, Sven. *Dostoevskij on Realism.* Stockholm Slavic Studies, I. Stockholm, 1976.

Magarsack, David. *Dostoevsky.* New York, 1962.

Magarsack, David, ed. *Dostoevsky's Occasional Writings.* New York, 1963.

Merezhkovskii, Dimitri S. *Dostoievsky.* Trans. G. A. Mounsey. London, 1910.

Mikhailovski, Nikolai Konstantinovich. 'Zhestokii talant'. *Sochinenie*, V, 1–78. St Petersburg, 1908.

Mirsky, D. S. *A History of Russian Literature.* New York, 1958.

Mochulsky, Konstantin. *Dostoevsky: His Life and Work.* Princeton, 1967.

Muchnic, Helen. *Dostoevsky's English Reputation, 1881–1936.* Smith College Studies in Modern Languages, 20 (1939).

Passage, Charles E. *Dostoevski the Adapter.* Chapel Hill, 1954.

Pereverzev, Valerian. *Tvorchestvo Dostoevskogo.* Moscow, 1922.

Poggioli, Renato. 'Dostoevsky or Reality and Myth'. *The Phoenix and the Spider.* Cambridge, 1957.

Polzinsky, Petr. *Detskii mir v proizvedeniakh Dostoeskogo.* Revel, 1891.

Reizov, B. G. 'O Zapadnom vliianii v tvorchestve Dostoevskogo (nekotorye zapadnye istochniki romana "Unizhennye i oskorblennye")'. *Izvestiia Severo-Kavkazskogo gosudarstvennogo universiteta* (Rostov-na-Done), 12, No. 1 (1926), 95–104.

Rowe, William Woodin. *Dostoevsky: Child and Man in His Works.* New York, 1968.

Seduro, Vladimir. *Dostoyevski in Russian Literary Criticism, 1846–1956.* New York, 1957.

Simmons, Ernest J. *Dostoevsky: The Making of a Novelist.* New York, 1940.

Steiner, George. *Tolstoy or Dostoevsky.* New York, 1951.

Vivas, Eliseo. 'The Two Dimensions of Reality in *The Brothers Karamazov*'. *Dostoevsky: A Collection of Critical Essays.* Ed. René Wellek. Englewood Cliffs, 1962.

Vogüé, E. M. de. 'The Religion of Suffering—Dostoevsky'. *The Russian Novel.* London, 1913.

Wasiolek, Edward. *Dostoevsky: The Major Fiction.* Cambridge, 1964.

Yarmolinsky, Avrahm. *Dostoevsky: His Life and Art.* New York, 1957.

IV. General Works

Brewster, Dorothy. *East-West Passage.* London, 1954.

Davie, Donald, ed. *Russian Literature and Modern English Fiction.* Chicago, 1965.

Forster, E. M. *Aspects of the Novel.* London, 1947.

Freud, Sigmund. *The Interpretation of Dreams.* Trans. Dr A. A. Brill. New York, 1950.

Frye, Northrup. *Anatomy of Criticism: Four Essays.* Princeton, 1957.

Guérard, Albert. *Stories of the Double.* Philadephia, 1967.

Kettle, Arnold. *An Introduction to the English Novel.* London, 1953.

Lubbock, Percy. *The Craft of Fiction.* New York, 1957.

Lukacs, Georg. *Studies in European Realism.* New York, 1964.

Miller, J. Hillis. *The Form of Victorian Fiction.* Notre Dame, 1968.

Rank, Otto. *Beyond Psychology.* New York, 1941.

—*The Double.* Trans. Harry Tucker. Chapel Hill, 1971.

Rogers, Robert. *The Double in Literature.* Detroit, 1970.

Rosenfield, Claire. 'The Shadow Within: The Conscious Use of the Double'. *Daedalus*, 92 (Spring 1963), 326–44.

Simmons, Ernest J. 'English Literature in Russia'. *Harvard Studies and Notes in Philology and Literature*, 13 (1931), 251–307.

Tillotson, Kathleen. *Novels of the 1840's.* Oxford, 1954.

Van Ghent, Dorothy. *The English Novel: Form and Function.* New York, 1953.

Wellek, René, *Concepts of Criticism.* Ed. Stephen G. Nichols Jr. New Haven, 1963.

V. Major Bibliographic Sources

DICKENS

Fridlender, Iu. and Katarsky, Igor M. *Charl'z Dikkens: Bibliografia.* Moscow, 1962.

Gold, Joseph, comp. *The Stature of Dickens: A Centenary Bibliography.* Toronto, 1971.

Kitton, Frederic G. *Dickensiana: A Bibliography of the Literature Relating to Charles Dickens and His Writings.* London, 1886.

Miller, William. *The Dickens Student and Collector.* Cambridge, 1946.

DOSTOEVSKY

Beebe, Maurice, and Newton, Christopher. 'Dostoevsky in English: A

Selected Checklist of Criticism and Translations'. *Modern Fiction Studies*, 4, No. 3 (Autumn 1958), 271–91.

Belkin, A. A., Dolinin, A. S., and Kozhinov, V. V., eds. *F. M. Dostoevsky : Bibliografiia proizvedeniia F. M. Dostoevskogo i litertury o nem, 1917–1965.* Moscow, 1968.

See also Muchnic, Helen and Seduro, Vladimir, above.

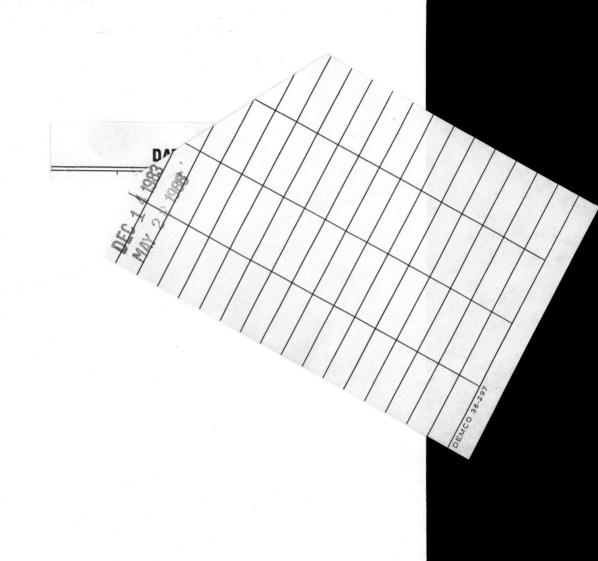